New Visions
for Metropolitan America

A N T H O N Y   D O W N S

New Visions
for Metropolitan America

The Brookings Institution
Washington, D.C.

Lincoln Institute of Land Policy
Cambridge, Massachusetts

Copyright © 1994 by
THE BROOKINGS INSTITUTION
1775 Massachusetts Avenue, N.W., Washington, D.C. 20036
and
LINCOLN INSTITUTE OF LAND POLICY
113 Brattle Street, Cambridge, Massachusetts 02138

Library of Congress Cataloging-in-Publication Data
Downs, Anthony
    New visions for metropolitan America / Anthony Downs.
        p.   cm.
    Includes bibliographical references and index.
    ISBN 0-8157-1926-4 (cl) — ISBN 0-8157-1925-6 (pa)
        1. Cities   and   towns—United   States—Growth.
2. Metropolitan areas—United States.   3. Urban policy—
United States.   I. Title.
    HT384.U5D68   1994
    307.76'0973—dc20   93-47483
                                                                CIP

9 8 7 6 5 4

The paper used in this publication meets the minimum
requirements of the American National Standard for Information Sciences—Permanence of Paper for Printed Library
Materials, ANSI Z39.48—1984.

Set in Palatino by Harlowe Typography, Inc.
Cottage City, Maryland

Printed by R. R. Donnelley & Sons, Co.
Harrisonburg, Virginia

Foreword

*F*OR much of this century, but especially since World War II, the American Dream has centered on owning a car and a detached house in the suburbs with lawn, garden, responsive government, good schools, a quick commute to work, and fresh air. But as we approach the twenty-first century this dream has been compromised. Private cars have clogged roads and polluted the air, open space has given way to shopping malls, and the affordable bungalow has soared beyond the reach of many would-be homebuyers.

The cause of many of these diverse problems is attributed to unplanned and unrestrained growth. The response in community after community has been stricter building codes, tougher zoning laws— what is called growth management. But these attempts to tame unrestrained growth have themselves created problems. Communities practicing growth management have become isolated from the cities around which they cluster, and they have become exclusionary. More important, these policies have not solved these problems; they have merely dumped them on others.

In this book Anthony Downs analyzes the problems growth management confronts—and creates. By girdling core cities with a ring of exclusionary suburbs, growth management compresses inner-city populations, concentrates poverty, crime, and their attendant problems, and threatens the long-term health of the suburbs themselves. The author proposes a new vision of metropolitan growth, a vision that could slow or stop unconstrained suburban sprawl. He discusses alternatives for managing growth and their chances of implementation, focusing particularly on the regionwide nature of metropolitan problems and the prospects for regionwide solutions.

This study is one of a series being copublished by the Brookings

Institution and the Lincoln Institute of Land Policy, which helped to underwrite project costs. Financial assistance was also provided by Peter B. Bedford of Bedford Properties, Inc., Thomas L. Lee of the Newhall Land and Farming Company, and Daniel Rose of the Daniel and Joanna S. Rose Fund, Inc. Their vital assistance is deeply appreciated.

The author wishes to thank the many people who read and commented on various drafts or parts of the manuscript. They are Henry J. Aaron, Larry P. Arnn, William A. Fischel, Philip B. Herr, Leanne Lachman, Thomas L. Lee, Christopher B. Leinberger, Michael S. McGill, Edward Marciniak, Edwin S. Mills, Arthur C. Nelson, Larry Orman, Richard B. Peiser, Douglas Porter, Ingrid W. Reed, Lloyd Rodwin, Lyn Sagalyn, Anita Summers, and Richard Tustian.

James R. Schneider edited the manuscript, David Bearce verified its factual statements, David Rossetti keyed in corrections, Susan Woollen prepared it for typesetting, and Max Franke compiled the index. Lisa L. Guillory provided staff assistance.

The views expressed in this book are those of the author and should not be ascribed to the persons acknowledged, the funding sources, or the trustees, officers, or staff members of either the Brookings Institution or the Lincoln Institute of Land Policy.

Bruce K. MacLaury, President
The Brookings Institution

March 1994
Washington, D.C.

To my wife, Kay,
who is my inspiration

Contents

Appendixes

Tables

Figures

Part 1
Perspectives

1

Why We Need a New Vision

FOR HALF A century America has had one dominant vision of how its metropolitan areas ought to grow and develop. It is best described as unlimited low-density sprawl. This vision encompasses personal and social goals—a home in the suburbs, a car, good schools, responsive local government—that most Americans cherish. Most metropolitan areas have successfully realized the vision. Yet this achievement has contributed to unexpected growth-related dilemmas that threaten the long-run viability of American society, something the American public and most leaders have yet to realize. They have not therefore even begun to confront the need to alter the vision to resolve its problems. Yet these problems must be resolved if American society is to prosper.

As a result of increasingly intrusive difficulties during the 1980s, a remarkable transformation occurred in the attitude of hundreds of local governments. They had for many years considered growth a source of economic benefits and welcomed more jobs and more people. But now many have come to regard growth as responsible for traffic congestion, air pollution, loss of open space, higher taxes to pay for additional infrastructure, and a lack of affordable housing. They have adopted policies designed to control growth in their communities. Known as growth management, the policies are explicit attempts to limit the proliferation of new housing and commercial and industrial buildings; the addition of roads, schools, and other social infrastructure; and increases in population and jobs within existing facilities.[1]

Growth management in some form is nothing new; communities have long tried to shape their development through zoning laws and other ordinances. But adopting policies specifically designed to restrict growth itself *is* relatively new. These policies have been advanced

3

mostly in the past two decades, and they have spread rapidly. One reason is that once a few local governments in a metropolitan area have adopted growth management policies, others nearby come under pressure to do likewise to avoid being swamped by the development their neighbors have excluded. Growth management has become important mainly where there has been economic prosperity and rapid expansion of population and jobs. This applies to a minority of metropolitan areas, probably containing less than 30 percent of the nation's people. But they include California, Florida, and the Northeast, traditionally America's economically most dynamic regions.

It is not easy to manage growth effectively—if at all. Most metropolitan areas have dozens or even hundreds of local governments that exercise sovereignty over land use within their jurisdictions. But the problems growth management is supposed to solve are mainly regional. And even policies that any one community adopts often have regional implications. For example, when Petaluma, California, limited the number of housing units that could be built there each year, neighboring Santa Rosa experienced spillover housing demand. Rents and home prices increased and vacancies fell. More important, almost all growth management efforts themselves increase housing costs, which reduces the number of houses and apartments available to low- and moderate-income people. Thus well-meaning local efforts to manage growth could make society as a whole worse off without doing much to solve growth-related problems.

The most dangerous result of growth management policies is that they help perpetuate the concentration of very poor households in depressed neighborhoods in big cities and older suburbs. These neighborhoods contain a small percentage of the U.S. population, but they are riddled with the most virulent forms of four problems that are undermining social cohesion and economic efficiency throughout the nation: exploding rates of crime and violence, increased numbers of children growing up in poverty, poor-quality public education, and failure to integrate workers into the mainstream work force. These problems affect every community in the nation, but many Americans still do not recognize how serious they are. One reason is that the problems have intensified and spread gradually. Dramatic incidents such as the 1992 Los Angeles riots have been rare. They have, however, diverted attention from the reality that these problems are worsening nationwide, not just in inner cities.

In America it normally takes a social crisis to overcome resistance to addressing conditions that are dangerous but that benefit large numbers of people. That is precisely the case with these four problems: they are aggravated by low-density growth and other practices that benefit a great many people. Thus they do not seem threatening enough to overcome the inertia of the status quo. Yet if the problems are not attacked vigorously, they will gravely impair the political unity, productivity, and economic efficiency of American society and the personal security of everyone. Carrying out such attacks will, however, require changing our vision of how growth ought to occur.

In this confusing environment, it is hard for individual communities to decide how best to respond to rapid growth. Are the undesirable conditions really caused primarily by growth? Which policies might succeed in ameliorating them? Which might have severe side effects or make conditions worse? Is limiting local growth desirable at all for either a given locality or society as a whole? If so, what should the goals of such limitations be? To what extent do communities need to coordinate growth management policies with other communities to achieve effective results? Can the multiplicity of governments in metropolitan areas manage growth effectively, or does that arrangement need to be modified? If so, how?

This book seeks to answer these questions. It considers the problems associated with rapid metropolitan growth from a perspective that encompasses inner-city problems. And it examines the effects of growth management in communities that have tried to alter the course of urban growth. The book also analyzes three other ways growth could occur, alternatives that might reduce the problems that have arisen from pursuit of unlimited low-density development. This analysis necessarily focuses on the relationships between the suburbs and central cities. Finally, the book attempts to identify the policies likely to be most effective in helping to resolve growth-related problems.

The Dominant Vision

Ironically, the underlying cause of recent hostility toward growth has been the overwhelmingly successful realization of Americans' common vision of how growth ought to occur. Unlimited low-density development has dominated nearly all American policies affecting metropolitan area growth for more than four decades.

The first element of this vision is ownership of detached single-family homes on spacious lots. A 1993 poll conducted by the Federal National Mortgage Association showed that 86 percent of American households believed owning a home was better than renting, 83 percent believed owning was a good investment, and 73 percent preferred a single-family detached home with a yard.[2] Owning such a home has become the heart of the American dream, the prevailing image of how a household succeeds. Realization of this dream implies low-density settlement.

The second element is ownership of automotive vehicles. Nearly every American wants to be able to leap into his or her car, van, or truck and zoom off on an uncongested road to wherever he or she wants to go, in total privacy and great comfort.

The third element is working in low-rise workplaces—offices or industrial buildings or shopping centers—in attractively landscaped, parklike settings. Each structure is of course to be accompanied by its own free parking lot.

The fourth element is residence in small communities with strong local governments. Americans want these governments to control land use, public schools, and other things affecting the quality of neighborhood life. This form of governance permits residents to have an influential voice in shaping their environment.

The fifth element is an environment free from the signs of poverty. Unlike the other four, this element is not acknowledged or even consciously desired. But it inevitably results from two conditions for housing production that are explicitly desired by most Americans: no construction of "substandard" housing and few housing subsidies for low-income households.[3] Thus the dominant approach to housing the poor in the United States is the trickle-down process. Low-income people are housed in older units formerly occupied by the nonpoor. The result is concentration of the poorest households in neighborhoods where the oldest, most deteriorated housing is located—usually central cities and older suburbs.

These five elements define much of what passes for the American dream in the minds of most suburbanites and many city dwellers. The elements add up to a relatively unconstrained individualism. In effect, each person, household, or business seeks an environment that maximizes its own well-being without very much regard to the possible effects on society as a whole. Pursuing the realization of each element reinforces achievement of one or more of the others. A community of single-family homes creates the need for private transportation. And once households own cars, they can commute to widely scattered low-density workplaces.

The value and attainability of this vision has been reinforced through constant promotion by the real estate industry and suburban communities. Homebuilders, realtors, advertisers, town governments, and local planning officials sing the praises of suburban life-styles and uncrowded, safe communities. This vision is now so strongly entrenched that it has become almost political suicide for elected officials to challenge any of its elements.

Problems of the Low-Density Vision

Unfortunately, this model of development is riddled with internal inconsistencies that have created severe disparities between vision and reality. The ubiquity of the private automobile and its needs, for instance, have compromised the dream of open roads and fresh air. These inconsistencies are now becoming more apparent because the vision's elements have been achieved more completely than ever. Automobile ownership and use greatly accelerated during the 1980s.[4] More cars meant more traffic congestion and air pollution and high costs for building and widening roads. However, most Americans do not realize that success in attaining their goals is responsible for other results they abhor. Even when confronted by overwhelming evidence, they find it much easier to blame traffic congestion and other urban ills on some scapegoat than to recognize that their own habitual behavior causes them.

Most suburbanites blame congestion and delay on real estate developers and the latest residents to arrive in their communities. They often adopt strong growth management policies in response to these problems. But most policies do not attack the problems' fundamental causes, so the policies cannot remedy them effectively.

Excessive Travel

A primary flaw in the dominant vision is that it generates excessive travel. A pattern of single-family housing and low-density workplaces spreads homes and jobs widely. People have to travel long distances from where they live to where they work, shop, or play. In theory, if jobs spread out as much as housing, dispersion would not increase average travel distances as long as people lived near where they worked. But jobs have not spread out as widely as housing, and cross-commuting is common because people do not choose homes near their jobs. In both 1980 and 1990, about 30 percent of all U.S. commuters traveled 30 minutes or more to their jobs, though the average time was 20 minutes.[5] From 1983 to 1990 the average household vehicle trip increased from 7.9 to 9.0 miles and the average commute from 8.6 to 10.9 miles. Average vehicle miles traveled per household rose 29 percent.[6]

These increases can be considered excessive only in relation to some standard. But more travel has generated more traffic congestion, expense, time spent driving, and air pollution than many Americans can tolerate easily.[7] Therefore it is reasonable to conclude that people are traveling much more than they would prefer. And expanding mass transit is not likely to remedy the problem. Buses or fixed-rail transit can operate efficiently only if at least one end of most journeys is concentrated in a few points of destination. But when both homes and jobs are widely scattered, concentration no longer prevails, even if there are a few major nodes, such as a downtown. Low-density settlements cannot efficiently support mass transit.

So single-family homeownership and low-density workplaces provide strong incentives for households to use private vehicles. In 1983, 87 percent of all U.S. households owned at least one motor vehicle, and 53 percent owned two or more. Even among households with incomes less than $10,000, more than 60 percent owned at least one car or truck; among those with incomes of $40,000 or more, 99 percent owned at least one, and 87 percent owned two or more.[8] Because of automobile ownership and low-density settlements, nearly all American workers commute by private vehicles. In 1990 only 5 percent of all rush hour commuters used public transit; 86 percent used private vehicles, and 73 percent drove to work alone.[9] The result, of course, is peak-hour traffic congestion.

Such congestion could have been mitigated if a lot more streets and roads had been built, or existing ones expanded, in the 1980s. But people wanted to avoid the expense and the disruptions of acquiring land and building more highways. Those costs were collective: bearing them required communities to raise public funds and choose rights-of-way. Suburban citizens could not, however, agree about who was to bear the costs, so no one did, and roads that might have better accommodated the explosion of the vehicle population were not built.[10]

Americans usually believe these problems are caused by high-density development. Because traffic is most congested near big-city downtowns, regional shopping centers, and large outlying office parks, they think high-density land use must cause the congestion. It is true that the most intense local congestion is often found near high-density sites because they generate many vehicle movements in a small area. In fact, some experts argue that the spreading out of jobs and housing around the edges of metropolitan areas has helped Americans adjust to massive increases in urban population, jobs, and vehicle use without creating even more local congestion.[11] But when large areas are developed with high average densities rather than low ones, total travel and general congestion are reduced.

Lack of Affordable Housing

The dominant vision's second flaw is that it focuses on relatively high-cost housing. Areas of new growth developed to its specifications provide few dwellings that low- and moderate-income households can afford. Yet these households are an integral part of American life, even in the suburbs. They provide workers for low-wage jobs essential to fast-food establishments, gas stations, laundries, hospitals, shopping centers, lawn care firms, and so on. And moderate-wage workers are often the backbone of police and fire protection, teaching, and other local government services.

Among the 92 million U.S. households in 1990, one-third did not live in single-family homes and one-third were renters.[12] But the low density of metropolitan development does not include dwelling units appropriate to these people. Although suburbs do contain multifamily dwellings, such housing is not part of the dominant vision, and its construction is often opposed by local residents. Besides, most low- and moderate-income people cannot afford to live in new housing. To maintain desirable environments, American communities require that new housing meet quality requirements that are very high by world or even Western European and Japanese standards. These requirements are designed by middle-class architects, planners, and citizens in conformity with what they believe is decent housing. But their concept of decency far surpasses what is necessary for human health and safety. Consequently, all new American dwellings are too costly for low-income people to occupy without direct subsidies. But subsidies are provided for only a few of the many households with incomes low enough to be eligible for them. So poor people live in unsubsidized older dwellings.

At first glance, nothing seems wrong with this practice; it has provided adequate shelter for millions for many years. However, trickle down only works in metropolitan areas with more housing units available than households to occupy them. Then when a household moves into a newly built unit it leaves a vacant unit behind that some less affluent household can occupy. That household in turn leaves another unit behind and so on. But when net housing construction is lower than net household formation, such chains of moves cannot occur as effectively. This happens nationally when housing starts are down and happens more often in fast-growing metropolitan areas such as many in California and Florida. By the time older units do become available they may be deteriorated and inadequate. Yet their rents may still be high in relation to the low incomes of the poor.

The trickle-down process also helps generate a socioeconomic hierarchy of neighborhoods that separates low-income households from moderate-, middle-, and upper-income ones. The poor become concentrated in the most deteriorated housing at the centers of cities because it is the cheapest. In 1990, 10.4 million people lived in census tracts where 40 percent or more of the residents had money incomes below the poverty level. Some 17 percent of black and 11 percent of Hispanic Americans lived in extreme poverty areas of America's one hundred largest central cities, compared with only 1 percent of whites. Three-fourths of the residents of these concentrations lived in the nation's central cities; less than 5 percent lived in suburbs.[13] High unemployment, crime, broken families, drug abuse, mental illness, disability, children born out of wedlock, gang membership, and structural deterioration are endemic there. Schools and other public services are of much lower quality than services in the rest of the metropolitan area. Young people find it difficult to escape from poverty.

These inner-city maladies have undermined the ability of central cities to perform economic and social functions crucial to the welfare of all residents, including suburban residents. This problem is the most harmful result of pursuing the dominant vision of metropolitan development, although that pursuit is not its only cause. Until America makes far more progress at coping with crime and other problems, especially in inner cities, the problems will cripple its ability to compete in a global economy and to function as a viable democracy.

In contrast to these inner-city neighborhoods, most suburbs have been built since World War II. Total suburban population rose from 41 million in 1950 to 115 million in 1990, an increase of 181 percent compared with a 65 percent increase in total population. The proportion of Americans living in suburbs rose from 27 percent to 46 percent.[14]

Historically, suburban employers of low- and moderate-income workers have relied on those living in older city neighborhoods. However, this arrangement has gradually deteriorated. Many more new jobs are being created in the suburbs than in central cities. And the sheer size of Los Angeles, northern New Jersey, and other fast-growing areas means that most older, less costly housing is many miles from where new jobs are located. Thus workers living in older, more central neighborhoods often have a hard time in looking for jobs, or commuting when they do find them.

Finally, the economic expansion of the 1980s drove the unemployment rate below 7 percent nationally.[15] This prosperity and demographic changes in the U.S. age distribution created a nationwide shortage of entry-level workers. As a result, before the 1990 recession, far-out suburbs of many metropolitan areas were experiencing acute shortages of low-wage and even moderate-wage labor. These shortages were gone by the 1990–91 recession, but they will reappear when unemployment rates fall as the economy expands. Thus the low-density vision's focus on relatively costly single-family housing and its reliance on trickle-down housing are inconsistent with the need for low- and moderate-wage workers in every community in every metropolitan area.[16]

Financing Infrastructure Fairly

Another flaw in the dominant vision is its lack of consensus about how best to finance new schools, roads, and sewage and water systems. There is also no consensus on how to pay for increasing the capacity of existing facilities in established areas through which new residents will pass on their way to and from work or shopping. The lack of consensus creates political conflicts, often resulting in gross underfunding of facilities and services. Residents of fast-growing areas want most of the added infrastructure to be paid for by newcomers through impact fees, exactions, proffers, and permit fees.[17] Residents regard these tactics as merely requiring newcomers to pay their fair share because they will be the main beneficiaries. Residents thus typically vote against most increases in general taxes or bonding powers to pay for expanded facilities. But developers and potential newcomers believe the entire community should share in the costs. Because existing residents benefited from past general financing of infrastructure, it is unfair for them to change the rules. Also, growth creates greater economic prosperity, which aids everyone. Finally, loading the marginal costs of growth onto new developments raises housing costs, unfairly reducing homeownership and rental opportunities of people with low and moderate incomes.

Political resolution of this controversy is inherently biased in favor of existing residents: potential newcomers cannot vote on local government policies that affect their welfare. Even so, it is difficult to force newcomers to pay all the marginal costs of growth. Some costs spring from more intensive use of existing facilities by both newcomers and previous residents.

Faced with this situation, residents often choose to hold down taxes by providing inadequate facilities for newcomers and even for themselves. New housing and commercial subdivisions may get built without adequate sewers, streets, and schools, as has been happening in Florida for some time. The dominant vision of how metropolitan areas ought to develop offers no guidance on how to resolve these problems.

Siting Locally Undesirable Land Uses

The dominant vision also contains no effective means of resolving conflicts between the welfare of a metropolitan area as a whole and the welfare of its parts. Government decisionmaking powers, especially those controlling land use, are divided among many communities, so each local government has a parochial viewpoint. Public officials are not primarily concerned with the welfare of the area as a whole or of society as a whole. Still, every society must have some facilities—airports, expressways, jails, garbage incinerators, landfills—that benefit society as a whole but have unpopular effects on their immediate surroundings. These essential facilities, known as locally undesirable land uses, or LULUs, promote an attitude called NIMBY, not in my back yard.

In an urban society designed in accordance with low-density growth, it is difficult to find a politically acceptable location for a needed but locally undesirable facility. Residents near every potential site pressure their local governments to oppose putting it there, and those governments have the power to reject the facility because controls over land use have been divided among myriad local entities. Officials are motivated to reject the facility because they are politically responsible only to their own residents. The resulting paralysis has virtually halted airport construction in the United States and blocked creation of thousands of other badly needed facilities. Low- and moderate-income households themselves are regarded as undesirable by many middle- and upper-income people who fear the market values of their homes will plummet and property taxes will skyrocket. Thus "not in my back yard" reinforces the dominant vision's failure to provide housing that low- and moderate-income people can afford.

Paying the Costs

Another flaw in the vision is its failure to compel people whose behavior generates significant social costs to pay for those costs directly. Every driver who enters a well-traveled highway during rush hour adds to congestion, slowing down all other drivers to some extent and costing them lost time. Drivers who make the same trip during nonpeak hours do not generate this cost. It would therefore be socially efficient if solo drivers on major roads were charged a direct fee for traveling during peak hours but not at other times. These charges would encourage more people to drive in nonpeak periods or to share rides. The money could be used to improve the nation's transportation system.[18] Politicians, however, have usually refused to adopt peak-hour road-use pricing because it would penalize low-income drivers. Also, time-differentiated road pricing runs counter to the "right" of citizens to use private vehicles to go anywhere anytime.

Another example of creating social costs without paying for them is the exclusionary zoning in many suburbs. Middle- and upper-income households often pressure local governments to adopt regulations that greatly increase the costs of homes. The residents believe such regulations help maximize home values. But exclusionary requirements force low- and moderate-income workers to live far from suburban jobs and commute long distances, which increases traffic congestion and air pollution and imposes time losses on all commuters. The people who lobby local governments to adopt exclusionary regulations do not have to pay the social costs they are generating for others.

Absorbing Too Much Open Space

The dominant vision encourages converting too much open space into urban uses. Of course, any settlement pattern accommodating additional population and economic development will convert some open space to urban uses, so conversion should not be considered excessive per se. But low-density settlement requires much larger areas to accommodate any given total population than higher-density settlement does. That in turn decreases the access of metropolitan area dwellers to open space. Some planners also criticize suburban sprawl because it swallows prime agricultural land and often encroaches upon environmentally sensitive areas. Because the United States produces agricultural surpluses, conversion of agricultural land probably does not diminish the nation's welfare much, but losses of accessible open space and environmentally sensitive areas clearly reduce the quality of life.

The pattern of development typical in U.S. metropolitan areas also bypasses parcels of vacant land, spreading development out farther than low net residential densities would otherwise require. This increases infrastructure costs. And many small pieces of open space that are skipped remain privately owned and are too scattered to be used as recreational areas. Local governments are not motivated to buy and set aside large parcels of land for open space accessible to people throughout the region. They may create parks for their own residents, but they do not want to spend money on people living elsewhere.

Finally, many environmentalists believe low-density growth threatens wetlands, forests, river basins, and habitats of threatened species. Developers, they contend, should be prohibited from converting such land to urban uses through regulatory procedures, rather than by having public authorities purchase it. The environmentalists oppose public purchase because they do not believe taxpayers will fund as many purchases as are socially desirable.

These social costs of the dominant vision are harder to quantify, even in theory, than its other flaws. It is impossible to establish scientifically just how much open space is necessary for a good quality of life or just how accessible it should be. But these criticisms have had a powerful political impact on growth management policies. In Oregon and Florida a major motivation for adopting statewide land use planning and urban growth boundaries was fear that development would convert open land in the Willamette River Valley and the Everglades to scattered urban uses.

The Dominant Vision and Social Inconsistencies

The flaws in the dominant vision have undermined the desirability of the environment produced by pursuing that vision: the results are inconsistent with the high quality of life it promises. These flaws threaten to weaken the economic and social functioning of many metropolitan areas and therefore of the entire U.S. economy and society.

This situation illustrates a fundamental problem in democracies. They have great difficulty solving the long-run problems created by policies that provide short-run benefits. Once people receive the benefits, they do not want to give them up. But they cannot agree how to distribute the long-run costs necessary to sustain the benefits. Each group of beneficiaries tries to shift as many of the costs as possible onto other groups. In some cases the costs are not paid at all. Ultimately, such a failure undermines or offsets the short-run benefits. Increased traffic congestion and air pollution offset some of the benefits people sought when they moved to low-density suburbs. Yet these problems are partly caused by the very low density these people insisted on.

A major focus of this book is how America can reduce the harm these social inconsistencies can do to the quality of life in metropolitan areas. But before that can happen, people must realize that the problems they associate with growth are in fact caused primarily by their own behavior. They cannot improve conditions without altering their vision of how metropolitan areas ought to develop. Achieving such a transformation is difficult and is made even more so because each person is part of a group, and the behavior of the group must change to affect the overall result. Consequently, each person believes what he or she does will make no difference, and the motivation to change remains weak.

Most Americans do not recognize their responsibility in causing the growth-related social problems they dislike. It will take strong and persistent leadership from those who do realize it to convince them. A primary goal of this book is to help public and private parties exercise such leadership.

2

Factors Affecting Growth

Visions of how metropolitan area growth ought to occur must be based on a realistic understanding of how growth actually occurs. This chapter describes key factors affecting growth and explains how some create conditions that are either inefficient for society as a whole or unfair to social subgroups or both. A primary cause of these outcomes—but also of benefits to millions of households—is the geographically splintered structure of governmental powers over land uses in most U.S. metropolitan areas.

Low-Income Households

In every large metropolitan area many residents are too poor to pay for housing and neighborhood conditions that meet middle-class definitions of decent quality. At least they cannot do so without financial aid from someone else. Yet these people are needed to perform low-wage jobs vital to restaurants, supermarkets, gas stations, and hospitals even in the most luxurious suburbs. And of course, low-wage workers are crucial to housecleaning, gardening, building maintenance, and other services. Yet many such jobs do not pay enough to lift these workers out of poverty. In 1981 there were about 5 million persons in poor families whose heads worked year-round; they comprised one-sixth of all persons officially defined as poor.[1] Many workers cannot earn enough to afford decent living standards without some form of subsidy, unless several live together. And some people cannot work at all.

The immigration of newcomers from abroad and from rural parts of the United States into metropolitan areas to perform low-wage jobs has always been part of America's normal economic and social life. If

the area's population is increasing, the number of low-income households grows absolutely larger. So every metropolitan area must contain
at least some housing units that are substandard by prevailing middle-
class definitions. When these households cluster together, their neighborhoods are called slums. As the total metropolitan population
grows, its slums also grow unless the rest of society provides subsidies
for the poor to live in decent housing. Few societies have ever funded
such costly subsidies for all their low-income households; the United
States has never come close to doing so.[2] Yet few urban planners, and
no elected officials, will admit publicly that metropolitan areas must
contain slums in order to operate efficiently and that slums must grow
if their metropolitan economies are growing.

Household Migration Patterns

How any metropolitan area grows is greatly influenced by the nature and size of migration into it. Rates of natural increase from a
metropolitan population are inherently limited, so rapid population
growth always involves high net immigration. The immigration can be
influenced by the level of housing prices, as described in the housing
price sensitivity principle. It states that the willingness of households
to move into a metropolitan area where jobs are available is affected
by the supply and prices of housing there and varies inversely with
their incomes, except among households with the very highest incomes.

Thus poor people are not inhibited from entering an area by high
housing prices. If decent affordable housing is not available where jobs
are located, they will occupy less-than-decent units. If permitted, they
will build shacks on vacant land. If such construction is prohibited by
local authorities, they will illegally overcrowd existing units, as immigrants from Latin America and Asia are doing now in southern
California.

Unlike very poor workers, people who earn middle- and upper-level
incomes refuse to occupy overcrowded dwellings. They would rather
reject a better job in an area with high housing costs than take the job
and radically reduce the quality of their families' housing. High prices
probably slowed overall population growth in the Boston and New
York City areas during the late 1980s, although that is hard to prove
statistically. At the highest income levels, housing prices are irrelevant

to job choices, except during wartime when existing units are rationed and building new ones is prohibited.

Establishing Separate Jurisdictions

The founders of every major U.S. city drew its initial boundaries to encompass what they thought would be enough land for expansion. But urban settlements last a long time, and many have grown well beyond their initial boundaries. The original city may respond by annexing surrounding territories when it has the legal power to do so. That has happened in Omaha, Albuquerque, and other metropolitan areas in the few southern and western states that give their central cities strong annexation powers.[3]

But in most U.S. metropolitan areas, residents outside the original city's boundaries establish separate communities legally independent of it. These people want separate jurisdictions in part because they do not want certain externalities affecting them that are regulated by some broad government that reflects the interests of persons living throughout the metropolitan area.[4] They may not, for instance, want commercial development in their neighborhood of single-family homes. Only some type of direct government regulation can take proper account of these wishes. In the United States, local governments control such regulations regarding land use, and those governments are very sensitive to their residents' desires. Therefore it is in the interest of residents to live in jurisdictions where most other citizens prefer regulations similar to the ones they approve of. That is most likely in small, relatively homogeneous localities.

Many suburban residents also want to live in independent jurisdictions to influence who their neighbors are. Most Americans want to live in neighborhoods occupied primarily by households with incomes equal to or higher than their own, similar cultural values and outlooks, and similar racial or ethnic backgrounds. Many associate lower incomes with cultural values and behavior patterns conflicting with their own, including a greater proclivity toward crime and violence. They also fear that the proximity of lower-income households will reduce the market values of their homes. And a large group of low-income households within their jurisdiction might cause their local government to raise taxes to provide the services needed by such households.

Preferences for racial segregation are based on prejudice and on beliefs that members of some racial groups exhibit less desirable behavior than others, especially criminal behavior. The beliefs are bolstered by studies of urban crime rates, although the conclusions of the studies are more ambiguous than many observers realize.[5]

Thus many middle-income and upper-income households establish independent jurisdictions to pass local zoning, building code, subdivision, and other regulations that raise the cost of housing high enough to exclude low-income people. It is much easier for middle- and upper-income residents to exert enough local political control to engage in exclusionary zoning if they live in small, relatively homogeneous localities. And in a related point, each individual can exert more influence over a small local government than over a large regional one. Their views are less likely to be ignored by bureaucracies or drowned out by the sheer number of other voices.

Supply-side factors also encourage separate jurisdictions. Builders cater to the preferences of middle- and upper-income households by creating large subdivisions of homes similar in size and price. Mass production of similar units is simpler and less costly than highly diversified development. And builders can usually market such subdivisions more easily. The result is neighborhoods that are relatively homogeneous internally in housing quality and price. Residents of several similar and adjacent suburban neighborhoods often band together to form a new political entity, particularly if they have higher average incomes than residents of the central city. That is likely because their housing units are generally more costly than the older units in the central city.[6] For these reasons, the growth of a metropolitan area beyond the boundaries of its founding city usually generates strong political pressures to create new, smaller suburbs independent of the city.[7]

In a few places suburbs themselves achieve very large populations. Either they are geographically extensive counties, as in the Washington, D.C., metropolitan area, or they have experienced high-density development, as in the Los Angeles and New York City areas. But in most places, suburbs remain relatively small in both area and population compared with the central cities they surround.

Demand-side motivations and supply-side forces thus generate fragmented local government structures in the suburbs of most metropolitan areas. This arrangement creates extremely parochial attitudes about land use policies on the part of individual households, local elected governments, and local government agencies. Each is motivated almost entirely by how its behavior affects its own welfare or the welfare of households living within its own locality. Some more broad-minded people form civic organizations to promote a regional perspective concerning land use policies, but they are always a minority. Local officials are particularly susceptible to parochialism, because only citizens who live within their locality's boundaries can directly influence their political survival. So nearly every citizen, official, agency, and community tries both to capture as many benefits of growth as possible for its own locality, and to shift as many costs of growth as possible onto other localities. This results in beggar-thy-neighbor policies of most localities and no attempt to maximize the welfare of the region as a whole.[8]

A Self-Reinforcing Hierarchy

The very existence of many independent suburbs surrounding central cities reinforces their separatism and establishes a hierarchy of prestige among them. Each presents a different combination of local tax rates and policies, public services, housing prices, and residents' socioeconomic levels and ethnicity. Tax rates and public services are controlled by local government; housing prices and the socioeconomic status and ethnicity of residents by individual decisions about where to live. Those decisions also affect local government policies because suburban governments are very responsive to residents' desires. In turn, local government policies affect households' decisions about where to live. These interdependent forces encourage the differentiation of suburbs.[9]

People considering where to live can choose from a broad spectrum of metropolitan localities. Although they can only consider places with housing prices they can afford, there is still usually a menu of possibilities. This choice increases social welfare because people can find places closer to their own preferences. But this benefit is available only to those with enough money to choose. Moreover, the benefit is diminished to the extent that racial or ethnic discrimination reduces the choices of minority groups.

The differentiation made possible by fragmented government is self-reinforcing. If people move where public policies are congenial, their arrival strengthens political support for those policies. So does the departure of residents whose preferences are different. If most households choose to live where residents have incomes similar to or slightly above their own or have an ethnic background like their own, their choices perpetuate local homogeneity. And many places further ensure uniformity by deliberately excluding households with incomes substantially below the average there.[10]

To the extent that each suburban income group segregates itself from others with notably lower incomes, it creates a hierarchy based on income levels: high-income households cluster in high-prestige areas, middle-income in middling-prestige areas, and so forth. But low-income households are compelled to gather in low-prestige areas because they cannot afford any alternatives. This produces neighborhood conditions reasonably congenial to all except the poorest. Of course, there is some heterogeneity in all communities, but such a socioeconomic hierarchy exists in most metropolitan areas.[11] At the top are a few high-prestige communities with expensive homes; at the bottom are a larger number of low-prestige communities of often deteriorated housing in the central cities or close-in suburbs.[12]

Unfortunately, this hierarchical structure reinforces the difficulties of the poor in trying to escape from poverty.[13] Some people, of course, do escape, but the conditions in their neighborhoods surely diminish their chances. Thus the institutional structure that provides comfortable living for most metropolitan area households does so in part by penalizing the households with the fewest resources.

Population Dynamics and Competition among Communities

Certain basic traits influence the economic strength of all communities. People and businesses are constantly being born, moving in, growing, dying, and moving out. From 1989 to 1990, for instance, 17 percent of all U.S. residents moved (ranging from 12 percent in the Northeast to 22 percent in the West).[14] Businesses and other organizations move less often than households but have much shorter life spans. The successful ones also expand and have a choice of where to locate their growth. To attain stability, every locality must attract newcomers to replace those who have left. Equally important, the newcomers must be at least as prosperous and desirable in the eyes of residents as the occupants who left. The community itself must remain alluring enough to keep attracting desirable replacements; failure to do so will cause residential and business composition to deteriorate economically and socially.

Consequently, all communities compete with all other communities in their vicinity and indirectly throughout the nation to attract new residents and other resources. Because most residents and firms have wide choices of where to locate and many frequently move, no locality can permit itself to become far less attractive than its competition. In particular, it cannot permit its tax rates to become much higher than theirs.[15]

Low-income residents, especially those who are not employable, weaken the economy of a community. Low-income areas typically absorb more per capita spending on police and fire protection, sanitation, welfare, and public health services than high-income areas in the same community. Low-income neighborhoods also have less valuable property and lower consumer expenditures, which means lower property tax and sales tax revenues. And many poor neighborhoods are physically and socially undesirable environments. Low-income residents cannot afford decent dwellings, so the resulting "blight" often reduces the entire community's attractiveness in the eyes of the potential residents and businesses. Similarly, public schools and school systems in which pupils from low-income households predominate tend to repel higher-income families, who regard the education as inferior to that available in more affluent communities.

The antisocial behavior of some low-income households reinforces the aversion of the nonpoor. Violent crimes occur at higher rates in low-income areas.[16] Although they reflect the behavior of only a small percentage of the residents in these areas, they damage the reputation of all. Thus a great many middle- and high-income Americans do not want low-income people living near them. They are even more strongly opposed to any sizable increase in the number of such households already present. Given the realities of average behavior by low-income people, this attitude is a rational means by others of protecting themselves from the deterioration of their neighborhoods. Unfortunately, it is unfair to most low-income people, but it is widespread and deeply rooted. These factors mean that most leaders, government officials, and nonpoor residents of nearly every locality strongly desire to minimize the number of low-income residents within their communities' boundaries. That includes preventing any more from entering, even though low-income persons perform services vital to the economic health of the entire metropolitan area and of every locality in it.

The only exception is where low-income people are themselves a majority and can elect officials sympathetic to their needs. These officials will have a vested interest in expanding the number of low-income constituents. But they also have an incentive to strengthen their local economies, so they will want to prevent the community's low-income population from growing much larger. This creates a conflict of policy goals. Mayors in many very poor cities, for instance, have often extended tax breaks to wealthy developers, high-income residents, or rich corporations to attract them, while denying similar benefits to the poor constituents who elected them.

This situation helps explain why local governments do not tax the nonpoor heavily so as to spend more aiding the poor. Competition to attract new resources inhibits every community from raising its tax rates very far above those of others nearby, unless it has some unique attractions.[17] Local tax rates can raise a lot of public funds only if the community has a high tax base. Therefore only wealthy communities can support major redistributive policies. And the residents of those localities have strong social and political motives to reject additional low-income residents and policies favorable to them.

If poor quality of life in low-income neighborhoods is a major cause of this exclusionary behavior, why not adopt public policies that provide better conditions there? Unfortunately, no one knows how to use public policies very effectively to remedy drug abuse, broken families, and other problems. And the remedies for other scourges are extremely expensive.

Thus an inherent tension exists within every growing metropolitan area between its need to use more low-wage workers and the desire of every locality in it to avoid having more low-income residents. Because nearly all metropolitan areas are growing, this tension is almost universal. It explains why formal areawide plans never indicate where poor people will live. No community wants to admit that it will be accepting more of them. However, public officials and many other citizens are equally reluctant to admit that they do *not* want them: blatant antipathy toward the poor would be undemocratic as well as uncharitable and unjust. So planners and leaders avoid all public discussion of where low-income people will live.

Racial Segregation in Housing Markets

The tendency of most middle- and upper-income households to separate themselves from poor households is aggravated by widespread racial segregation. This segregation can be measured by a *racial dissimilarity index*. It is the percentage of blacks who would have to move from one census tract (or other measurement zone) to another in order to produce a uniform percentage of black residents in all tracts. In the thirty metropolitan areas with the largest black populations in 1990, the average racial dissimilarity index was 75.3 in 1970, 68.3 in 1980, and 66.5 in 1990.[18] Eight metropolitan areas—all in the Northeast or Midwest—still had 1990 indexes exceeding 80. These indexes are much higher than indexes for Hispanics or Asians. Moreover, blacks are highly separated from whites at all income levels. In the thirty metropolitan areas, the average black-white dissimilarity index was 74.4 for households with incomes of less than $25,000; 66.7 for those with incomes of $25,000 to $27,500; and 72.8 for those with incomes of $50,000 or more.[19] Clearly, black-white residential segregation is primarily racial, not economic.

Such segregation results from two types of behavior. The first is deliberate discrimination against blacks in housing market transactions. This has been illegal since 1968 but remains widespread. The federal government has tested the presence of this discrimination by sending comparable white and black couples ostensibly seeking housing into the offices of realtors and landlords and recording how they were treated.[20] Across the nation in 1977, blacks received less favorable treatment than whites in 48 percent of sales transactions and 39 percent of rentals. Similar tests conducted in 1988 showed favoritism toward whites in 34 percent of sales transactions and 45 percent of rentals.[21] Blacks were shown fewer available units, steered away from white or integrated neighborhoods, given less information about possible financing, or refused services outright. Analyses of how potential borrowers have been treated by mortgage lending agencies has revealed similar patterns of discrimination.[22] Moreover, in many metropolitan areas, some blacks moving into mainly white areas have been greeted by violence. All these illegal but still widespread actions make it difficult for black people at all income levels to move into mainly white neighborhoods.

The second cause of racial segregation in housing is a basic difference in how blacks and whites feel about living with members of the other group. Most blacks would like to live in neighborhoods that were half black and half white.[23] But most whites would not like to live in neighborhoods more than 33 percent black, and a majority would try to move out of neighborhoods that were 50 percent black.

These preferences ultimately lead to totally segregated neighborhoods, even if both whites and blacks prefer what they view as racially integrated living.[24] Once a neighborhood becomes more than 33 percent black, few whites will move in. But blacks continue to move in because it still seems desirably mixed. The average residential neighborhood has a turnover of 10 to 20 percent a year for reasons unconnected with racial change. When nearly all newcomers are black, it does not take long for the neighborhood to become almost totally black, even if no whites move out for purely racial reasons. This process is not universal, but it is widespread enough to make achievement of stable, racially integrated neighborhoods extremely difficult.

Residential segregation, combined with a higher poverty rate among blacks, tends to isolate poor black households in concentrated-poverty areas much more than would occur if no racial segregation existed. So the separation of low-income households from middle- and upper-income ones is much greater among blacks than among whites. In 1990 the proportion of all poor persons living in concentrated poverty areas was 16.6 percent among blacks but only 1.9 percent among whites.[25] This concentration of poor blacks is a major cause of the development of an "oppositional culture" among some inner-city residents. Their social values are opposite those held by most Americans. They deliberately "do poorly in school, denigrate conventional employment, shun marriage, and raise children outside of marriage."[26] Once such values appear in these neighborhoods, the hostility of all whites and many middle-class blacks to accepting any low-income blacks as neighbors is strengthened. So residential segregation by race creates results that intensify support for its continuance, even though it is tremendously destructive to society as a whole.

The Regional Nature of Growth-Related Problems

Although many local governments try to deal with them in isolation, growth-related problems are regional rather than local in nature.

Traffic Congestion

Peak-hour traffic congestion arises because vehicles from all parts of a metropolitan area are trying to move to destinations in all parts at the same time and on the same roads.[27] The road and street network on which they move crosses all local boundaries and does not differentiate among communities. Therefore anticongestion policies adopted in any one locality will not be very effective—even within that locality itself—unless they are closely coordinated with policies adopted simultaneously in other communities. This is true even for most central cities. By 1980 only about 8 percent of all workers in an average metropolitan area were employed in its central business district; the proportion is probably lower today.[28] Even large cities, then, cannot control their regions' traffic flows through adoption of strictly local policies.

Lack of Affordable Housing

The shortage of housing affordable to low- and moderate-income households has two aspects. One is an absolute shortage of units they can afford. The other is the distance separating affordable units from areas where new jobs are being created. The absolute shortage arises because of disparity between the incomes of poor families and the minimum cost of "decent" housing. Curing this is beyond the scope of any growth management policies, local or regional. But the distance of affordable housing from outlying locations where many low- and moderate-income workers are employed results from local ordinances that prohibit construction of relatively low-cost units. Changing those ordinances would allow developers to build at least some affordable housing in all parts of a metropolitan area. Other regulatory changes would encourage owners of existing single-family units to rent accessory apartments. Both changes would permit many more low- and moderate-income workers to live closer to their jobs. The result would be less severe suburban shortages of low-wage workers, shorter average commuting journeys for many, and better educational opportunities for their children.

But this is not happening. Although each suburb has the legal authority to change its housing regulations without waiting for a regional housing strategy, the situation discourages unilateral action because most citizens do not want more low-income neighbors. Few suburban governments have voluntarily removed their regulatory obstacles to affordable housing.[29] The barriers will fall only if there is external pressure to remove them or to change local officials' incentives. Only state governments have the constitutional power to alter the rules under which local governments operate. But states must exert such pressures on all the suburban communities within their jurisdictions, not just one or a few. Besides, local resentment against state removal of barriers would be greatly diminished if residents of each community realized the same requirements were being imposed on all other communities. Only a policy encouraging the development of affordable housing throughout an entire region can effectively attack this problem.

The Isolation of the Inner Cities

The poorest people are concentrated in a few neighborhoods in the central city and some older suburbs, but their socioeconomic isolation results from the regionwide hierarchy of neighborhoods caused by deliberately exclusionary policies of the suburbs distant from these inner-city neighborhoods. Thus the responsibility for creating impoverished inner-city neighborhoods is to some extent regional.

Air, Water, and Solid Waste Pollution

The inherently regional nature of pollution problems is obvious for air pollution. But although flows of water within a region can be more effectively channeled than flows of air, communities often draw water from the same lakes, rivers, or aquifers, and the behavior of each necessarily affects the supply available to the others. Similarly, the way each community treats its liquid wastes can directly affect the welfare of surrounding communities. Because management of solid wastes permits more discretionary control, purely local policies have a better chance of being effective. Yet appropriate sites for solid waste disposal are usually found in just a few places, so that regional management of its disposal is more likely to be effective and socially efficient than purely local management.

Siting Locally Undesirable Land Uses

If all policymaking regarding the siting of locally undesirable land uses that produce vital regional benefits were left to individual communities, each would reject every proposed site and no facilities would be built. Only decisionmaking that places high priority on the interests of the entire region and either overrides the objections of individual localities or compensates their citizens can find socially efficient sites.

Infrastructure Finance

Most localities believe shopping centers, office parks, and other commercial land uses and expensive, single-family residences generate more local revenues than they absorb, so the localities try to capture such facilities.[30] Most localities also believe the expenditure demands of multifamily and high-density single-family housing are larger than the revenues they produce. So most local governments try to prevent the development of such housing or hold it to a minimum. Yet such housing must be located somewhere to accommodate the workers running the commercial facilities every community wants. These policies breed local competition inconsistent with efficient regional development. Resolving this inconsistency requires a regional perspective and regional policy.

Excessive Loss of Open Space

Retaining open land imposes obvious costs. By blocking more intensive development, it prevents the land's owners from realizing higher prices, prevents the local government from collecting higher property taxes and possibly sales tax revenues, and does nothing to create jobs. For society as a whole, these costs may be unimportant; the intensive development that might have occurred will move somewhere else nearby. But that does not offset the losses of potential gains endured by the landowners and the local government. Therefore, where private land ownership and public governance are fragmented, landowners and local officials will fight against having their land designated as community open space serving the entire metropolitan area.

Conclusions

Effective public policy responses to growth-related problems are inhibited by three factors stemming from the fragmentation of government powers over land use. The first is the disparity between the regional scope of growth-related problems and the localized scope of government land use powers. The second is that the incentives facing households, local elected officials, and local government agencies encourage them to support parochial perspectives. The third is that the socioeconomic hierarchy of neighborhoods and localities generated by development creates radically unequal qualities of environments for different social groups. To achieve effective policy responses to growth-related problems, each factor must be thoroughly altered or offset. But this structure is intrinsic in low-density growth. Each factor directly serves what middle- and upper-income Americans, who comprise a majority of households, perceive to be their best interests.

In a democracy, institutions that directly and significantly benefit a large majority are extremely difficult to change through political action. Politicians are strongly motivated to continue supporting what most of their constituents want. Overcoming the joint effects of these three factors will therefore not be easy; it may not even be possible. Yet unless the effects of fragmented government structures are effectively counteracted, the growth-related problems described in chapter 1 cannot be significantly remedied.

3

Local Growth Management Policies

L OCAL GOVERNMENTS have adopted many different growth
management policies to respond to growth-related prob-
lems.[1] But each jurisdiction tends to adopt policies designed to benefit
its own residents and disregards their effects on the rest of the metropolitan area. This parochial viewpoint causes serious discrepancies
between the welfare of individual communities and that of the entire
metropolitan area. This chapter analyzes the effects of such policies
on growth patterns in metropolitan areas.

Growth Management and Social Welfare

What are the effects of local growth management policies on social
welfare? Answering this question is not easy. It is difficult to measure
the effects of specific policies on different groups. Moreover, various
"communities" are involved: the locality adopting the policies, surrounding localities, the metropolitan area, and the nation. And nearly
all policies that affect growth benefit some people and harm others,
so their distributional effects are also important. Finally, weighing the
social desirability of benefiting one group at the expense of another
requires making comparisons of personal welfare that involve subjective value judgments.

Nevertheless, some important conclusions can be drawn about the
effects of familiar growth management policies. In analyzing these
effects I will use the following principles.

—Analysis of social welfare must take into account the private and
social benefits and costs created by specific policies, rather than focusing only on benefits, or only on costs, or only on private or social
forms of either.

31

—Many policies adopted by one locality have detectable impacts elsewhere. Thus some minimum spillover threshold is necessary to bring the welfare of members of other localities into consideration in evaluating the desirability of any one locality's policies. Normally, however, the persons and communities whose welfare is relevant in evaluating each locality's growth management policies include the residents of the entire metropolitan area.

—If groups having dominant political power within a locality can benefit by approving growth management policies that impose costs mainly on others, the dominant groups are likely to carry such policies too far. They may, for instance, sharply restrict the number of new housing units that can be built, which may drive up the prices of both new and existing units. Higher prices benefit local homeowners and impose costs mainly on renters, whether they live in the locality that has approved the policy or elsewhere in the metropolitan area. Because the beneficiaries bear few of the costs of their actions, they will tend to ignore those costs in deciding how stringent to make the regulations.

—To prevent unfairness, growth-related policies should be designed so that people making specific choices under those policies must bear private marginal costs equivalent to the social marginal costs resulting from their choices. This will motivate them to make only those choices for which they are willing to pay those social costs. For example, solo drivers using congested roads during peak hours should be charged tolls because they impose delays on others.

—Growth-related policies that rely on voluntary market transactions are usually preferable to those that rely on regulations. Unfortunately, however, voluntary market transactions will often not equate private marginal costs and benefits with social marginal costs and benefits. For example, the noise and air pollution from a busy highway harm nearby residents, even though they have not entered into any transactions with people using the highway. Regulatory remedies may be required in many cases of such direct effects.

—Growth management policies that benefit high-income groups but impose significant costs on similarly sized or larger lower-income groups are to that extent socially undesirable. Lower-income people cannot provide for the necessities of life as easily as those with higher incomes.

Goals of Growth Management Policies

Local governments adopt growth management policies to achieve one or more of the following goals:

—limiting the total amount of new development to reduce increases in traffic congestion on roads and in other public facilities and to restrict added infrastructure costs;

—slowing the pace of new development;

—shifting the costs of added infrastructure to new development to avoid raising the taxes of existing residents;

—regulating local pollution sources more effectively;

—preventing low-income households from entering the locality so as to maintain local home values, limit additional taxes, and maintain the socioeconomic status of existing residents.

Economic Effects of Growth Management Policies

The substance and enforcement of growth management policies vary enormously, so measuring and comparing their effects is difficult. However, all have one or more of the following economic effects. Some policies restrict allowable uses of specific sites to those that are less than the most profitable to developers. They may, for instance, prohibit commercial structures taller than five stories. Growth management policies often limit annual additions to the supply of various types of property in the adopting community. This slows the pace of development and inevitably diverts potential new development to other localities nearby. Restrictions on supply also increase the prices of the types of property concerned without increasing development costs, thereby increasing developers' profits.

Many growth management policies—those requiring large lots, for example, or minimum floor areas for new housing—impose higher costs on developers, lengthen the time required to complete a project, or reduce permissible densities. Such cost increases can often exceed $20,000 a unit. These actions raise product prices and reduce the profits of developers.

Some growth management policies require governments to build adequate streets or sewer systems to serve a proposed subdivision before housing can be built there. The reluctance of governments to

TABLE 3-1. *Local Growth Management Policies*

Residential policies
  Population growth caps
  Residential building permit caps
  Infrastructure adequacy requirements
  Residential downzoning
  Voter approval for upzoning
  Super majority approval for upzoning
  Residential land rezoned exclusively for other uses
  Requirement for developer infrastructure contributions before approval
  Requirement for environmental impact study
  Exclusion of multifamily uses
  Historic district designation
  Designation as critical environmental area
  Requirement to include low- or moderate-income housing
  Water or sewer or permit moratorium
  Special assessments
  Restrictive covenants on design, use
  Requirement for endangered species offset

Commercial and industrial policies
  Commercial square footage limits
  Industrial square footage limits
  Infrastructure adequacy requirements
  Commercial or industrial locational restrictions
  Building height limits

pay these added costs often causes them to delay projects, which also raises developers' costs.

Table 3-1 lists various types of local growth management policies. All of these economic effects raise the market prices of new and existing housing and other types of properties in the localities adopting the policies.

Housing Price Responsiveness to Growth Management

The extent to which local growth management policies increase housing prices varies in accordance with the principle of housing supply substitutability. This principle states that the effect of any locality's growth management policies on its housing prices will depend on how easily people priced out of living there can find similar housing available in nearby localities. Assume city A adopts stringent limits on how

TABLE 3-1. *Continued*

Commercial downzoning
Requirement for developer to provide infrastructure contributions before approval
Requirement for environmental impact study
Historic district designation
Designation as critical environmental area
Linkage fees for housing, art, and so forth
Water or sewer or permit moratorium
Special assessments
Restrictive covenants on design, use
Requirement for endangered species offset

Planning measures and other policies
Growth management element in general plan
Urban growth limit line, greenbelt
Public acquisition of land (including land banks)
Preferential taxation of farmland
Transfer of development rights
Exclusive agricultural zoning
Planned unit development zoning

Sources: Derived from classifications by David R. Godschalk and others, *Constitutional Issues of Growth Management* (Chicago: ASPO Press, 1977), pp. 240–47; and Madelyn Glickfeld and Ned Levine, "The New Land Use Regulation 'Revolution': Why California's Local Jurisdictions Enact Growth Control and Management Measures," Graduate School of Architecture and Urban Planning, University of California at Los Angeles, June 22, 1990.

many new housing units can be built in it each year. If people can easily buy almost identical homes in adjacent cities B or C, which have no limits, prices of homes in city A will not rise much above what they were before growth management, other things being equal. But if there are no nearby markets similar to those in city A, or nearby markets also have exclusionary regulations, potential buyers will be unable to substitute units nearby. They will bid against each other for the smaller supply of available units in city A, driving up prices.

Dozens of studies have attempted to determine just how much local growth management policies increase the prices of land and housing, under widely varying conditions, with almost equally varying results.[2] Among the highest estimates are those from a 1987 study done in the San Francisco Bay area. It contended that a locality adopting a growth management program or a housing moratorium for at least one year from 1973 through 1979 experienced home prices 17 to 38 percent higher than prices of similar housing in localities without such policies.[3]

After Petaluma, California, placed an annual cap on building permits in 1972, prices were 9 percent higher than prices of similar units in nearby Santa Rosa.[4] And a study of Davis, California, concluded that housing prices were almost 9 percent higher in 1980 than they would have been if growth management policies had not been adopted.[5]

A study conducted by David Segal and Philip Srinivasan used a subjective restrictiveness index as one variable to explain variations in housing prices among fifty-one metropolitan areas. Areas that had withdrawn 20 percent or more of their suburban land from development because of growth controls, they concluded, experienced 6 percent greater inflation in housing prices than areas that had not.[6] A study of the impact of growth controls in Santa Cruz, California, concluded, "after ten years of growth control, the prices of owner-occupied houses were 10 percent higher than they would have been in the absence of controls."[7]

In San Diego County the median price of new homes rose from $150,000 in late 1987 to $245,000 in late 1989. This 63 percent increase occurred shortly after the five largest jurisdictions in the county drastically reduced the number of units they permitted to be built each year. The inventory of unsold homes fell by 60 percent from January to September 1988 as a result of strong demand.[8] William A. Fischel calculated that the early and widespread adoption of growth controls by California localities caused housing prices in the state to be 33 to 43 percent higher than prices elsewhere.[9] Several of these studies concluded that growth management policies raised housing prices 10 percent more than they would have risen without such policies. Other studies found much greater impacts.[10]

A 10 percent increase in the U.S. median price of existing homes in late 1991 would have made it impossible for about 4 percent of U.S. households to buy a median-priced home.[11] Any policy that reduces the availability of a locality's housing for 4 percent of the households in a metropolitan area should be considered socially significant. If local growth management policies increase housing prices much more than 10 percent, their effects would be much worse. And if many localities in a metropolitan area adopt such policies, as often happens, their combined effects will be still greater.

Higher Housing Prices and Social Welfare

Even if housing prices rise soon after a community adopts growth management policies, the policies cannot be labeled socially undesirable without further consideration. Such a conclusion is not necessarily justified even if all other causes for the increase—general inflation, increased population, higher incomes—can be ruled out. The increase might have occurred because the growth management policies made the locality more desirable and increased the demand for housing. In that case higher prices would reflect social benefits to the community.

If greater demand rather than restricted supply is the main cause of higher housing prices, the production of new housing in a community will normally increase as builders respond to the stronger market. Yet the failure of new housing construction to rise would not be an infallible sign that demand has not risen. Demand could increase even if these policies themselves raised development costs or otherwise restricted additions to supply. Then production would not necessarily increase too; it might very well decrease.

Stronger demand for the housing caused by a locality's greater exclusiveness benefits its homeowners. But it also causes higher rents there and elsewhere and generates higher home prices that prevent homeowners living elsewhere from moving into that locality. Unless the adopting locality is very large, the number of people benefited by growth management policies is likely to be much smaller than the number living elsewhere whose housing choices are restricted. (The relative size of the benefits and costs per household are difficult to judge a priori, but the benefits for each household aided are probably larger than the costs imposed on each household restricted.) And the people who benefit almost surely have higher incomes than those who are penalized. Restricting the housing choices of low- and moderate-income people also reinforces the socioeconomic hierarchy of neighborhoods, unjustly isolating those with the lowest-incomes from the remainder of society, with effects detrimental to the poor and to society generally.

Considered from the viewpoint of society as a whole, local growth management policies that raise housing prices by increasing the exclusivity of the community rather than by creating more parks, better schools, and other amenities are likely to have net harmful effects on social welfare even though they provide net benefits to homeowners in the adopting localities. Housing prices in the adopting locality may also have risen solely because local policies increased development costs or limited additions to supply without raising demand. Higher prices then reflect a pure social cost because the efficiency of society's resource allocations has decreased.[12]

The Principle of Competitive Land Supply

Another factor influencing the effects of growth management policies on housing prices is the amount of land available for development in the regulating jurisdiction. The principle of competitive land supply states that for land use regulation to avoid significantly increasing the final price of developed property, the total supply of land of each type designated as available for development in any given period must be a multiple of the amount likely to be absorbed during that period. If a locality limits to certain sites the land that can be developed within a given period, it confers a preferred market position on those sites. In economists' terminology, any such limitation shifts the demand curve for developable land upward and to the left, raising land prices.[13] If the limitation is stringent enough, it may also confer monopolistic powers on the owners of those sites, permitting them to raise land prices substantially.

For example, assume a community designates a certain 1,000 acres as the only land legally developable for housing during the next five years. But housing construction there has been absorbing 200 acres a year. Therefore, the owners of these 1,000 acres control 100 percent of the land likely to be demanded for housing there in the next five years. They could charge developers very high prices for sites, which would compel the developers to charge higher prices for the housing there.

Exactly how large the available supply of land must be in relation to average annual absorption rates has not been empirically determined. My guess is that it must be at least two or three times as large and probably more. In Oregon a multiplier of twenty has been built into land use regulation laws. Every Oregon locality must draw an urban growth boundary indicating the area where development will be permitted. It is required to include a twenty-year supply of vacant and usable land, based on recent absorption rates. It must also redraw its boundary every five years. This multiplier seems high enough to create a good cushion in case land absorption rates should speed up right after the boundary is drawn or updated.

Not all land in this large supply has the same locational qualities or prestige, however. Shortages of parcels with unusual qualities can still occur while the total supply of developable land remains adequate. For example, prices of single-family lots in the prestigious Lake Oswego area outside Portland, Oregon, have risen much more than average land prices in the entire metropolitan area. It is probably impossible to prevent such effects in small areas because no one can make reliable predictions of housing demand at the micromarket level.

Growth Management Policies and Metropolitan Growth

Local growth management policies have significant impacts on the overall growth of metropolitan areas. In the long run they restrict the supply of new properties or increase the costs of producing the supply or both. The resulting higher prices and rents of newly built housing units cause the prices and rents of existing units to rise because some demand will be diverted to them. Higher prices and rents reduce the supply of housing that low- and moderate-income households can afford. Outside of the adopting locality itself, the extent of the injury per household caused by any one locality's growth restrictions is usually small. But the impact over the metropolitan area may be sizable, especially if many localities adopt growth limits concurrently, as has frequently happened.[14]

True, higher housing prices benefit owners of existing units, who make up most of U.S. households and a majority of households in most metropolitan areas. So higher prices do not necessarily cause a net welfare loss to an entire metropolitan area. But higher prices do cause a net regressive redistribution of incomes or wealth or both within the metropolitan area. To that extent such policies are socially undesirable.

Growth management policies also tend to spread urban development in a metropolitan area over a larger territory than would otherwise have been the case. This effect could be avoided if other localities accept the demand diverted from the adopting communities by permitting higher densities. But that is not likely. Most suburbs resist increases in density; many have down-zoned permissible densities. So growth diverted from a locality to its neighbors tends to spread the metropolitan area's growth. This is especially likely if the localities adopting limits cover a substantial portion of the metropolitan area.

Territorial spreading generates both benefits and costs to residents. It benefits those who prefer low-density settlement patterns and open space. Thus spreading does not in itself necessarily cause a net loss of welfare to society. However, it does increase total travel in the area, adding to total traffic movements and air pollution, which are costly to residents outside the adopting locality. A single locality's adopting growth management would, of course, add only marginally to those costs. But hundreds of localities are adopting such limits, and their collective effects can be enormous, even within a single metropolitan area.

Limitations of Growth Management Policies

Growth management policies are typically adopted by one or a few localities acting independently, not by entire metropolitan areas. As a result, the effectiveness of the policies is limited by the dynamics of metropolitan areas. These limitations can be expressed as two principles: imperviousness and growth diversion.

The principle of imperviousness is that the total job or population growth in a metropolitan area cannot be significantly changed (that is, altered enough to affect the welfare of area residents in ways they notice) by policies adopted in any one suburban locality. This is true even though individual localities can greatly influence their own population and job growth rates, either positively or negatively, through various local ordinances. According to one study using data from 1970–75, what does affect population growth is the metropolitan area's rate of job growth, its average January temperature, its rate of natural increase (the excess of births over deaths as a percentage of total population), its unemployment rate, and the percentage of Hispanic people in its largest city. Factors most affecting job growth include an area's overall rates of natural increase and immigration, its industry mix (the more nationally fast-growing industries it contains, the higher its rate of job growth), whether it is a state capital, the estimated cost of living there, income per capita, the rate of growth of income per capita, and the total number of jobs there in 1970 (the larger the total, the smaller the job growth from 1970 to 1975).[15] Most of these factors are not controllable by public policy, and none can be directly influenced by any one suburban government's policies.

A central city can influence the total growth of its metropolitan area under some circumstances. The city's population must be a large proportion of the entire area's population, and the city's land area must represent a large proportion of the metropolitan area's territory. But the policies of such large central cities influence areawide rates of job growth mainly in the long run. For example, New York City's adoption of high tax rates motivated many businesses to move out of the New York metropolitan area altogether, or not to move into it, or to shift expansion to other areas. But these effects were not felt until long after the passage of those policies.

In theory, if most of the suburban governments in a metropolitan area simultaneously adopted coordinated ordinances to limit growth, they could reduce the area's growth within its initially defined boundaries. Such cohesive action has never occurred in the United States.[16] But even then, as long as the economic and other factors stimulating the area's growth remained unchanged, people would continue to move into the area. Defying local laws, they would occupy sites in unincorporated areas, move into adjacent counties, or overcrowd existing housing within the metropolitan area.

Thus particular suburbs cannot escape some effects of growth in their metropolitan area by limiting growth within their own boundaries. Very rapid overall growth clearly reduced the quality of life in southern California during the 1980s. Many residents are appalled by the prospect of even worse degradation from further growth. But they cannot prevent more overall growth by prohibiting further entry into their own localities. Although some localities virtually halted growth within their own boundaries, the area's total population soared during the late 1980s. Because of continued heavy immigration—legal and illegal—from Latin America, this trend is likely to continue.

A corollary of the imperviousness principle is the principle of growth diversion. It states that successful efforts by any individual suburb to limit growth within its own boundaries will merely shift all growth that would have occurred there to other parts of its metropolitan area. Such beggar-thy-neighbor policies do not resolve basic social difficulties but instead try to change who must cope with them. Effectively dealing with the problems of metropolitan area growth requires regional policy responses, not just local ones.

A second implication of the principle of growth diversion is that when any locality reduces its own average residential density, unless other localities increase their permissible densities, the built-up portions of the metropolitan area will eventually occupy a larger territory than they would have before the density reduction. Such spreading could be offset if older localities close to the center of the metropolitan area increase the density of their development at the same time that new-growth localities decrease density. Close-in suburbs typically experience an increase in the intensity of development as the frontier of growth passes beyond them. But they do so mainly by adding more commercial, industrial, and other nonresidential buildings. And there is no inherent link between decreased density in new-growth communities and intensified development in older ones. So it is still reasonable to conclude that growth management policies which reduce densities in new-growth localities spread the development of the metropolitan area over a larger territory.

Part 2
Relations between Cities and Suburbs

4

Links between Central Cities and Suburbs

*P*OWERFUL FORCES have been weakening the ties between central cities and their surrounding suburbs. Some observers even proclaim that big cities are now functionally obsolete or will soon become so.[1] At the very least, these forces threaten to persuade many suburbanites and other people to withhold the economic and other supports that cities need to perform their basic social functions. This chapter explores the links between central cities and suburbs and recent trends affecting them.

The Attenuation of the Ties

The first force weakening links is the evolution itself of large and growing metropolitan areas. When U.S. metropolitan areas grow larger, they evolve from a center focus toward a low-density network (see appendix A). Suburbs become more urban, assuming more of the functions and services formerly performed only in the central city. Fewer suburban residents need to visit central cities or even to interact indirectly with them. At the fringes of the few very large metropolitan areas that have nearly arrived at the ultimate low-density form, suburban residents may almost never interact with the city.

Many central cities have also been losing population, particularly in the Northeast and Midwest. Among the forty-four metropolitan areas in 1990 with more than 1 million residents, the suburbs of forty-two gained population from 1980 to 1990; the central cities of eighteen lost population.[2] As a result, the political power of cities in state legislatures and Congress has deteriorated and that of suburbs has strengthened. This has weakened the ability of cities to influence the share of government spending allocated to them and their residents.

Changes in Communications and Transportation

Developments in communications and transportation are also causing suburbanites to believe they can get along without central cities.
The widespread availability of personal computers, modems, fiber op-
tic networks, and fax machines has meant that millions of workers no
longer need to gather every day at one location with other members
of their organizations to work effectively. Many people work at home
at least part of the time, and a growing number of large organizations
have moved routine operations to lower-cost quarters not only in the
suburbs but as far away as South Dakota, Puerto Rico, Hong Kong,
and Ireland. More and more executives manage their firms from thousands of miles away through electronic means. Intensifying this decentralization is that the product of many enterprises is some form of
information rather than physical objects or personal services.[3] Information can be transmitted nearly instantly almost anywhere at very
low cost.

Under these conditions, physical proximity no longer seems necessary for interaction with other people. When it is, the increasing use
of automobiles and air transport has facilitated it. The centrality of
central cities has thus lost a lot of its importance for maintaining economic efficiency.

Job Losses in Cities

Because of these developments, cities are losing jobs to their suburbs, and suburban employment is growing faster than central city
employment. Decennial censuses do not gather information about
where jobs are located, so it is difficult to measure the loss of jobs. But
a study that analyzed the locations of jobs in the sixty largest PMSAs
from 1970 to 1986 using postal district boundaries instead of municipal
boundaries showed that the central postal zones contained 52 percent
of all metropolitan area jobs in 1976, but only 47 percent in 1986 (table
4–1). Two-thirds of all jobs added in these metropolitan areas after
1976 were in the outer postal zones. They captured 93.5 percent of
manufacturing jobs added in the metropolitan areas from 1976 to 1980,
and all of those jobs added from 1980 to 1986. The central zones lost 6
percent of their 1980 manufacturing jobs, while the outer zones gained
5 percent, with the biggest gains occurring outside metropolitan areas
altogether.[4]

TABLE 4-1. *Location of Jobs in Metropolitan Areas, 1976, 1980, 1986*[a]

Year	Central city[b]		Suburbs[c]		Total metropolitan	
	Thousands	Percent	Thousands	Percent	Thousands	Percent
1976	17,418	52	15,991	48	33,409	100
1980	19,041	49	19,541	51	38,581	100
1986	21,243	47	23,996	53	45,238	100
1976–80	1,623	9	3,550	22	5,172	15
1980–86	2,202	12	4,455	23	6,657	17

Source: Mark Alan Hughes and Julie E. Sternberg, "The New Metropolitan Reality: Where the Rubber Meets the Road in Antipoverty Policy," Urban Institute, Washington, 1992, p. 10.

a. Sixty largest PMSAs in 1980.
b. Employment in PMSA central postal zones.
c. Employment elsewhere in metropolitan area.

Another study of urban decline computed changes from 1960 to 1989 in the number of employed residents in each of the seventy-seven largest U.S. cities.[5] Eighteen had fewer residents employed in 1989 than in 1960, and seven—Pittsburgh, Newark, St. Louis, Louisville, Buffalo, Cleveland, and Detroit—had lost more than 25 percent between 1965 and 1989.

Thus the cities identified in chapter 5 as severely declining are suffering from relative job losses compared with their suburbs, and many are experiencing absolute losses. The suburbanization of jobs decreases the dependence of many suburban residents on their central cities, since they now both live and work outside those cities.

Geographic Separation of Income Groups

Another force weakening ties between central cities and suburbs is an increasing geographic separation of socioeconomic groups. In 1990, median household income was 38 percent higher in the suburbs than in the central cities. In metropolitan areas of 1 million or more residents, household income was 45 percent higher in suburbs; in smaller metropolitan areas the difference was 26 percent.[6] Low-income people are becoming more and more concentrated in central cities, where the least costly housing is located. Cities also typically provide more services aimed directly at the poor than most suburbs provide because they have many more poor voters and are politically more sensitive to their needs. Some poor people prefer living where access to these services is convenient.

As a metropolitan area's population grows, the concentration of low-income households differentiates its central city from the suburbs. The area of the central city is normally fixed because it is surrounded by independent suburbs that resist annexation. As suburbs expand, the percentage of the area's population living in the central city dwindles. If low-income households remain a roughly constant proportion of all households in the metropolitan area but become concentrated in the central city, they will inevitably become a larger proportion of all households there than in the suburbs. The proportion of all city residents who had incomes below the poverty line expanded from less than 15 percent in 1970 to 19 percent in 1990. In all the suburbs combined, the share increased from 8.1 percent in 1970 to 8.7 percent in 1990 (figure 4–1). In addition, poor residents are more concentrated in destitute neighborhoods in cities than in suburbs. In 1990, 10 percent of all central city residents but a much smaller proportion of suburban residents lived in census tracts where 40 percent or more of the people had incomes below the poverty line.[7] The proportion of all U.S. poor people living in central cities increased from 1970 to 1990; the percentage in suburbs rose along with the suburbs' share of the nation's total population (figure 4–1).

Poverty among children is more concentrated in central cities than elsewhere. Of all persons younger than 18 years of age living in central cities in 1990, 30.5 were in households below the poverty level. The proportion was 13.3 percent in suburbs and 22.9 percent in nonmetropolitan areas. For the entire nation, one out of five children lived in poverty, more than in either 1970 or 1980.[8]

Neighborhoods in which poor people are concentrated are more seriously plagued by crime, drug abuse, unemployment, births out of wedlock, and other social ills than are higher-income neighborhoods. Residents of suburbs tend to associate these conditions with central cities per se. This strengthens their desire to avoid visiting central cities and to prevent low-income central city residents from moving into their communities.

Expenditures and revenues also separate city and suburb. The costs of providing police and fire protection, judicial systems, public hospitals, and jails are much higher in low-income areas than in higher-income ones. For example, a city with "a poverty rate 1 percentage point higher than another city's will have police costs that are 5.5 percent higher."[9]

FIGURE 4-1. *Share of Population with Incomes below the Poverty Line, by Type of Area, 1970, 1980, 1990*

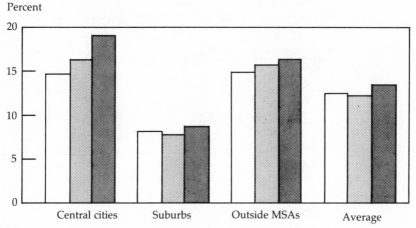

Proportion of residents in each type of area who are poor

Percent

Central cities   Suburbs   Outside MSAs   Average

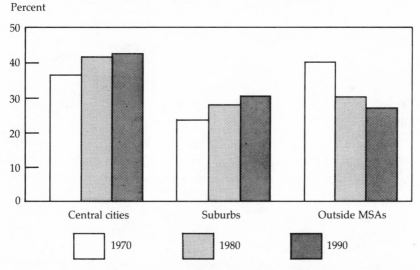

Proportion of all U.S. poor residents in each type of area

Percent

Central cities   Suburbs   Outside MSAs

1970   1980   1990

Sources: Author's calculations using data from Bureau of the Census, *State and Metropolitan Area Data Book: 1986* (Department of Commerce, 1986), pp. 364, 366; Bureau of the Census, *Statistical Abstract of the United States: 1984* (Department of Commerce, 1984), p. 26; and Department of Housing and Urban Development, *The President's National Urban Policy Report: 1978* (1978).

FIGURE 4-2. *City Expenditures and Revenues per Capita, 1988, by Population in 1986*

Population

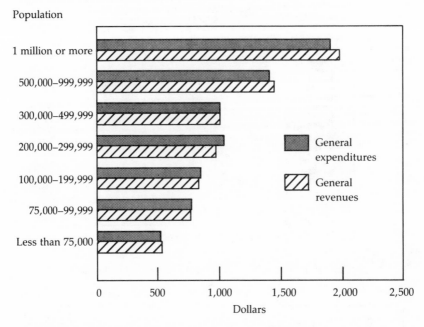

Source: Bureau of the Census, *Statistical Abstract of the United States: 1991* (Department of Commerce, 1991), p. 301.

Meanwhile, the revenues raised per 1,000 residents in large cities tend to be lower than those in smaller cities. In 1982, cities with populations over 1 million had an average revenue-raising capacity 15 percent smaller than the average for the seventy-eight cities studied; cities with populations less than 100,000 had a capacity 11.6 percent above the average.[10]

Because they have heavier expenses and weaker revenue-raising capacity, central cities also typically have higher property and other tax rates than do surrounding suburbs. That decreases their attractiveness for higher-income residents. In 1988, cities with 1 million or more residents had per capita spending 82 percent higher than did cities with 200,000 to 300,000 residents and per capita revenues 101 percent higher (figure 4–2). And cities with 200,000 to 300,000 residents had per capita revenues 78 percent higher than did cities with populations less than 75,000 and per capita expenditures 92 percent higher. Most suburban communities have populations smaller than 75,000, and most cities with 200,000 or more residents are central cities.

The growth of large metropolitan areas increasingly separates poor from nonpoor residents not only spatially but also jurisdictionally. This permits residents of relatively high-income suburbs to isolate themselves doubly from the problems of low-income citizens.

Increasing Ethnic and Cultural Diversity

The ethnic diversity of central cities is growing because of larger net immigration in the past two decades than at any time since the first decades of the century. Most recent immigrants have come from Latin America or Asia and have a wide variety of cultural backgrounds—children attending the Los Angeles public schools, for example, speak more than one hundred languages. Newly arrived immigrants settle in central cities and older suburbs because most are poor. In Los Angeles, Chicago, Philadelphia, Miami, and Baltimore, some neighborhoods have become ethnic islands of Koreans, Vietnamese, Cubans, Haitians, and so on.

This increase in ethnic diversity, added to the large black populations in many cities, has produced high overall proportions of minorities. Meanwhile, most new suburbs are predominantly white, although there are growing enclaves of black residents in the suburbs of big cities with large black populations. In six of the ten largest U.S. cities in 1990, blacks, American Indians, Asians, and Hispanics comprised 60 percent of total population; in only one were minorities less than 42 percent. (These groups made up 24.8 percent of the total U.S. population in 1990.) The combined minority population of the thirty-one largest central cities was more than 50 percent of their total population.[11]

Although minority groups have become economically much more integrated with whites in workplaces, they are not much more integrated residentially or socially. The resulting lack of social contacts between suburbs and central cities increases feelings of alienation for both.

How Independent Are the Suburbs?

As a result of all these forces, many suburban residents, especially in higher-income and new-growth suburbs, believe their own welfare is less and less connected to the welfare of city residents and the fiscal condition of city governments. Moreover, suburban residents are gaining more political power in both state legislatures and Congress as their share of the nation's population increases. Thus their ability to ignore or disregard the problems of central cities is not only psychological and social but increasingly extends to the allocation of federal resources.

But the long-run welfare of suburban residents is still closely linked to how well central cities and their residents perform significant social and economic functions in each metropolitan area. The belief among suburbanites that they are independent of central cities is a delusion. So is the belief that central cities are obsolete. Both fallacies have consequences dangerous to America's economic and social health.

Social and Economic Functions of Central Cities

Some social and economic functions crucial to the prosperity of every metropolitan area as a whole can be performed only within its central city, at least given the present structure of American metropolitan areas.

Creative Contacts among Top Leaders

First, face-to-face contacts of community leaders in a central city's downtown stimulate creativity. Cities have always been cultural centers, partly because of the stimulation provided by the day-to-day mingling of diverse residents. Business executives, politicians, journalists, educators, scientists, labor leaders, and government officials still need to meet each other regularly. Only such personal contacts provide spontaneous stimulation and permit them to conduct confidential business. Although a few suburban edge cities also have large agglomerations of facilities, only one spot within each region can be the habitual gathering place of most movers and shakers.

Undoubtedly, advances in communications have diminished the importance of face-to-face contacts. But electronic contacts cannot be randomized or accidental in the same way as meetings at offices, restaurants, stores, churches, or just on the street. Nor can electronic meetings convey the same completeness of meaning as face-to-face contacts in which each person is exposed to the body language and full expressional nuances of the others.[12] And because electronic contacts are susceptible to interception, they cannot be entirely entrusted with the confidential communications so important in politics and government affairs.

Specialized Activities and Facilities

One of Adam Smith's basic economic principles was that the extent of specialization that can be supported concerning any activity varies directly with the size of its market. The more clients the activity serves, the greater the investment in specialized processes and machinery justified to serve them. High-fashion retail outlets, major medical centers, operas and other cultural activities, and specialized wholesale suppliers serving a thin but widely spread market need the combination of one location accessible to the entire metropolitan area and the area's large market to thrive. Central cities or sites near them remain the most effective locations for such facilities.[13]

Hubs for Area Networks

Central cities also contain nodes or central switching facilities in technological networks—sewage purification systems, electrical power grids, telephone networks, water supply systems, railroads, and highway systems—serving entire metropolitan areas. In many cases these nodes were originally located near the downtown, and the networks that serve the remainder of the metropolitan area grew up around them. An entire network may have been constructed to converge in the central city, as major highway systems do. Although it would be technically possible to move these nodes into the suburbs, doing so would be expensive and disruptive. Even many airports serving entire regions are located within central cities, as in New York, Los Angeles, Washington D.C., Minneapolis, Atlanta, and Miami.

Housing for Low-Wage Workers

A major function of cities is to provide housing and related services for low-wage workers employed in the suburbs and those employed in the central city whose activities are vital to the prosperity of the suburbs. Suburban housing is often too costly to be occupied by these workers, but suburban communities need these people. Central cities not only provide affordable housing, but also provide associated public services such as schools and police protection.

Social and Economic Mobility for Immigrants

Cities traditionally provide upward mobility for recent immigrants. Many do not speak English and have few marketable skills, but in older city neighborhoods they find low-cost housing and opportunities for economic and social improvement through unskilled jobs and free public schools.

The proportion of unskilled jobs has, however, steadily shrunk in central cities, and most job growth has been in the suburbs. These changes have made it hard for immigrants to find suitable jobs in central cities. Many economists believe the United States should focus employment strategies on high-technology manufacturing and specialized services. That would send low-technology manufacturing to lower-wage facilities abroad and permit most Americans to perform higher-wage tasks. But to perform more skilled jobs, U.S. workers must have a high level of technical competence. This can be achieved only if economic opportunities and effective educational systems remain open in someplace easily accessible to new immigrants.

Such chances for upward mobility must occur mainly in central cities, with their affordable housing and clusters of persons from similar backgrounds with whom immigrants can establish family or cultural ties in spite of not knowing English. If this function is not performed effectively, the public sector will be saddled with providing expensive services that the taxes poor people pay cannot support. Income will have to be transferred to central cities from elsewhere. So suburban residents and all other taxpayers have a direct stake in the ability of central cities to continue turning immigrants into well-educated, self-supporting workers.

Other City Functions

Some social and economic functions crucial to the prosperity of entire metropolitan areas and now performed mainly in central cities could in theory be moved to the suburbs. But a huge investment in necessary facilities has already been made, and moving them to the suburbs would be extremely costly and disruptive. Although some functions have migrated to the suburbs, for a long time to come it will remain more economical to perform them in central cities.

Many of the nation's largest and best universities, including the University of Chicago, the University of California at Los Angeles,

Columbia, Georgetown, Yale, Brown, and Michigan are in central cities. Most important medical centers are, too, as are state legislatures, state agency offices, federal government offices, courthouses, and jails. These facilities are used extensively by people from suburbs and small towns. Each facility has generated an entourage of nearby services, firms, and facilities that make contributions essential to its success and support thousands of local residents. Although there is no intrinsic reason why these facilities must remain in central cities, moving them would require duplicating a great many structures and abandoning existing ones to less productive uses.

Businesses in central cities also employ suburban residents. In 1990, cities contained 78 million residents and their suburbs 115 million. Cities thus contained 40 percent of all metropolitan area residents but close to 50 percent of all metropolitan area jobs.[14] This means that one out of four employed persons who lived in suburbs still worked in central cities.

In theory most city jobs could be moved to the suburbs, and many cities have indeed been losing jobs to the suburbs for a long time. In fact, most new jobs are being created in the suburbs. Still, it would be costly to society to move all remaining city jobs to the suburbs. So the prosperity of America's suburbs will still depend heavily on employment located in central cities.

City Health, Suburban Welfare

Cities provide social and economic functions of great value for suburbs. But the welfare of suburbs also depends on the general health of central cities.

The City as a Good Site for Business

Many businesses and other organizations are not inherently tied to a specific metropolitan area. They can choose where to operate, or at least where to locate future growth. They will avoid metropolitan areas with bad reputations as places to do business. A metropolitan area's business reputation is heavily influenced by conditions in its central city. New York City, for instance, has high municipal and state taxes, high crime rates, short working hours, a very high cost of living, and many poorly trained graduates of its troubled public schools. Many businesses have either moved out, or refrained from moving activities into it. And when Philadelphia's city government had severe fiscal and managerial troubles in the late 1980s, 40 percent of the firms that moved out of the city abandoned the whole metropolitan area.[15]

Spillover of Bad Conditions

Some problems within central cities can reduce the quality of life in nearby suburbs. City air pollutants can drift, a common water source, such as one of the Great Lakes, can be polluted, and city traffic may clog surrounding communities. City criminals may operate in suburbs: certainly drug trafficking headquartered in cities feeds the addiction of suburban residents.

Central City Residents and Suburban Home Sales

The main wealth of most Americans consists of equity in their homes. Suburban households have high rates of homeownership, and when they try to sell their homes, they will need a pool of buyers to form a strong market. Because of the baby boom, a great many home-owners now 30 to 50 years old will want to sell their homes in the decades after 2000. But the number of younger buyers will be much smaller because of the baby bust of the 1960s and 1970s. To find ready demand, baby-boom homeowners will have to count on people who are presently less affluent and live in central cities. Only if these people have sufficient purchasing power and upward mobility to change residence will there be a strong market for millions of suburban homes. And that will in turn depend on the economic vitality of central cities.[16]

Federal and State Government Transfers to Cities

Because suburban residents have higher average incomes than city residents, they also pay higher federal income taxes. If cities are plagued by serious social problems that require financial assistance beyond their own means, they have to ask the federal government or their state governments to help them. Even though cities' political power in federal and state legislatures is weakening, if their problems become bad enough, the governments will be compelled to aid them. The worse those problems become, the more outside aid will have to be supplied, and a disproportionately large share of financing it will come from households with above-average incomes. This means greater federal and state tax burdens on suburban residents.

The Prosperity of the Nation's Economy

The economic welfare of American households is heavily influenced by general economic conditions. This includes the prosperity of the 78 million persons living in central cities, almost one-third of the nation's population. If any large share of them experiences economic adversity, that will cause a recession. During the regional recessions of 1985–89 and 1990–91, major layoffs by large American corporations affected thousands of suburban-dwelling, white-collar and executive workers in the Southwest, New England, and California. Home prices in California and northeastern suburbs fell sharply after 1988, though they remained higher than before the price run-up in the middle 1980s.

A study of incomes from 1979 to 1989 in the nation's seventy-eight largest metropolitan areas showed a high correlation between changes in the suburban and central city median incomes in each metropolitan area.[17]

The economic welfare of the 46 percent of the nation's population living in suburbs in 1990 will continue to be greatly affected by what happens to the 31 percent living in central cities. Moreover, if cities have such inadequate school systems that they cannot produce competent workers, that will weaken the ability of the U.S. economy to compete in global markets.

The Final Equation

Although the factors connecting the welfare of suburbs to the prosperity and general welfare of the cities are being gradually weakened, they will remain important for a long time. Unfortunately, although suburban residents can see every day the forces that weaken these links, the most vital remaining links are not apparent on a daily basis. The resulting illusion of independence from central cities is strongest among suburbanites who live and work in the suburbs, shop and play there, and may only rarely have contact with central cities and poorer people.

This link between cities and suburbs implies a broader meaning for the term community. When a suburban government, for example, adopts a growth management policy, it justifies doing so as "protecting the community's welfare." The community referred to consists of all persons living within that one jurisdiction and excludes everyone else.[18] Potential harm to outsiders is not considered relevant as long as the policy seems to benefit the adopting jurisdiction's insiders.

But as I have shown, no jurisdiction is an island. Every suburb is linked to its central city and to other suburbs. Therefore policymaking arrangements that do not consider the welfare of people who may be significantly affected by the policies created are not morally legitimate. True, there must be some practical geographic limit to how broadly *community* is defined for purposes of creating public policies. But the definition appropriate for evaluating the desirability of growth-related policies in a metropolitan area is the entire area. Yet the legal structure of U.S. metropolitan areas does not require decisionmakers in a jurisdiction to pay attention to the effects of their actions on people in other parts of the area. Thus the legal dimensions of the concept of community prevailing in the United States differ sharply from its ethical and moral dimensions.

This situation violates the basic axiom of democracy stated in the Declaration of Independence that "governments . . . deriv[e] their just powers from the consent of the governed." Everyone who is significantly affected by some public policy has a right to have a voice in determining that policy. This does not mean exercising sole power over the policy. But it does mean being included within the community whose welfare is explicitly considered in the formation and adoption of policies.

This sense of community must, however, extend beyond the ideal of not hurting other people. Growth-related and other policies adopted by each jurisdiction must do what they can to help those in other jurisdictions as a way of ultimately helping themselves. In terms of city-suburb links this means that revenue-strapped cities will need increased transfers of income, through state and federal government tax revenues, from the wealthier suburbs.

This conclusion does not imply that more money is all that would be necessary to improve conditions in central cities. Fundamental reforms of many aspects of city life from school systems to law enforcement to family structures to city bureaucracies are more important than additional funds. Without such reforms, more money will not be very effective. This is clear from the high levels of current spending on public schools in many low-quality big-city education systems.

But carrying out the required reforms is likely to require at least some additional external funding for nearly every endeavor. Without it, cities will increasingly have to compromise their functions, links between cities and suburbs will be further attenuated, and everyone's life will be poorer.

5

Urban Decline and Inner-City Problems

*E*VERY CITY performs functions crucial to the economic and social life of its entire metropolitan area. It is a focus of business and higher education and the arts, it provides medical centers and other specialized facilities, it is a major metropolitan employer, it houses thousands of low-wage workers, and it determines the uniqueness and tone of the area. But the accelerating deterioration of inner-city neighborhoods is undermining cities' ability to perform these functions and encouraging city residents to flee the resulting blight. This deterioration is both a cause and a result of seemingly endless low-density suburban sprawl. Any useful analysis of managing metropolitan area growth must therefore take inner-city problems into account.

These problems are many, interrelated, and not easily attacked. Population declines and often the loss of jobs located in central cities are "rooted in certain persistent long-range social trends that many people regard as desirable. These include rising real incomes, greater use of cars and trucks, widespread desire for living in relatively new low-density settlements, economic advantages of homeownership, and strongly entrenched tendencies for people to segregate themselves socioeconomically and racially by neighborhood."[1] Other irreversible trends aggravating central city problems are the expanding use of computers and electronic communications and a shrinking share of the work force in manufacturing. Both give businesses more liberty in choosing locations than ever before, so they can easily select sites outside central cities.

Thus the same forces that have successfully produced the suburban American dream of single-family homes, two cars in every garage, and a better life have left many of the poor behind in central-city isolation.

60

Poverty breeds deterioration and despair, which feed on themselves in the form of crime, ignorance, and poor health. And so a downward spiral in quality of life perpetuates itself.

As deterioration proceeds, the fiscal resources available to city governments shrink even though their needs increase. They become less and less able to provide opportunities for their residents that are equal to those provided in suburbs. So a great many people in inner cities fail to develop the skills, knowledge, basic values, and behavior patterns that would enable them to be productive members of society. This outcome imposes huge costs on the rest of society.

Society as a whole must therefore develop an effective strategy to attack inner-city problems. Doing so would not be necessary if each city could remedy its problems through its own efforts. But it cannot. In fact, most big cities would have difficulty providing adequate services even if they were not losing population because they contain such high proportions of very poor households. This chapter analyzes the most crucial inner-city problems in selected detail. Chapter 6 then discusses strategies that may ameliorate the consequences of urban decline.

Demographic Diversity

In 1990 the 194 cities in the United States with populations of 100,000 or more contained 63.4 million residents, or 25.5 percent of the nation's total population.[2] These cities range from relatively small, fast-growing suburbs such as Irvine, California, to sprawling urban centers such as New York City. Those most likely to encounter severe inner-city problems have large populations and high proportions of blacks, Hispanics, Asians, and other minorities.

My analysis focuses on the sixty-three cities that had 1990 minority populations of 100,000 or more. Each city includes some concentrated-poverty neighborhoods occupied primarily by minority groups. These cities contained 42.5 million persons, or 17.1 percent of the nation's residents.[3] Table 5-1 lists them in order of the size of their minority populations; table 5-2 summarizes the most important data about them.

The cities included 11.9 million black residents, or 39.5 percent of the nation's total, and 8.7 million Hispanic residents, or 39.1 percent of the total.[4] About 28 percent of the cities' population was black and

TABLE 5-1. *Population Characteristics of Sixty-Three Cities with Minority Populations of 100,000 or More, by City, 1990*

City[a]	Total population[b] 1980	Total population[b] 1990	Percent change 1980–90	Minority population 1990[b]	Percent minority Black	Percent minority Hispanic	Percent minority Other	Percent minority Total
New York	7,072	7,323	3.5	4,430	28.7	24.4	7.4	60.5
Los Angeles	2,969	3,485	17.4	2,237	14.0	39.9	10.3	64.2
Chicago	3,005	2,784	−7.4	1,746	39.1	19.6	4.0	62.7
Houston	1,595	1,631	2.2	980	28.1	27.6	4.4	60.1
Detroit	1,203	1,028	−14.6	819	75.7	2.8	1.2	79.7
Philadelphia	1,688	1,586	−6.1	768	39.9	5.6	2.9	48.4
San Antonio	786	936	19.1	600	7.0	55.6	1.5	64.1
Dallas	905	1,007	11.3	535	29.5	20.9	2.7	53.1
San Diego	876	1,111	26.8	472	9.4	20.7	12.4	42.5
Baltimore	787	736	−6.4	453	59.2	1.0	1.4	61.6
Washington	638	607	−4.9	444	65.8	5.4	2.0	73.2
San Jose	629	782	24.3	403	4.7	26.6	20.2	51.5
San Francisco	679	724	6.6	394	10.9	13.9	29.6	54.4
El Paso	425	515	21.2	381	3.4	69.0	1.6	74.0
Memphis	646	610	−5.5	345	54.8	0.7	1.0	56.5
New Orleans	558	497	−10.9	335	61.9	3.5	2.1	67.5
Miami	347	359	3.4	326	27.4	62.5	0.8	90.7
Phoenix	790	983	24.5	283	5.2	20.0	3.6	28.8
Honolulu	365	365	0.1	280	1.3	4.6	70.8	76.7
Atlanta	425	394	−7.3	276	67.1	1.9	1.0	70.0
Oakland	339	372	9.7	272	43.9	13.9	15.4	73.2
Cleveland	574	506	−11.9	266	46.6	4.6	1.3	52.5
Milwaukee	636	628	−1.3	249	30.5	6.3	2.8	39.6
Boston	563	574	−2.0	241	25.6	10.8	5.6	42.0
Newark	329	275	−16.4	237	58.5	26.1	1.4	86.0
Santa Ana	204	294	44.0	229	2.6	65.2	10.2	78.0
Long Beach	361	429	18.8	221	13.7	23.6	14.2	51.5
St. Louis	453	397	−12.4	198	47.5	1.3	1.1	49.9
Fort Worth	385	448	16.2	197	22.0	19.5	2.4	43.9
Jacksonville	541	635	17.9	191	25.2	2.6	2.2	30.0
Denver	493	468	−5.1	184	12.8	23.0	3.6	39.4
Fresno	217	354	62.9	183	8.3	29.9	13.6	51.8
Indianapolis	701	731	4.3	181	22.6	1.1	1.1	24.8
Austin	346	466	34.6	181	12.4	23.0	3.4	38.8
Sacramento	276	369	34.0	176	15.3	16.2	16.2	47.7

	Change 1980–90					Metro area growth 1980–90 (percent)
Black		Hispanic		Non-Hispanic white		
Number[b]	Percent	Number[b]	Percent	Number[b]	Percent	
319,557	17.9	379,484	27.0	−448,041	−11.5	3.29
−16,830	−3.3	574,040	70.3	−41,210	−2.5	18.54
−107,446	−9.0	124,964	29.7	−238,518	−17.2	0.16
13,675	3.1	166,620	58.8	−144,295	−16.6	20.75
19,103	2.5	−88	−0.3	−194,015	−46.7	−2.36
−5,250	−0.8	24,672	38.5	−121,422	−12.3	2.98
6,390	10.8	85,446	19.6	58,164	19.9	21.45
30,995	11.6	99,148	89.1	−28,143	−5.3	30.44
26,470	34.0	99,453	76.2	109,077	16.3	34.17
4,436	1.0	−510	−6.5	−54,926	−15.8	49.22
−49,108	−10.9	14,914	83.5	3,194	1.9	20.69
7,820	27.0	67,745	48.3	77,435	16.8	15.63
−7,317	−8.5	17,119	20.5	35,198	6.9	7.71
3,910	28.8	89,725	33.8	−3,635	−2.5	23.3
26,784	8.7	−898	−17.4	−61,886	−18.6	7.47
−931	−0.3	−1,577	−8.3	−58,492	−25.4	−1.42
11,269	12.9	30,402	15.7	−29,671	−45.0	19.17
13,196	34.8	79,680	68.1	100,124	15.8	40.61
329	7.5	−2,346	−12.3	2,017	0.6	9.7
−18,676	−6.6	1,536	25.8	−13,860	−10.2	32.52
4,317	2.7	19,164	58.9	9,519	6.5	18.23
−15,616	−6.2	5,482	30.8	−57,866	−19.0	−3.57
44,624	30.4	13,488	51.7	−66,112	−14.3	2.51
20,832	16.5	25,960	72.0	−35,792	−8.9	3.3
−30,603	−16.0	10,581	17.3	−33,978	−44.5	−2.92
−516	−6.3	100,908	111.2	−10,392	−9.9	24.71
17,980	44.1	50,704	100.3	−684	−0.3	18.54
−17,993	−8.7	−275	−5.1	−37,732	−15.7	2.8
10,780	12.3	38,850	80.1	13,370	5.4	36.9
22,606	16.5	6,772	69.5	64,622	16.4	25.5
744	1.3	14,956	16.1	−40,700	−11.9	13.6
5,822	24.7	47,318	80.8	83,860	62.2	29.7
12,388	8.1	1,732	27.5	15,880	2.9	7.1
12,278	27.0	37,429	53.7	70,293	30.5	45.6
19,473	52.7	20,586	52.5	52,941	26.5	34.7

TABLE 5-1. *Continued*

City[a]	Total population[b] 1980	Total population[b] 1990	Percent change 1980–90	Minority population 1990[b]	Percent minority Black	Percent minority Hispanic	Percent minority Other	Percent minority Total
Birmingham	284	266	−6.5	171	63.3	0.4	0.7	64.4
Hialeah	145	188	29.4	169	1.9	87.6	0.6	90.1
Columbus, O.	565	633	12.0	166	22.6	1.1	2.6	26.3
Albuquerque	332	385	15.6	162	3.0	34.5	4.7	42.2
Kansas City, Mo.	448	435	−2.9	153	29.6	3.9	1.7	35.2
Tucson	331	405	22.6	151	4.3	29.3	3.8	37.4
Jersey City	224	229	2.2	150	29.7	24.2	11.7	65.6
Cincinnati	385	364	−5.5	145	37.9	0.7	1.3	39.9
Corpus Christi	232	257	10.9	145	4.8	50.4	1.3	56.5
Charlotte	315	396	25.5	140	31.8	1.4	2.2	35.4
Seattle	494	516	4.5	139	10.1	3.6	13.2	26.9
Nashville	456	488	6.9	131	24.3	0.9	1.6	26.8
East Los Angeles	110	126	14.9	123	1.4	94.7	1.7	97.8
Stockton	150	211	42.3	123	9.6	25.0	23.8	58.4
Oklahoma City	404	445	10.1	123	16.0	5.0	6.6	27.6
Buffalo	358	328	−8.3	123	30.7	4.9	1.8	37.4
Norfolk	267	261	−2.2	117	39.1	2.9	3.0	45.0
Tampa	272	280	3.1	117	25.0	15.0	1.7	41.7
Anaheim	219	266	21.4	117	2.5	31.4	9.9	43.8
Laredo	91	123	34.4	116	0.1	93.9	0.6	94.6
Richmond	219	203	−7.4	116	55.2	0.9	1.1	57.2
Jackson	203	197	−3.1	112	55.7	0.4	0.6	56.7
Paterson	138	141	2.1	111	36.0	41.0	1.7	78.7
Pittsburgh	424	370	−12.8	105	25.8	0.9	1.8	28.5
Baton Rouge	220	220	−0.4	104	43.9	1.6	1.8	47.3
Inglewood	94	110	16.4	103	51.9	38.5	2.9	93.3
Gary	152	117	−23.2	101	80.6	5.7	0.4	86.7
Hartford	136	140	2.5	101	38.9	31.6	1.7	72.2

Source: Author's calculations based on data from Bureau of the Census, *Statistical Abstract of the United States: 1991* (Department of Commerce, 1991), pp. 34–36.

n.a. Not available.

a. Ranked by total minority population.

b. Thousands.

Change 1980–90						Metro area growth 1980–90
Black		Hispanic		Non-Hispanic white		
Number[b]	Percent	Number[b]	Percent	Number[b]	Percent	(percent)
8,806	5.5	−1,232	−53.7	−25,574	−20.9	2.7
1,397	64.2	56,953	52.9	−15,350	−43.7	19.2
18,193	14.6	2,443	54.0	47,364	10.9	10.7
3,250	39.2	20,609	18.4	29,141	13.8	14.4
6,008	4.9	2,181	14.8	−21,189	−6.8	9.3
4,872	38.8	34,254	40.6	34,874	14.9	25.5
5,965	9.6	13,754	33.0	−14,719	−12.2	−0.7
7,826	6.0	−532	−17.3	−28,294	−11.2	3.7
402	3.4	20,484	18.8	4,114	3.7	7.3
24,868	24.6	1,958	54.6	54,174	25.8	19.6
5,186	11.1	5,732	44.6	11,082	2.6	22.7
12,336	11.6	744	20.4	18,920	5.5	15.8
1,764	n.a.	119,322	n.a.	−105,086	n.a.	n.a.
4,656	29.8	19,600	59.1	36,744	36.3	38.4
12,216	20.7	10,938	96.7	17,846	5.3	11.4
5,468	5.7	6,406	66.3	−41,874	−16.5	−4.6
8,067	8.6	1,428	23.3	−15,495	−9.3	20.3
6,080	9.5	5,824	16.1	−3,904	−2.3	28.2
4,022	153.0	45,856	121.7	−2,878	−1.6	24.7
27	28.1	26,217	29.4	5,756	n.a.	n.a.
−291	−0.3	−363	−16.6	−15,346	−14.7	13.7
14,319	15.0	−633	−44.5	−19,686	−18.5	9.2
3,702	7.9	18,204	46.0	−18,906	−36.8	n.a.
−6,300	−6.2	−62	−1.8	−47,638	−14.9	−7.3
16,280	20.3	−440	−11.1	−15,840	−11.7	6.9
3,228	6.0	24,302	134.7	−11,530	−52.2	18.5
−13,314	−12.4	−4,123	−38.2	−17,563	−52.3	−5.9
8,356	18.1	16,640	59.7	−20,996	−33.9	7.3

TABLE 5-2. *Aggregate Population Characteristics of Sixty-Three Cities with Minority Populations of 100,000 or More, 1990*

Characteristic	Sixty-three cities	U.S. total
U.S. total		
1990 population	42,509,000	248,709,843
Percent of total	17.1	100.0
1980 population	40,474,000	226,545,805
Percent of total	17.9	100.0
Percent change	5.0	9.8
Black		
1990 population	11,854,918	29,986,000
Percent of all U.S. blacks	39.5	100.0
Percent of cities' population	27.9	12.1
1980 population	11,302,037	26,495,000
Percent change	4.9	13.1
Hispanic		
1990 population	8,738,392	22,354,000
Percent of all U.S. Hispanics	39.1	100.0
Percent of cities' population	20.6	9.0
1980 population	6,048,744	14,609,000
Percent change	44.5	53.0
Other minorities		
1990 population	2,757,099	9,233,000
Percent of all U.S. other minorities	29.9	100.0
Percent of cities' population	6.5	3.7
1980 population	n.a.	5,257,000
Percent change	n.a.	75.6
Total minorities		
1990 population	23,350,409	61,573,000
Percent of all U.S. minorities	37.9	100.0
Percent of cities' population	54.9	24.8
1980 population	n.a.	46,549,000
Percent change	n.a.	32.3
Non-Hispanic whites		
1990 population	19,158,591	187,136,843
Percent of all U.S. non-Hispanic whites	10.2	100.0
Percent of cities' population	45.1	75.2
1980 population	n.a.	179,996,805
Percent change	n.a.	4.0

Sources: Author's calculations using data from table 5-1 and Bureau of the Census, *Statistical Abstract of the United States: 1992* (Department of Commerce, 1992), p. 17.
n.a. Not available.

20.6 percent Hispanic. Minorities made up 55 percent of their combined population and 25 percent of the nation's total population.[5] The proportion of minorities ranged from 25 percent in Indianapolis to 93 percent in Inglewood, California.

From 1980 to 1990 the cities gained 2 million residents, or 5 percent, half the growth rate of the nation as a whole. They lost 1.2 million white, non-Hispanic residents, 5.2 percent of their 1980 total.[6] Thirty-eight cities lost white population, and twenty-four had declining total populations. Detroit, Newark, Gary, Miami, Hialeah, and Inglewood lost more than 43 percent of their 1980 white populations. Fourteen had declining black populations, and the combined black population of all sixty-three rose only 4.9 percent. Thirteen cities had declining Hispanic populations, but the combined Hispanic population of all sixty-three soared 44.5 percent.

These are the cities in which the main problems of the American inner-city "underclass"—however it is defined—are to be found.[7] I have classified the cities into four groups based on their rates of population change from 1980 to 1990. *Rapidly declining cities* lost more than 4.9 percent of their population; *slowly declining cities* lost 0.1 to 4.9 percent; *slowly growing cities* gained population but less than 10 percent; and *rapidly growing cities* gained 10 percent or more (table 5-3).[8]

Thirty-four cities experienced their first rapid growth before automobiles became the dominant form of urban movement. Twenty-one of the twenty-five cities in which blacks comprised more than 30 percent of the total population fell into this older category. Twenty-three of them are located in regions other than the West, and twenty lost population in the 1980s. The fourteen cities in which Hispanics made up more than 30 percent of the population were mainly located in the West, the Southwest, or Florida. Every one gained population during the 1980s; the average increase was 18.1 percent.

This disparity between heavily black and heavily Hispanic cities reflects the growth rates of these two groups. During the 1980s the Hispanic population shot up 7.7 million, or 53 percent; the black population grew only 3.3 million, or 12 percent. The non-Hispanic white population grew 7.1 million, or 4.0 percent. The Hispanic gains were due to heavy immigration and higher birth rates.[9]

TABLE 5-3. *Population Growth and Decline in Sixty-Three Cities with 1990 Minority Populations of 100,000 or More, 1980–90*

City[a]	Population[b] 1980	1990	Change 1980–90 (percent)	Minority population 1990[a]	Minority percent of total population	Non-Hispanic white population 1980–90 Number[a]	Percent	Metro area growth 1980–90 (percent)
Rapidly declining (loss of 4.9 percent or more)								
Gary	152	117	−23.2	101	86.7	−18	−52.3	−5.9
Newark	329	275	−16.4	239	86.0	−34	−44.5	−2.9
Detroit	1,203	1,028	−14.6	819	79.7	−19	−46.7	−2.4
Pittsburgh	424	370	−12.8	105	28.5	−48	−14.9	−7.3
St. Louis	453	397	−12.4	198	49.9	−38	−15.7	2.8
Cleveland	574	506	−11.8	266	52.5	−58	−19.0	−3.6
New Orleans	558	497	−10.9	335	67.5	−58	−25.4	−1.4
Buffalo	358	328	−8.3	123	37.4	−41	−16.5	−4.6
Chicago	3,005	2,784	−7.4	1,746	62.7	−239	−17.2	0.2
Richmond	219	203	−7.3	116	57.2	−15	−14.7	13.7
Atlanta	425	394	−7.3	276	70.0	−14	−10.2	32.5
Baltimore	787	736	−6.4	453	61.6	−55	−15.8	49.2
Birmingham	284	266	−6.5	171	84.4	−26	−20.9	2.7
Philadelphia	1,688	1,586	−6.1	768	48.4	−121	−12.3	3.0
Memphis	646	610	−5.5	345	56.5	−62	−18.6	7.5
Cincinnati	385	364	−5.5	145	39.9	−28	−11.2	3.7
Denver	493	468	−5.1	184	39.4	−41	−11.9	13.6
Washington	638	607	−4.9	444	73.2	3	1.9	20.7
Total	12,621	11,536	−8.6	8,333	59.2	−1,086	...	...
Slowly declining (less than 4.9 percent loss)								
Jackson	203	197	−3.1	112	56.7	−20	−18.5	9.2
Kansas City, Mo.	448	435	−2.9	153	35.2	−21	−6.8	9.3
Norfolk	267	261	−2.2	117	45.0	−15	−9.3	20.3
Milwaukee	636	628	−1.3	249	39.6	−66	−14.3	2.5
Baton Rouge	220	220	0.4	104	47.3	−16	−11.7	6.9
Total	1,774	1,741	−1.9	735	42.2	−138	...	...
Slowly growing (less than 10 percent growth)								
Honolulu	365	365	0.1	280	76.7	2	0.6	9.7
Boston	563	574	2.0	241	42.0	−36	−8.9	3.3
Paterson	138	141	2.1	111	78.7	−19	−36.8	n.a.
Jersey City	224	229	2.2	150	65.6	−15	−12.2	−0.7
Houston	1,595	1,631	2.2	980	60.1	−144	−16.6	20.8
Hartford	136	140	2.5	101	72.4	−21	−33.9	7.3
Tampa	272	280	3.1	117	41.7	−4	−2.3	28.2
Miami	347	359	3.4	326	90.7	−30	−45.0	19.2
New York	7,072	7,323	3.5	4,430	60.5	−45	−11.5	3.3
Indianapolis	701	731	4.3	181	24.8	16	2.9	7.1

TABLE 5-3. *Continued*

City[a]	Population[b] 1980	1990	Change 1980–90 (percent)	Minority population 1990[a]	Minority percent of total population	Non-Hispanic white population 1980–90 Number[a]	Percent	Metro area growth 1980–90 (percent)
Seattle	494	516	4.5	139	26.9	11	2.6	22.7
San Francisco	679	724	6.6	394	54.4	35	6.9	7.7
Nashville	456	488	6.9	131	26.8	19	5.5	15.8
Oakland	339	372	9.7	272	73.2	9.6	6.5	18.2
Total	13,381	13,873	3.7	7,854	56.6	−624	...	...
Rapidly growing (growth 10 percent or more)								
Oklahoma City	404	445	10.1	123	27.6	18	5.3	11.4
Corpus Christi	232	257	10.7	145	56.5	4	3.7	7.3
Dallas	905	1,007	11.3	535	53.1	−28	−5.3	30.4
Columbus, O.	565	633	12.0	166	26.3	47	10.9	10.7
East Los Angeles	110	126	14.9	123	97.8	−105	n.a.	n.a.
Albuquerque	332	385	15.6	162	42.2	29	13.8	14.4
Fort Worth	385	448	16.2	199	43.9	13	5.4	36.9
Inglewood	94	110	16.4	103	93.3	−12	−52.2	18.5
Los Angeles	2,969	3,485	17.4	2,237	64.2	−41	−2.5	18.5
Jacksonville	541	635	17.9	191	30.0	65	16.4	25.5
Long Beach	361	429	18.8	221	51.5	−7	−0.3	18.5
San Antonio	786	936	19.1	600	64.1	58	19.9	21.5
El Paso	425	515	21.2	381	74.0	−4	−2.5	23.3
Anaheim	219	266	21.4	117	43.8	−3	−1.6	24.7
Tucson	331	405	22.6	151	37.4	35	14.9	25.5
San Jose	629	782	24.3	403	51.5	77	16.8	15.6
Phoenix	790	983	24.5	283	28.8	100	15.8	40.6
Charlotte	315	396	25.5	140	35.4	54	25.8	19.6
San Diego	876	1,111	26.8	472	42.5	109	16.3	34.2
Hialeah	145	188	29.4	169	90.1	−15	−43.7	19.2
Sacramento	276	369	34.0	176	47.7	53	26.5	34.7
Laredo	91	123	34.4	116	94.6	6	n.a.	n.a.
Austin	346	466	34.6	181	38.8	70	30.5	45.6
Stockton	150	211	42.3	123	58.4	38	36.3	38.4
Santa Ana	204	294	44.0	229	78.0	−10	−9.9	24.7
Fresno	217	354	62.9	183	51.8	84	62.2	29.7
Total	12,698	15,359	21.0	7,929	51.6	650	...	...

Source: See table 5-1.

n.a. Not available.

a. Ranked by declining or increasing population.

b. Thousands.

Two Types of Inner-City Neighborhoods

Inner-city neighborhoods fall into two categories. *Stagnant or declining neighborhoods* have stable or falling populations, decreasing local employment, and are mainly black. Because they are gradually emptying out as people who can afford to live elsewhere move away, they often contain abandoned housing and large tracts of vacant cleared land. Such neighborhoods are found primarily in Philadelphia, New York, Newark, Chicago, Detroit, Atlanta, and other big northeastern, midwestern, and southern cities. Blacks are the main minority group. Most of these cities are losing population; even their black populations are falling. The number of people living in the concentrated-poverty areas of such cities in the Midwest rose sharply during the 1980s.

Dynamic and still growing inner-city neighborhoods have increasing population because of immigration, low but stable levels of local employment, and mainly Hispanic and Asian residents, though some contain many black residents too. These neighborhoods are usually overcrowded; they contain few vacant housing units, and many units designed for one household are occupied by two or more. Even though people who can afford to live elsewhere often move out, they are immediately replaced by new immigrants. Such areas are found primarily in Houston, Los Angeles, Santa Ana, San Antonio, and other large western and southwestern cities. Most have declining non-Hispanic white populations but growing total populations.

Neighborhoods in both categories have high percentages of poor people and high rates of crime, drug abuse, unemployment, births out of wedlock, single-parent households headed by women, and truancy. In the remainder of this chapter, *inner-city neighborhoods* refers to both types unless otherwise indicated.

Some researchers classify inner-city neighborhoods into two groups that are not mutually exclusive. *Underclass neighborhoods* are census tracts with above-average rates of four variables that indicate poor integration of potential workers into the mainstream economy. These variables measure male detachment from the labor force, percentage of households receiving public assistance, percentage of households headed by women with children, and teenage high school dropout rates. All four must be one standard deviation above the national mean for the tract to be considered an underclass area. Ronald B. Mincy and Susan J. Wiener of the Urban Institute have estimated that 2.48 million

FIGURE 5-1. *Share of Population Living in Underclass Neighborhoods, by Region and Ethnic Distribution, 1990*

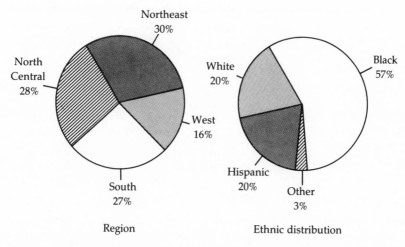

Region   Ethnic distribution

Source: Ronald B. Mincy and Susan J. Weiner, "The Under Class: Changing Concept, Constant Reality," Urban Institute, Washington, July 1993.

people lived in such neighborhoods in 1980 and 2.68 million in 1990, an increase of 8 percent.[10] The regional distribution of these in 1990 is shown in figure 5-1. The mainly minority distribution of the residents of these areas combined is also shown in figure 5-1; it remained stable in the 1980s. Only 1.37 percent of the total U.S. population lived in these areas in 1980 and 1.08 percent in 1990.

In contrast, *extreme poverty neighborhoods* are census tracts in which 40 percent or more of the residents have money incomes below the official poverty level. Many of these areas are the same as those classified as having underclass status. But in 1990 there were nearly four times as many extremely poor census tracts as underclass ones. The number of people living in extreme poverty neighborhoods rose from 5.57 million in 1980 to 10.39 million in 1990.[11] Three-fourths lived in the nation's central cities (figure 5-2). In 1990, 4.18 percent of the U.S. population lived in these extreme poverty areas. The South had the highest proportion of this total (figure 5-3).

From 1980 to 1990 the proportion of non-Hispanic blacks shrank in extreme poverty areas and that of non-Hispanic whites and Hispanics expanded. By 1990 whites formed a much higher percentage of the residents in extremely poor neighborhoods than in underclass neigh-

FIGURE 5-2. *Share of Population Living in Two Types of Poverty Areas, by Location, 1990*

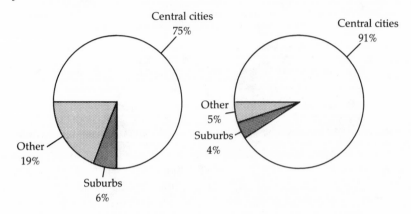

Extreme poverty neighborhoods   Underclass neighborhoods

Source: Author's calculations using data from Mincy and Weiner, "Under Class."

borhoods. Nevertheless, extremely poor neighborhoods as a whole were 48 percent black, 22 percent Hispanic, and 26 percent non-Hispanic white. They contained only 7 percent of all poor persons who were white, compared with more than 30 percent of all poor blacks and 21 percent of all poor Hispanics.[12]

In 1990 one-fifth of persons residing in extremely poor neighborhoods lived in New York, Chicago, and Los Angeles; another one-sixth lived in the six other metropolitan areas with 2 million to 4.99 million residents. The proportion of blacks in extreme poverty neighborhoods was very high.

Many of these low-income areas are not neighborhoods in the sociological sense because they lack the mediating institutions found in other communities. That is particularly true of census tracts containing very large public housing projects. They often have no churches, no retail outlets, no community organizations, few fully employed workers, few middle-income households, and few two-parent households. The absence of these elements compounds the difficulties that residents have in escaping poverty.

The percentages of city residents living in underclass and extremely poor neighborhoods, including both poor and nonpoor persons, in ten large central cities is shown in figure 5-4. In all these cities except

FIGURE 5-3. *Share of Population Living in Extreme Poverty Neighborhoods, by Region and Ethnic Distribution, 1990*

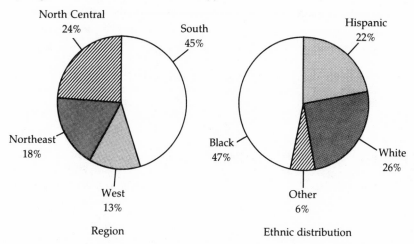

Source: Author's calculations using data from Mincy and Weiner, "Under Class."

Philadelphia the proportion living in extremely poor areas is at least double that living in underclass areas. It ranges from a high of 36.5 percent in Detroit to a low of 4.3 percent in Seattle.[13] The proportion is highest in older, relatively stagnant cities with mainly black minority populations. In all of the one hundred largest cities as of 1990, 10.7 percent of the total population lived in extremely poor neighborhoods compared with 7.9 percent in 1980 and 5.2 percent in 1970.[14] For the proportion of people in such areas in sixty-three cities with large minority populations see table 5-4.

Four important conclusions can be derived from these data. The number and percentage of central-city residents living in concentrated-poverty neighborhoods rose sharply during the 1980s. Nevertheless, poor inner-city neighborhoods, however defined, contain a small proportion of the U.S. population and even of the central-city population in most cities. In addition, although most residents in 79 percent of inner-city neighborhoods are minorities, the number and percentage of non-Hispanic whites in extremely poor neighborhoods increased in the 1980s. Yet poor blacks and Hispanics remain far more concentrated in inner-city and other high-poverty neighborhoods than do poor non-Hispanic whites.

TABLE 5-4. *People in Poverty in Sixty-Three Cities with Minority Populations of 100,000 or More, 1990*

City[a]	Population[b]	Population in extreme poverty tracts		Population with poverty income	
		Number	Percent of total population	Number	Percent of total population
Rapidly declining (loss of 4 percent or more, 1980–90)					
Gary	117	9,589	8.18	34,398	29.4
Newark	275	49,189	17.89	72,325	26.3
Detroit	1,028	375,548	36.53	333,072	32.4
Pittsburgh	370	58,985	15.40	79,180	21.4
St. Louis	397	80,842	15.33	97,662	24.6
Cleveland	506	100,422	19.85	145,222	28.7
New Orleans	497	151,624	30.51	157,052	31.6
Buffalo	328	61,277	18.68	83,968	25.6
Chicago	2,784	381,866	13.72	601,344	21.6
Richmond	203	22,257	10.96	42,427	20.9
Atlanta	394	91,944	23.34	107,562	27.3
Baltimore	736	104,212	14.16	161,184	21.9
Birmingham	266	45,505	17.11	65,968	24.8
Philadelphia	1,586	191,515	12.08	321,958	20.3
Memphis	610	126,866	20.80	140,300	23.0
Cincinnati	364	68,376	18.78	88,452	24.3
Denver	468	22,796	4.87	80,028	17.1
Washington	607	20,609	3.40	102,583	16.9
Total	11,536	1,941,402	16.83	2,714,685	23.5
Slowly declining (less than 4.9 percent loss, 1980–90)					
Jackson	197	31,748	16.12	44,719	22.7
Kansas City, Mo.	435	24,049	5.53	66,555	15.3
Norfolk	261	36,749	14.08	50,373	19.3
Milwaukee	628	140,831	22.43	139,416	22.2
Baton Rouge	220	59,040	26.84	57,640	26.2
Total	1,741	292,417	16.80	358,703	20.6
Slowly growing (less than 10 percent growth, 1980–90)					
Honolulu	365	6,811	1.87	30,660	8.4
Boston	574	28,738	5.01	107,338	18.7
Paterson	141	0	0	26,085	18.5
Jersey City	229	8,445	3.69	43,281	18.9
Houston	1,631	156,223	9.58	337,617	20.7
Hartford	140	n.a.	0	38,500	27.5
Tampa	280	31,426	11.22	54,320	19.4
Miami	359	90,644	25.25	112,008	31.2
New York	7,323	952,484	13.01	1,413,339	19.3
Indianapolis	731	23,297	3.19	91,375	12.5

TABLE 5-4. *Continued*

City[a]	Population[b]	Population in extreme poverty tracts		Population with poverty income	
		Number	Percent of total population	Number	Percent of total population
Seattle	516	22,283	4.32	63,984	12.4
San Francisco	724	12,127	1.68	91,948	12.7
Nashville	488	32,834	6.73	65,392	13.4
Oakland	372	18,626	5.01	69,936	18.8
Total	13,873	1,383,938	9.98	2,545,783	18.4
Rapidly growing (growth 10 percent or more, 1980–90)					
Oklahoma City	445	27,623	6.21	70,755	15.9
Corpus Christi	257	26,222	10.20	51,400	20.0
Dallas	1,007	80,383	7.98	181,260	18.0
Columbus, O.	633	74,889	11.83	108,876	17.2
East Los Angeles	126	0	0	30,492	24.2
Albuquerque	385	6,478	1.68	53,900	14.0
Fort Worth	448	31,202	6.96	77,952	17.4
Inglewood	110	0	0	18,150	16.5
Los Angeles	3,485	230,338	6.61	658,665	18.9
Jacksonville	635	27,005	4.25	82,550	13.0
Long Beach	429	0	0	72,072	16.8
San Antonio	936	152,420	16.28	211,536	22.6
El Paso	515	82,197	15.96	130,295	25.3
Anaheim	266	1,041	0.39	28,196	10.6
Tucson	405	38,965	9.62	81,810	20.2
San Jose	782	0	0	72,726	9.3
Phoenix	983	56,036	5.70	139,586	14.2
Charlotte	396	24,756	6.25	42,768	10.8
San Diego	1,111	38,739	3.49	148,874	13.4
Hialeah	188	0	0	34,216	18.2
Sacramento	369	18,466	5.00	63,468	17.2
Laredo	123	0	0	45,879	37.3
Austin	466	26,988	5.79	83,414	17.9
Stockton	211	23,492	11.13	45,154	21.4
Santa Ana	294	0	0	53,214	18.1
Fresno	354	81,765	23.10	84,960	24.0
Totals	15,359	1,049,005	6.83	2,672,168	17.4

Source: Author's calculations based on data from John D. Kasarda, "Inner-City Concentrated Poverty and Neighborhood Distress: 1970–1990," in *Fannie Mae Annual Housing Conference 1993: Housing Policies for Distressed Urban Neighborhoods* (1993), pp. 31–33.

a. Ranked by declining or increasing population.

FIGURE 5-4. *Share of Population Living in Underclass and Extreme Poverty Neighborhoods, Ten Cities, 1990*

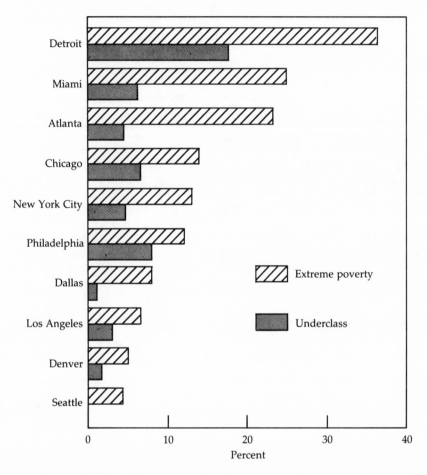

Sources: Author's calculations based on data from Bureau of the Census, *Statistical Abstract of the United States: 1991* (Department of Commerce, 1991), pp. 34–36; and Kasarda, "Inner-City Concentrated Poverty," pp. 31–33.

Urban Decline and Local Government Spending

A 1993 study by Stephen Moore and Dean Stansel claims that urban growth and decline are caused primarily by local government fiscal policies, not by high rates of poverty or other urban social or economic conditions. "We find significant and consistent patterns of higher spending and taxes in the low-growth cities than in the high-growth cities. . . . Cities with high spending and taxes in 1980 lost population in the 1980s; cities with low spending and taxes gained population. High spending and taxes are a *cause*, not just a consequence, of urban decline."[15]

The authors reject the contention that higher spending in slow-growth cities is caused by the large proportion of low-income residents. Instead, they claim that high state and local taxes drive away businesses and households, and the cities hire too many workers. Declining cities are not suffering from underfunding but from over-funding. Therefore, if urban governments raise and spend less money, such cities can be restored to economic health and vigorous growth. "Through an aggressive agenda of budget control, tax reduction, privatization, and deregulation, America's declining cities can rise again in prominence and prosperity."[16]

This argument has some initial plausibility because city governments use their resources with varying efficiency. The conclusions are fatally flawed, however, by the method of analysis. The authors do not test the relative contribution of the independent variables they discuss to their dependent variable of rates of growth or decline. And they ignore other variables likely to influence growth rates. Understanding these flaws requires some technical discussion.

To correct these shortcomings, I conducted a multiple regression analysis of the same cities using the data in their report and data on other relevant variables (appendix B). The dependent variable was not their composite index of growth or decline, but simply city population change, either from 1980 to 1990 or from 1970 to 1990. The results show that their fiscal variables have some impact on city growth or decline but nothing like the dominant causality they claim.

For example, when percentage population growth from 1980 to 1990 is the dependent variable, a regression using nine of the most statistically significant independent variables produces a multiple R^2 adjusted for degrees of freedom of 0.70. Only one of their fiscal variables remains (increase in per capita city expenditures from 1965 to 1990). In contrast, four of the five most significant independent variables (those with t-statistics above 2.0) are objective characteristics of city population that are not directly affected by local fiscal policies. They are the percentage point increase in households headed by women, the percentage of poor persons in 1979, the percentage of total primary metropolitan statistical area (PMSA) population formed by the central city's population, and the percentage growth rate of the city's suburbs from 1980 to 1990.

These results suggest that growth or decline is more heavily influenced by each city's demographic characteristics than by its fiscal policies. Large numbers of low-income households headed by women are associated with population decline; small numbers are associated with population gains. This may mean that people may be fleeing from declining cities more because of pervasive poverty or an absence of viable neighborhood schools and other institutions than because of fiscal policies.

Similar results occur when population change from 1970 to 1990 is the dependent variable. Moreover, regressions using city expenditures per capita (excluding health, education, and welfare spending) and city workers per 10,000 residents as the dependent variables imply that both are strongly influenced by each city's population traits, not only or even mainly by its fiscal policies.

Changing fiscal policies, then, would not by itself turn around losses of population and jobs. Too many social and economic characteristics that are difficult to change influence cities' growth or decline and their fiscal policies. Fiscal policies are themselves strongly responsive to such local conditions as poverty rates and whether the city also has responsibilities as a county government. It is noteworthy that the percentage of black or Hispanic residents has little influence on city rates of growth or decline.

Cities might very well profit from reducing taxes, cutting bureaucracy, and privatizing some services. But such policies are not sufficient to cope with the problems society has loaded onto cities by concentrating so many poor people in them. The conclusion that declining cities are overfunded in relation to their capabilities rather than underfunded is not supported by Moore and Stansel's study and probably cannot be supported by any other study.

National Problems and Inner-City Neighborhoods

The economic prosperity and political viability of American society depend on resolving four problems: lack of civil order, poverty among children, poor public education, and incomplete integration of workers into the economy. These problems are nationwide in scope but occur most intensively in inner cities.[17] They interact in ways that aggravate all four.

America cannot remain a healthy democratic society unless these problems are overcome for the vast majority of citizens. Many Americans still suffer from one or more of them. In fact, the problems are becoming more widespread than ever, but they are most intense in inner-city neighborhoods. And because they are generated locally, they must ultimately be dealt with locally, although often with resources from the national level.

The Threat to Personal Security

Americans are amazingly more violent than the people of other economically developed societies. The U.S. murder rate was 9.4 per 100,000 people in 1990, double that of France, three times that of the United Kingdom, and nine times that of Japan.[18] Partly because gun ownership is much more widespread here than elsewhere, 34,471 persons were shot to death in the United States in 1990 (less than 50,000 were killed in motor vehicle accidents).[19] The number murdered by handguns per million people was 3 times greater in the United States than in Switzerland, 60 times greater than in Japan, and 111 times greater than in the United Kingdom.[20] In 1990 there were also 732 violent crimes and 5,089 property crimes reported per 100,000 residents. The rate of violent crime was the highest recorded in the United States in this century and more than double the rate in 1970.[21] Polls show that Americans have long considered crime and violence high-priority social problems.[22]

Inner-city residents are afraid to venture onto their streets and sidewalks. Many families will not allow their children to walk to school unescorted. Homes and stores are routinely burglarized or robbed at gunpoint. In many cities, gunshot wounds are the leading cause of death among black males age 14 to 24. In some inner-city neighborhoods, more than half of all young men are either in jail, on parole, or awaiting trial.[23]

These conditions grotesquely mock the personal freedoms a democratic society supposedly guarantees. If people cannot walk outside their homes without fear of robbery, attack, or injury, they are not free. This extreme insecurity in inner-city neighborhoods results to a large extent from the concentration of low-income households there. That in turn is caused by the trickle-down urban development process described in chapter 2.

But personal insecurity is spreading to other parts of metropolitan areas, too—downtown districts, the parking lots of suburban shopping centers, subway trains, and parks and forest preserves. Moreover, the expanding ownership of handguns by people living in all parts of the nation is increasing the risk of being killed or injured almost everywhere.[24]

Children in Poverty

In 1990, 20 percent of all U.S. children younger than age 18 lived in households with incomes below the official poverty level (13.5 percent of persons of all ages lived in such households). About 30 percent of children under 18 living in central cities were poor.[25] The proportion of children under age 18 living in poverty has been rising for the past two decades; it was 14.9 percent in 1970 and 17.9 percent in 1980. Among black children under age 18, 44.2 percent lived in poor households in 1990; among Hispanic children, 39.7 percent.

Many children growing up in poverty suffer serious handicaps. In 1990, 60 percent lived in households with only one parent present; 95 percent of those households were headed by women.[26] Recent evidence shows that children who grow up in one-parent households have more psychological and educational difficulties than those in two-parent homes.[27] This tendency is undoubtedly compounded by the general difficulties of living in poverty. Yet in 1989, 27 percent of all U.S. births occurred out of wedlock, 19 percent among whites and 64 percent among blacks.[28] These rates are higher in central cities than in the nation as a whole.

Poverty and the lack of education associated with it often cause prospective mothers to avoid getting proper medical care for themselves and their offspring, both before and after birth. Many babies born to poor mothers have low birth weights, which are associated with malformation of brain cells, high rates of disease, learning deficiencies, and mental illness. Thousands of babies are now being born to mothers who are addicted to cocaine or heroin. They start life similarly addicted and immediately suffer withdrawal traumas. Many mothers of poor children are teenagers who are still children themselves; they are ill-equipped to provide the constant nurturing and care healthy children need.

All these factors cause a significant percentage of babies born in poverty to achieve inadequate brain cell development during their early years. This restricts them in all phases of their later lives. Society often must bear huge costs to deal with criminal behavior, severe physical and mental handicaps, and other problems associated with their later development.

No modern society can develop its full economic, social, or intellectual potential if one-fourth of its children are growing up under such conditions. America must either substantially reduce the proportion of children growing up in poor families or provide compensating benefits to those families that would eliminate most of the ill effects of their poverty.

The Failure of Public Education

The inadequacies of the American elementary and secondary education systems have been studied intensively and publicized widely during the past two decades. It is therefore hardly necessary to set forth a detailed description of this problem here. But a few points should be emphasized.

American young people are not being well educated in comparison with their parents, their counterparts in other nations, or their own potential. This is true of children across the entire nation, in all types of communities, and from all socioeconomic and ethnic groups. Some black and Hispanic children are spending more years in elementary and secondary school than their parents did. But scholastic achievement test scores for most groups show weakening performance during the past two decades. And comparative test scores from examinations administered to students in many developed or developing nations consistently put U.S. children at or near the bottom of the heap.[29]

American children could learn a lot more. They go to school fewer days each year than most foreign children, spend more hours watching television, and spend far fewer hours doing homework.[30] These inadequacies are magnified in many city school systems by the large

number of children from very poor homes, especially in schools serving inner-city neighborhoods. For example, according to Gary Orfield,
in metropolitan Chicago high schools,

> the correlation between the percentage of black and Hispanic stu-
> dents and the percentage of low-income students was .92 in 1986.
> And nine-tenths of the elementary schools that are 90 to 100 percent
> black and Hispanic are predominantly poor. Not a single predomi-
> nantly white elementary school has as many as one-third low-
> income children.
>
> Across the metropolitan area there was a .81 correlation between
> the percentage of a school's students who were poor and the per-
> centage whose math scores were below the national norm. Those
> schools that ranked in the top tenth academically had an average of
> 4 percent low-income students, while those in the bottom tenth
> academically averaged 89 percent low-income students.
>
> There is, in other words, an overwhelming problem of isolation
> of black and Hispanic students in schools of concentrated poverty
> and low achievement.

This combination of segregation and poverty concentration produces abysmal performances by the products of many public schools.
As Orfield goes on to point out, "a 1985 study of high schools within
Chicago showed that only 8 percent of the students of the 'nonselective
segregated high schools' in the city graduated and were reading at the
national norm level. These schools served about two-thirds of the city's
students." He notes that "a fourth of high school *graduates* read at the
sixth-grade level or lower; the average school scores on the ACT test
(the dominant college admissions test in the Midwest) place half the
city's schools in the bottom one percent of all U.S. schools."[31]

Although Chicago's public schools were among the worst in the
nation, the combination of segregation and concentrated poverty was
typical of public school systems in the nation's largest cities. The
percentages of minority students in the elementary and secondary
public school systems of the sixty-three U.S. cities in 1990 with minority populations of 100,000 or more are shown in table 5-5. In all
fifty-five districts combined for which the proportion of minority students was reported, minorities made up 73.4 percent of public school

students. This racial concentration is accompanied by poverty concentration in many schools, especially in inner-city areas.

The impact of the inadequate education received by many minority and poor children in central cities will be felt for years. For example, in the 1990–91 school year 1.06 million students were enrolled in Chicago public schools: 66 percent in the suburbs, and 34 percent in the city. Of the total, 54 percent were white, 26 percent black, 16 percent Hispanic, and 4 percent Asian. Minority students comprised 88 percent of all Chicago public school students (and 25 percent of suburban public school students.) More than half the region's potential future labor pool from public schools will soon consist of minority group members. Even though these data exclude Catholic schools, there will be an immense impact on the capabilities of the whole Chicago metropolitan area labor force because of the poor quality of education now being provided to minority-group members. This will surely affect the desirability of the Chicago metropolitan area as a place to do business. It will also affect the ability of white suburban homeowners to sell their homes when they want to retire because half the potential market will consist of minorities. If few of them can afford to own a home because of their low incomes, the market for home resales will be crippled. Thus the quality of education in central city public schools is not just an irrelevant or academic matter for white suburban residents. It has direct implications for their economic welfare.

No Entry into the Mainstream Work Force

Millions of unskilled workers across the nation have had difficulty finding work. In 1991 the unemployment rate was 5.5 percent for people older than age 25. But the rate varied inversely with educational attainment (figure 5-5). Ten percent of workers with only an elementary school education were unemployed, but only 2.4 percent of those with five or more years of college. The three educational categories with 10 percent unemployment rates made up 26 percent of all unemployed workers but only 13 percent of all workers. The figure omits 20.6 million workers age 16 to 24, who had an unemployment rate of 13.4 percent. Many of these young people also had relatively little education. So if lack of advanced education indicates a low level of worker skills, unemployment connected with inadequate skills was widespread in 1991.

Many people who were fully employed earned incomes that did

TABLE 5-5. *Minorities in Public Schools in Sixty-Three Cities with Minority Populations of 100,000 or More, 1990*
Percent

City[a]	Minority population			Minority public school enrollment
	Black	Hispanic	Total	
New York	28.7	24.4	60.5	69.4
Los Angeles	14.0	39.9	64.2	86.3
Chicago	39.1	19.6	62.7	88.2
Houston	28.1	27.6	60.1	85.6
Detroit	75.7	2.8	79.7	92.2
Philadelphia	39.9	5.6	48.4	76.9
San Antonio	7.0	55.6	64.1	93.5
Dallas	29.5	20.9	53.1	83.0
San Diego	9.4	20.7	42.5	62.6
Baltimore	59.2	1.0	61.6	82.2
Washington	65.8	5.4	73.2	96.1
San Jose	4.7	26.6	51.5	59.2
San Francisco	10.9	13.9	54.4	86.1
El Paso	3.4	69.0	74.0	78.8
Memphis	54.8	0.7	56.5	80.7
New Orleans	61.9	3.5	67.5	92.1
Miami	27.4	62.5	90.7	81.0
Phoenix	5.2	20.0	28.8	18.5
Honolulu	1.3	4.6	76.7	77.4
Atlanta	67.1	1.9	70.0	n.a.
Oakland	43.9	13.9	73.2	91.6
Cleveland	46.6	4.6	52.5	79.2
Milwaukee	30.5	6.3	39.6	68.1
Boston	25.6	10.8	42.0	77.8
Newark	58.5	26.1	86.0	90.1
Santa Ana	2.6	65.2	78.0	93.1
Long Beach	13.7	23.6	51.5	72.0
St. Louis	47.5	1.3	49.9	n.a.
Fort Worth	22.0	19.5	43.9	65.9
Jacksonville	25.2	2.6	30.0	40.7
Denver	12.8	23.0	39.4	66.2
Fresno	8.3	29.9	51.8	66.9
Indianapolis	22.6	1.1	24.8	52.3
Austin	12.4	23.0	38.8	56.4
Sacramento	15.3	16.2	47.7	65.0

TABLE 5-5. *Continued*

City[a]	Minority population			Minority public school enrollment
	Black	Hispanic	Total	
Birmingham	63.3	0.4	64.0	89.0
Hialeah	1.9	87.6	90.1	n.a.
Columbus, Ohio	22.6	1.1	26.3	50.4
Albuquerque	3.0	34.5	42.2	51.3
Kansas City, Mo.	29.6	3.9	35.2	n.a.
Tucson	4.3	29.3	37.4	46.9
Jersey City	29.7	24.2	65.6	87.9
Cincinnati	37.9	0.7	39.9	63.9
Corpus Christi	4.8	50.4	56.5	74.1
Charlotte	31.8	1.4	35.4	43.3
Seattle	10.1	3.6	26.9	56.5
Nashville	24.3	0.9	26.8	41.2
East Los Angeles	1.4	94.7	97.8	n.a.
Stockton	9.6	25.0	58.4	78.8
Oklahoma City	16.0	5.0	27.6	55.5
Buffalo	30.7	4.9	37.4	59.4
Norfolk	39.1	2.9	45.0	n.a.
Tampa	25.0	15.0	41.7	35.4
Anaheim	2.5	31.4	43.8	55.1
Laredo	0.1	93.9	94.6	97.5
Richmond	55.2	0.9	57.2	n.a.
Jackson	55.7	0.4	56.7	80.7
Paterson	36.0	41.0	78.7	90.6
Pittsburgh	25.8	0.9	28.5	53.6
Baton Rouge	43.9	1.6	47.3	57.2
Inglewood	51.9	38.5	93.3	n.a.
Gary	80.6	5.7	86.7	98.5
Hartford	38.9	31.8	72.4	92.1

Source: Author's calculations using data from National Center for Education Statistics, *Digest of Educational Statistics, 1992*, NCES 92-097 (Department of Education, 1992), pp. 97–101.

n.a. Not available.

a. Ranked by total minority population.

FIGURE 5-5. *Unemployment Rates of Workers Age 25 and Older, by Educational Attainment, 1991*

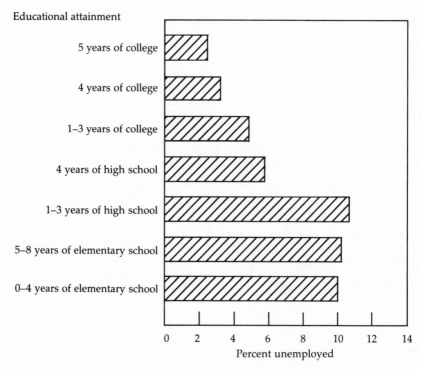

Source: Author's calculations using data from Bureau of the Census, *Statistical Abstract of the United States: 1992*, p. 400.

not raise their living standards above the poverty level. Twenty percent of all families with incomes below the poverty level in 1987 included members who worked fifty or more weeks a year.[32] So even a full-time job does not guarantee workers a decent living standard. And the real earnings of young men have been falling in the past decade, although earnings of young women have risen somewhat. Year-round, full-time male workers age 25 to 34 who had completed four years of high school earned an average of $28,000 in 1975 in constant 1990 dollars but only $24,000 in 1990.[33] Only male workers age 25 to 34 with four or more years of college had rising real earnings from 1975 to 1990.

The link between education and incomes is further illustrated by median household incomes in 1990 for households with heads 25

FIGURE 5-6. *Median Incomes of Households with Heads Age 25 and Older, by Educational Attainment, 1990*

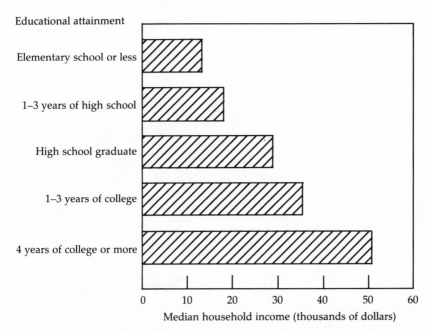

Source: Bureau of the Census, *Statistical Abstract of the United States: 1992*, p. 446.

years old or older (figure 5-6). Median incomes increased with educational attainment. Households with heads who went no further than elementary school had median incomes only one-fourth of those with heads who completed four or more years of college. On the average, younger households have higher average levels of educational attainment than much older ones because rates of school attendance have increased in the past few decades. Thus in 1991, 23.7 percent of all persons 25 to 34 years old had completed four or more years of college, but only 13.2 percent of those 65 to 74 years old.[34]

Of course, increasing the educational attainment of all Americans to four or more years of college would not increase their incomes to the level for their age group. But it does suggest the importance of increasing the educational levels of the American work force enough to integrate nearly all workers into the mainstream economy so they can enjoy reasonable prosperity.

FIGURE 5-7. *Changes in Adjusted Real Household Income, by Income Percentile, Selected Periods, 1967–87*

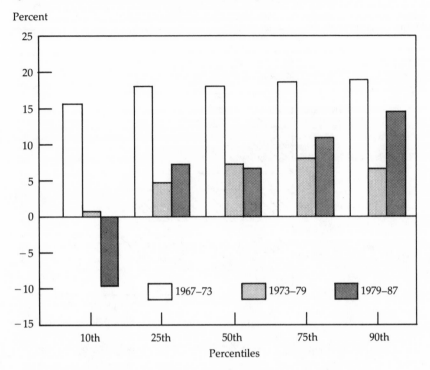

Percent

Source: Unpublished data from Lynn A. Karoly, adjusted for household size.

These data partly confirm the analysis of Robert B. Reich that low-skilled U.S. mass production workers have suffered a relative loss of economic power, both domestically and globally, because of intensifying competition with low-wage workers around the world.[35] True, the U.S. economy as a whole stands to gain from any increase in the wealth of other nations that trade with it. But many low-wage U.S. workers may lose their jobs. Most will eventually find other employment, especially if they continue their education and improve their skills. But they may suffer long periods of economic hardship in the meantime.

One result of these factors has been an increasing divergence in incomes between the poorest people in society and the wealthiest (figure 5-7). The households with pretax, pretransfer incomes in the

lowest quintile became worse off absolutely as their adjusted real incomes shrank in the 1980s. And the decrease occurred even though
the average number of persons in each household working outside the
home increased. Although this poorest quintile does not include exactly the same households over time, the figure indicates that much of
the U.S. work force is failing to maintain even constant low standards
of living. And its members are not learning the skills necessary to do
well in a high-technology economy.

Not being effectively integrated into the mainstream work force is
more prevalent in cities than in suburbs. In the fourth quarter of 1991
the unemployment rates for blacks were 13.9 percent in cities and 10.6
percent in suburbs; among whites they were 6.7 percent and 5.4 percent. And labor force participation rates were lower in central cities
than in suburbs.[36] The unemployment rate in New York City among
black teenagers in early 1993 was 40 percent, the highest ever recorded
in twenty-five years of collecting data.[37]

The percentage of dysfunctional workers in the labor force will
increase as more poor and unskilled immigrants enter. Not all move
into central cities; many suburban communities are also serving as
ports of entry. So as time passes, higher and higher proportions of the
labor force and of American society generally will be made up of
minorities. If the proportion of minorities who are inadequately
trained remains constant, the proportion of all workers who are not
properly prepared for a high-technology economy and global competition will inevitably increase.

It would clearly be desirable to integrate low-skilled workers into
sectors of the economy most likely to prosper. That would require
greatly improving their skills and education. If such an integration
is not carried out, the U.S. economy will have more and more workers who cannot earn enough to sustain the high standard of living
enjoyed by most workers. Political pressures could then arise for the
middle class to subsidize the poor more heavily. This pressure
would be stronger the larger the percentage of the labor force in the
substandard category. Social friction between the middle class and
the poor could increase and weaken the performance of the economy. Therefore the integration of underskilled and underemployed
workers into the mainstream economy is vital to the welfare of U.S.
society.

The Interaction of Basic Problems

The basic problems I have discussed interact in ways that aggravate all of them and undermine the fiscal and economic strength of cities. High rates of crime discourage companies that offer good jobs from locating or remaining in central cities. The best public school teachers choose schools outside such neighborhoods, reducing the quality of education available there. Young people have a harder time acquiring the skills and work habits necessary to become attractive workers.

In addition, the absence of good jobs and the high short-term payoffs from illegitimate ones lure many young people into crime, which aggravates the lack of personal security. Illegal activities also prevent many young people from developing legitimately marketable skills and work habits.

The inadequate nurturing, nutrition, and health care received by many children in inner-city families reduces their mental, physical, and emotional potential. And their parents' failure to emphasize the importance of getting a good education reduces their motivation to try hard in school. These conditions make it more difficult for public schools to educate them effectively and for them to qualify for and hold good jobs.

The poor quality of public schooling in inner cities aggravates all the other problems. It handicaps young people trying to get good jobs, which drives many into illegal activities. Young women who are not doing well in school and have few job prospects are more likely to accept becoming pregnant and going on welfare as a life pattern. Yet such women often make poor mothers because of ignorance, poor judgment caused by lack of life experience, and lack of proper example from their own mothers.

The concentration of poor households in inner cities that helps generate each of these problems also causes them to interact with each other. And as the reputation of central cities becomes tainted by all these conditions, fewer economically viable households and businesses are willing to stay. The economies of the cities are further undermined, and they are forced to raise tax rates to finance even minimal social services. Higher taxes induce the further withdrawal of prosperous businesses and households, and so on.

In the long run, deteriorating conditions in central cities will require at least some remedial spending by the entire nation. This is especially likely under a national health care system with·uniform benefits for all, since health deficiencies are worst in inner cities. Remedial spending is currently most obvious in the increased budgets for crime prevention and prison construction and operation. "Crack babies" and "AIDS babies" will also absorb large amounts of federal funds. These outcomes will weaken the fiscal position of the entire federal government and reduce the national savings rate.

Politics and Inner-City Problems

Although the basic problems occur most intensively in inner cities, policies targeted for remedying them are not likely to gain enough political support to become effective. For one thing, inner cities do not have large populations. In 1990 the number of people living in all census tracts with 40 percent or more poor persons was less than 5 percent of the total U.S. population. These inner-city areas contained about 8 million people, about 10 percent of the total population of all central cities. To gain broad enough support in Congress or state legislatures, remedial programs must spread at least some benefits over a large number of people and congressional or legislative districts. Therefore, the problems must be perceived as at least present in most districts. And they are.

Equally important, many inner-city neighborhoods, especially in cities that are losing population, are black. Programs that mainly benefit blacks, especially poor blacks, have a hard time garnering political support from white citizens and their representatives. So they rarely receive significant federal funding or attention.

To be politically feasible, strategies for resolving basic social problems should define them in national terms and conceive of the remedies as societywide. Yet such strategies should also be designed so the remedies have the most intensive effects in inner cities. This amounts to an indirect rather than a direct attack on inner-city problems.

Unfortunately, indirect attacks rarely focus enough resources or attention to make much headway in solving problems. By the time the resources have been spread around enough congressional or legislative districts to ensure adoption, little is left for the inner cities. That is why attacking these problems mainly by allocating more general resources to central city governments and hoping the resources will trickle down rarely works.

The racial aspect of inner-city problems poses another profound political difficulty. Continuing antiblack behavior patterns among whites are key causes of the lower average incomes, lower occupational and social status, and worse living conditions of blacks.[38] These patterns include white behavior concerning housing markets, schools, and job markets. Such racially discriminatory behavior is not the only causal factor, but it is extremely significant.

Remedying this situation would require policies aimed at redressing black-white disparities and inequalities. But explicitly race-oriented policies would require direct compensatory and integrative actions. These could include transferring more of the best public school teachers to mainly black schools, spending more money per pupil in black schools than in white, transporting black inner-city students to mainly white suburban schools (as is done successfully in the St. Louis area), enabling black inner-city households to move into subsidized housing units in mainly white suburban neighborhoods (as has been done successfully in the Chicago area Gautreaux program), setting up more effective job information and selection programs in inner cities that tap opportunities throughout metropolitan areas, and much more vigorously enforcing antidiscrimination laws against white realtors, landlords, and homeowners by means of large fines and damage awards.

Many whites oppose such policies because they believe that civil rights laws and other antidiscrimination policies have already eliminated any need for more public policies to improve the opportunities available to blacks. The persistence of problems among blacks, they believe, is mostly caused by blacks themselves. There is some truth in that view. Many inner-city problems cannot be remedied without major changes in the behavior of inner-city residents. And these changes cannot be forced on them by outsiders, especially white ones. Yet the inequalities caused by long-term and continuing residential and school segregation, housing and job discrimination, and other penalties imposed on blacks by whites are still so powerful that they will not disappear without explicit attacks upon them.

Some whites oppose these remedies because they do not want to change their own behavior. Especially repugnant would be accepting more blacks in their neighborhoods and local schools, particularly low-income blacks. Yet how can poverty concentrations be dispersed without encouraging at least some people living in inner cities to move into neighborhoods where poverty is not so concentrated? Poverty among whites is far more geographically dispersed than among blacks; even just replicating the dispersion of poor whites would require considerable movement of black households out of inner cities.

In addition, explicitly racial remedies are also opposed by many black politicians because the policies would weaken their political strength. Even many middle-class blacks who have moved out of inner cities would oppose policies designed to help poorer blacks do the same thing. They do not want poor neighbors any more than other middle-class households do.

Altogether, therefore, little political support exists for race-oriented remedies for the handicaps long imposed on blacks by whites. Yet without at least some such remedies, the scourge of inner-city conditions cannot be ended. Unfortunately, few elected politicians of any color or ethnicity are willing even to discuss this dilemma, let alone deal with it effectively.[39]

The Social Responsibility of Suburbs

The usual response to inner-city problems by people living outside central cities is to withdraw as far as possible geographically, fiscally, and psychologically. Many have moved out of central cities precisely to escape threatening inner-city conditions. They deny that they have any moral or other responsibility for dealing with such problems, which they blame on inner-city residents themselves.

But people who do not live in cities have a direct moral responsibility to help solve inner-city problems. First, suburban residents have partly caused the problems by supporting exclusionary laws that result in concentrations of very poor households in the most deteriorated older city neighborhoods. Second, all Americans benefit economically from the effective functioning of central cities and the low-wage workers living in them. Therefore people who do not live in cities have some responsibility to ensure that such functioning continues.

There are also indirect reasons why people living outside cities have a moral obligation to help inner-city residents. All members of any society have a responsibility to help preserve the conditions necessary for a civilized life in the society. Those conditions ensure that children grow up with adequate nurture and nutrition, civil order prevails, public education prepares a person for working life, and people can achieve a decent basic standard of living through working.

Finally, if a significant part of the labor force is unable to work effectively in a high-technology globalized economy, America will be unable to remain competitive with other developed societies. Living standards will fall relative to those of other nations, and perhaps absolutely as well.

Altogether, therefore, everyone has a responsibility to help remedy inner-city problems. And because those problems are threatening the quality of life, self-interest reinforces everyone's moral obligations. Exactly how much commitment of resources and effort this responsibility entails is of course highly debatable. Those matters cannot be fully dealt with in this book.

6

Policy Strategies for Large Cities

*H*AVING an overall strategy for dealing with urban decline or other domestic problems is considered un-American by many people. Past American social policy has often been left to market and other "spontaneous" forces. Such a seemingly laissez-faire approach has been especially important in determining land use. Households and businesses make many individual decisions, and government makes little attempt to deal with the results by trying to influence their choices.

But calling this process laissez-faire is disingenuous, even hypocritical. It disguises the fact that certain groups of households and businesses dominate land use decisionmaking both politically and economically. They use their influence to ensure that the results serve their goals at the expense of preventing other groups, especially poorer people, from achieving their goals. Yet this influence is exerted through such highly decentralized institutional structures that, on the surface, no one overall plan or blueprint is visible.

The dominance of these groups is revealed by the way they manipulate the trickle-down process of providing housing for low-income people. They use their political control over local zoning and building codes to exclude poor people from many suburbs, thereby overloading central cities and some older suburbs with them. These practices have greatly contributed to inner-city deterioration. In the past the dominant groups partly offset their actions by politically supporting federal programs aiding cities. According to Peter Salins,

what American urban policy really [has amounted] to is a kind of Faustian bargain struck by the leaders of the cities and the residents of the expanding suburbs: the cities agree to serve increasingly as

95

the poorhouses of the metropolitan community, as long as the suburbanites—with Washington and the state capitals acting as brokers
and intermediaries—underwrite the extra costs this role imposes.
This bargain has, after three decades of fitful implementation, broken down. . . . Both [federal and state] governmental levels [have
reneged] significantly on their part of the bargain.[1]

For the long-run health of its society, then, America must create a
new, coherent, and comprehensive response to urban decline.

Preliminary Considerations

Before examining strategies in detail, it is important to set forth
basic considerations relevant to their likely effectiveness.

Classifying Cities

The diversity of conditions among cities makes it hard to devise a
single strategy applicable to all of them. But to create a strategy for
each would require effective regional institutions. That is a cogent
reason to urge their creation, as discussed in chapter 9. However, it is
impractical to wait until the institutions are created before undertaking
action to reverse urban deterioration.

One way to begin would be to divide cities into a few categories,
with a different strategy for each category. Chapter 5 presented a
simple scheme based on city population growth rates in the 1980s.
The category of *rapidly declining* includes cities in some danger of becoming occupied by a high proportion of people with very low incomes. The cities' average percentage of poor people is higher than in
the other three categories, and the average percentage living in concentrated-poverty neighborhoods is more than double that in rapidly
growing cities. Federal and state strategies for arresting urban deterioration should focus on these rapidly declining cities and their close-
in suburbs. That might mean providing them with more federal assistance per capita than is provided to faster-growing areas. But any
federal formula for distributing assistance should also take into account
the relative tax efforts being made by individual cities.

Because inner-city neighborhoods in all categories have similar adverse traits, strategies should not ignore cities in any category.

The Need for State and Federal Assistance

Governments in declining cities cannot raise taxes on their businesses and nonpoor residents to finance remedial policies without motivating many to move to nearby localities with lower taxes. This is also true of state governments, although to a lesser extent. It is harder for a household or business to move from one state to another to avoid taxes without significant disruption.[2] Some reliance on federal funding is therefore probably essential. But relatively wealthy states, as measured by average per capita incomes, could successfully engage in some redistributive spending.

Therefore the federal and state governments must help develop effective strategies to deal with urban problems. Because the federal government will be involved with many large cities, it should formulate general principles for responding. Such a national strategy would have many dimensions. One would be an insistence that strategies be conceived and implemented on a metropolitan-wide basis. Effective remedies cannot be carried out without the multifaceted involvement of the suburbs. Therefore, the spending of federal funds to remedy urban deterioration needs to be planned and carried out at a regional level. As discussed in chapter 9, federal insistence on this point could be the most important element in creating effective regional institutions to guide urban development.

Similarly, state governments in states that contain more than one declining city need to develop a general approach to dealing with deterioration. Each state government should also insist that the suburbs participate in devising and implementing such policies.

The Implications of the Level of Resources

The best mix of strategies to deal with urban problems will depend on the resources available. The more there are, the more diversified and comprehensive the remedial effort can be. If only a few resources are available, they should be concentrated on strategies with the best chances for success.

In this era of scarce federal resources, it is critical to reexamine the flows of funds already focused on inner cities. If those flows can be made more effective, the impact of federal aid can be increased without increasing deficit financing. One of the biggest current flows of funds—$28 billion in fiscal year 1990 from federal, state, and local governments ($10 billion from the federal government alone)—is for the war on drugs.[3] The vast majority of the money is aimed at interdicting the flow of illegal drugs into the United States and reducing the supply in local markets. Yet drugs remain abundant and easily accessible. This massive effort is not producing many successes, and it has created serious problems. The number of people imprisoned for drug-related crimes has skyrocketed, and the criminal justice system has become clogged with drug-related cases. Crime rates have increased because of the needs of drug addicts and conflicts among dealers. And far too many young men from inner cities are building criminal records. I make no claim to expertise in this complex policy area. But it appears that much of this money could be used more effectively if it were redirected into community-based policing and drug rehabilitation programs.

Another large flow of federal funds into inner cities is intended for the rehabilitation of public housing projects. High-rise public housing projects in many big cities have vacancy rates of 30 percent or more because of vandalized and deteriorated units and high crime rates. Much of this funding could be better used to tear down the worst structures and provide the occupants with vouchers for private housing. Drastically reducing the size of public housing projects would also remove a major cause of neighborhood blight in many cities. But Department of Housing and Urban Development regulations prohibit such uses of federal public housing money.

Other programs putting a lot of federal money into inner cities include food stamps; medicare; medicaid; the women's, infants', and children's assistance program (WIC); mass transit subsidies; and even highway funding. How these funds might be better used would be a good subject for research.

A Comprehensive Attack on National Problems

Ideally, a comprehensive attack on inner-city problems would have multiple dimensions, coordinated as much as possible. The attack would be sustained for at least ten years and preferably twenty because shorter periods would not bring about the social changes required. The effort would involve significant participation by local residents, and not be just a top-down program. Finally, it would have access to substantial federal funds. Unfortunately, few government efforts in U.S. domestic policy have exhibited even two or three of these traits, and none that I know of has exhibited all. This shows how difficult it will be to attack urban decline effectively.

Basic Policy Strategies toward Central Cities

At least six comprehensive federal or state strategies for helping central cities have been advocated by various experts. Two do not try to remedy current problems. The other four propose specific remedial tactics. Those four are not mutually exclusive; each could be used by itself, or elements of two or more could be combined. The six are listed below.

—The present-policies strategy would do nothing more than whatever is being done now.

—The adjustment strategy would make little attempt to remedy present problems but would seek to offset their inadequacies with various forms of assistance to city governments and residents.

—The area development strategy would seek to improve target areas or the amenities or opportunities they offer in hopes of retaining residents or attracting new ones. Its two major subforms would focus on areas of concentrated poverty or spread aid throughout cities experiencing severe overall decline.

—The personal or human capital development strategy would aid the present residents of inner-city areas through various forms of human capital development, even if the residents then moved elsewhere.

—The household mobility strategy would help current residents move permanently out of inner-city areas to other neighborhoods, either in the central city or its suburbs.

—The worker mobility strategy would help residents of the target area gain access to jobs outside the area while they remained living in it.

Continuing Present Policies

However existing federal and state policies for treating urban decline are described, they are certainly not stopping the deterioration, nor are they likely to do so. Twenty-eight of the thirty-one cities that lost 4.9 percent or more of their population from 1980 to 1990 also lost population in the 1970s.[4]

The direct costs of retaining this strategy are very low; that is one reason its political feasibility is great. This feasibility can be seen from the results of a 1993 public opinion poll conducted by the *Wall Street Journal*. Respondents were asked whether they would be willing to pay higher taxes to support various specific uses of the funds. Seventy-eight percent said they would pay to improve the quality of education, 75 percent to improve access to health care, and 58 percent to reduce the federal deficit. Only 30 percent were willing to provide aid to city and state governments; 66 percent were opposed.[5]

In the long run the indirect costs of permitting unchecked urban decline could be very high indeed. But it is extremely difficult even to estimate those costs.

The Adjustment Strategy

The adjustment strategy seeks to help compensate declining city governments for the loss of revenues suffered because of shrinking population and employment. Some idea of the potential cost of this approach can be gained by computing how much more revenue the cities that lost 4.9 percent or more of their populations from 1980 to 1990 would have received in 1990 if they had the same populations as in 1980.[6] Separate computations were made by population category. The decrease in population among the thirty-one cities was calculated for each population category and multiplied by average 1990 per capita total revenues and average 1990 per capita tax revenues for that category. Together the cities would have collected $900 million more in taxes and $2 billion more in total revenues.

Of course, these cities also had fewer residents to serve in 1990 than in 1980. So it would not be sensible to try to make up fully for their revenue losses. Yet many operating costs do not fall in proportion with population losses.[7] Some part of the losses—perhaps 25 to 50 percent—might be made the target for adjustment assistance, on the theory that the cities were probably not providing adequate services to begin with.

Adjustment assistance should not be provided through direct unconstrained fund transfers from federal or state governments, such as general revenue sharing.[8] Instead, transfers should take the form of more categorical assistance, like that in the Community Development Block Grant program, to prevent municipal employees from capturing the added funding as higher wages without performing more efficiently. In theory, in a pure adjustment strategy few constraints would be placed on local governments' use of outside money. But prudence would suggest transforming some assistance into elements of an area development strategy, not pure adjustment.

The biggest drawback of an adjustment strategy is its political unacceptability at all levels of government. Every local official in any declining city is strongly motivated to call for reversing current deterioration rather than passively adjusting to it. Tactics aimed at halting decline would introduce more resources into the community than those aimed at adjusting to it. An explicit adjustment strategy would also force local officials to admit that they could not stop the city from losing more people and jobs, a defeatism few would admit publicly, even if privately they believe it is true. Besides, most residents of deteriorating cities advocate job and population increases because they would benefit from growth.

Similarly, the president and Congress cannot publicly admit that they want the declining cities to accept continued shrinkage, even if that is what they believe is necessary. Such a stance is particularly difficult for Democrats, for whom the residents and governments of big cities have been a traditional constituency. And even though the Republican administrations in the 1980s espoused large cuts in direct assistance to big-city governments and, to some extent, their residents, the administrations did not admit they were adopting an adjustment strategy. Instead, they justified their policies as transferring certain social functions to administrative levels "closer to the problems themselves." In reality, what the federal government does rather than what its leaders say determines its true urban strategy.

Area Development Strategies

The area development strategy has been referred to as "gilding the ghetto" by John Kain and Joseph Persky and "ghetto enrichment" by me.[9] The basic idea is to add jobs and improve education, job training, personal security, and the physical environment in inner cities. This was one of the three strategies described in the *Report of the National Advisory Commission on Civil Disorders* (the Kerner commission) in 1968.[10] The commission, however, recommended adopting what it called the integration strategy, which combined ghetto enrichment with policies aimed at greater mixing of blacks and whites residentially, in the communications media, and in workplaces.

The main argument for an inner-city development strategy is that existing patterns of segregation by race and income are too powerful to overcome. Any breakup of inner-city poverty areas or extensive out-movement of their residents is unlikely. The only way to improve conditions for current residents is to do so where they live. Jobs could be attracted by establishing enterprise zones that offer businesses operating there special tax and deregulation incentives.[11] Improvements in other conditions would require complex sets of other policies, some of which are described later in this chapter.

Attacking urban decline primarily through an area development strategy has two major drawbacks. First, it would perpetuate the geographical isolation of many minority and low-income people from better neighborhoods, jobs, schools, and other public facilities. The Supreme Court has repeatedly held that maintaining separate but equal public facilities is unconstitutional when applied to race. Legal separation in itself creates a stigma of inequality. And the facilities provided for separated groups are almost always inferior to those enjoyed by the dominant majority. The same conclusions apply to the de facto isolation of inner-city neighborhoods.

Second, attracting good jobs to the inner cities and providing better public facilities and services is extremely difficult. The high crime rates and other forces that caused businesses to abandon these neighborhoods in the first place will prevent them from being lured back. And such additional factors as shortages of large vacant sites for modern plants and warehouses, high insurance costs, and a long-range trend toward decentralization of all types of activities reinforces their choice.

This conclusion is borne out by experience with enterprise zones in both the United Kingdom and the United States. Such zones have been at best modestly effective, and then only when they have encompassed areas where significant activities and numbers of residents are already located. In the United Kingdom, most jobs created in enterprise zones were relocated from other parts of the metropolitan area. In the United States more new jobs can be attributed to the zones themselves, but they have mainly been the result of the expansion of firms already there. Tax abatement and other financial incentives provided by the zones seem to have had little effect in generating jobs. But professional management of the zones by entrepreneurial organizations did increase their effectiveness.[12]

A vital lesson from this experience and other attempts at urban renewal is that inner-city development is likely to succeed best in neighborhoods that contain or are close to at least some viable businesses, as well as strong churches, established community organizations, successful public or private schools, and major hospitals or universities or other employment centers. Following this principle, Chicago is gradually being redeveloped from its downtown outward in all directions through incremental improvements.[13] This strategy permits new projects to draw on the strengths of previous development rather than having to start from scratch in totally destitute areas.[14]

Yet trickle-down development that focuses investment on areas far outside inner-city neighborhoods in hopes that it will indirectly aid inner-city residents is ineffective. Inner-city neighborhoods usually contain less than 20 percent of a big city's population.[15] The residents are normally the poorest and least politically powerful. Local elected officials will thus disperse resources to all parts of the city or focus them on wealthier areas. Many jobs created in downtowns and other relatively prosperous parts of the city are taken by workers with higher skill levels, including suburban residents, rather than by unemployed inner-city residents. Finally, generalized aid provided to city governments is often captured by municipal workers, especially if their unions are strong.

If the federal government wants to focus resources on inner-city improvements, it must require local officials to use the funds for that. This does not mean spending funds only on the most destitute neighborhoods. More likely to succeed would be targeting the aid on inner-city neighborhoods one or two steps up from the bottom of the socioeconomic ladder. Investments there would be more likely to help residents gain economically viable jobs and create lasting physical improvements.[16]

In spite of the many drawbacks of inner-city development strategies, it is politically impossible to help residents get jobs and move out without trying to improve the areas themselves. Such a strategy would be resisted by city politicians and local community development organizations because it would undermine their constituencies. And the residents and local organizations remaining in inner-city neighborhoods would feel betrayed. So at least some inner-city development must be included in any viable overall strategy.

The Personal Development Strategy

If aid focuses mainly on helping people in the most deteriorated neighborhoods, many will move out as soon as they can. They will take most benefits of the aid with them and may even leave the neighborhoods in worse shape than before because their presence constitutes both an example and an economic asset.[17] That is what happened in the War on Poverty and Model Cities programs in the 1960s and 1970s. Even if job training, income assistance, and housing vouchers create net benefits for society, they can still reduce the long-run resources in the low-income neighborhoods at which they were originally aimed.

Yet many of the worst problems of inner-city areas involve personal poverty, poor health, low levels of skill, inadequate nutrition, and lack of safety and security. It would not serve the residents or society to restrict aid to people who cannot take the benefits with them if they decide to leave. In fact, funding direct personal empowerment that improves social and geographical mobility should be a high priority in any assault on urban decline. An example of a brilliantly successful form of such aid was the G.I. Bill for education adopted after World War II. Similar means of helping poor households enter mainstream society through their own choices should be emphasized.

Because any effective personal development strategy would allow many living in inner-city neighborhoods to move out, it would closely resemble a household mobility strategy. Certain elements of both are discussed later, and elements of both should be included in any overall approach to combating urban decline.

Some of the worst conditions in inner cities stem from destructive behavior patterns that probably cannot be changed by exhortation from outsiders. These patterns include young men's sexually exploitative attitudes toward young women and unwillingness to help support the children they produce, the willingness of teenagers to engage in active sexual lives at very early ages (although among young women the activity is not always started voluntarily), unwillingness to use contraceptives, failure to nurture children, and hostility among teenagers toward those who perform well in school.[18] Changing this behavior is crucial to improving life in these neighborhoods.

But such change will not be easy. "The major enemy of black survival in America," Cornel West has commented, "has been and is neither oppression nor exploitation but rather the nihilistic threat—that is, the loss of hope and absence of meaning." He believes this threat has grown in the past two decades because of weakening black religious and civic institutions and increased pressure from a commercialized culture.

> Like all Americans, African Americans are influenced greatly by the images of comfort, convenience, machismo, femininity, violence, and sexual stimulation that bombard consumers. These seductive images contribute to the predominance of the market-inspired way of life over all others and thereby edge out nonmarket values—love, care, service to others—handed down by preceding generations. The predominance of this way of life among those living in poverty-ridden conditions, with a limited capacity to ward off self-contempt and self-hatred, results in the possible triumph of the nihilistic threat in black America.[19]

As West states, American commercialized culture has had a terrible effect on inner-city minority-group behavior. Quick resort to violence, early engagement in sexual activity, fascination with expensive consumer goods, and indifference to human rights and life represent extreme versions of values constantly propagated by white-dominated media and business firms. The most violent and inhumane behavior reflects the actions of movie and television macho killer-heroes who gun down opponents by the score without a qualm and without legal retribution to the applause of the good guys in these stylized epics. Recently, popular black rap musicians have also been glorifying violent, antipolice, antifemale behavior for young black men. Inner-city teenagers are constantly seduced by these images because they are too often without the benefit of strong families, positive male role models, religious values, and other mediating institutions.

West believes that a combination of renewed black institutions, stronger black leadership, more outside assistance to poor black neighborhoods, and white willingness to attack remaining racist behavior is necessary to change destructive behavior. It is hard to believe government policies would have much effect, especially if administered from outside mainly by white officials. Efforts to change sexual behavior and child-nurturing activities in such neighborhoods have not been very successful, even when well funded by persistent and energetic sponsors.[20] Thus a crucial part of the responsibility for altering self-destructive behavior rests with inner-city residents themselves. The best public policy to support their efforts may be to continue attempts to cope with basic social problems through various forms of assistance. That would include strengthening and expanding the private schools that already effectively serve many inner-city black neighborhoods.

The Household Mobility Strategy

The household mobility strategy would offer low-income households greater opportunities for self-improvement by helping them move out of the inner city. They would then enjoy something closer to equality with the opportunities available to nonpoor people. Up to now this has not been possible for poor people, in part because so many communities have blocked the construction of low-cost housing.[21] Advocates of household mobility do not propose to pressure anyone to move out of inner-city neighborhoods. Rather, they believe more poor people, especially members of minority groups, ought to have a realistic opportunity to move if they want to as part of a general expansion of their opportunities. Members of many ethnic and racial groups have already taken advantage of such opportunities, as shown by the massive migration of middle-class households from cities to suburbs since 1950.

The household mobility strategy would create tension with any area development strategy because it encourages people to move out of the areas in which the other strategy invests. Yet elements of a household mobility strategy must be included in any approach to remedying inner-city problems in the long run. One reason is that it is unrealistic to believe that private businesses will voluntarily move into inner cities. Only public or publicly financed facilities could be located there on any large scale. No doubt these facilities could improve conditions in inner-city neighborhoods, but it is access to private sector jobs, facilities, and opportunities, not public facilities, that is crucial for rejuvenating the lives of inner-city residents.

Inner-city residents must also be exposed to environments that are not dominated by extreme poverty and its attendant conditions. That means sending their children to schools where most students are from working-class or middle-class homes. It means giving them job opportunities in businesses where most other workers have enough skills to earn decent incomes. It means giving them the chance to live in neighborhoods not dominated by juvenile gangs, drugs, and fear of violence. Only these can constitute real opportunities.

Concentrating on developing inner-city neighborhoods without also encouraging residents to move to better areas would be perpetuating the "two societies . . . separate and unequal" that the Kerner commission warned about in 1968.[22] In 1990 extremely poor inner-city neighborhoods were 47 percent black, 22 percent Hispanic, and 26 percent non-Hispanic white.[23] In spite of great improvements in civil rights enforcement since the 1960s, Hispanics and blacks are still strongly discriminated against, especially in housing markets. In the long run it is impossible to create truly equal opportunities for all Americans while continuing the geographic isolation by race or ethnicity. Furthermore, more than a century of American experience, including that since the civil rights acts of the 1960s, proves that a political system dominated by white majorities will not allocate equal resources to separate facilities intended for nearly exclusive use by minorities. The idea of "separate but equal" life opportunities is doomed from the start.

In the long run, then, society must deliberately help some poor inner-city residents achieve access to suburban homes, schools, and jobs if America's most serious domestic national problems are to be resolved. It will simply not work for suburban residents to continue dealing with central cities entirely at arm's length, such as by paying more taxes, although taxes are necessary too.

Some observers have objected that the household mobility strategy removes minority or low-income households from locations where welfare, subsidized health care, counseling, and other public services they depend on and are familiar with are most readily available. Low-income people may have difficulty moving around in the suburbs if they cannot afford cars. But experience with the Gautreaux plan in Chicago shows that sizable distances and not owning a car are not serious obstacles to gaining the benefits of moving out of inner-city neighborhoods.[24]

The main problems with the household mobility strategy are political. Suburban residents have mounted widespread resistance to permitting sizable numbers of low-income residents of central cities, especially blacks, to move into communities that are not already mainly minority. And some city politicians do not want to lose constituents; they attack out-movement policies as deliberate strategies of white racists to reduce the political power of minority groups and to displace poor minority city dwellers with high-income gentrifying whites. Another obstacle is that enabling large numbers of poor people to occupy housing in expensive new-growth areas would require substantial housing subsidies.

But these obstacles are not immovable. Far more members of minority groups, especially blacks, could move into suburban homes if they were not discriminated against by white realtors, lenders, and homeowners.[25] Just drastically reducing present discriminatory practices would permit more out-movement from cities in general and even from inner-city neighborhoods. If more suburbs allowed construction of lower-cost units and development of accessory apartments in existing single-family homes, many low-cost housing units could be made accessible in suburbs without public subsidies. If low-income renters were also provided with housing vouchers, the volume of out-movement would increase sharply. And this could be done without building subsidized housing units, which are so vehemently opposed by suburban residents.

The movement of households out of inner cities could be carried out on a significant scale. In the Gautreaux program, the Leadership Council for Metropolitan Open Communities administered vouchers to more than 4,000 mainly black low-income inner-city Chicago households, which they used to rent scattered dwellings, mostly in white suburban neighborhoods. They were also provided with assistance in locating the housing and counseling to help them adjust to suburban living. Follow-up studies have shown that members of most households improved their living conditions, level of employment, and school performance, and were satisfied at having made the move.[26] In St. Louis a school program bused inner-city black students to mainly white suburban schools, where they notably improved their academic performance. However, these experiments have not been conducted on a large scale anywhere.

A simple quantitative analysis of conditions in the Chicago and Atlanta metropolitan areas shows that greater use of household mobility would be feasible. Table 6-1 shows the effects on inner-city populations of devoting certain percentages of newly built suburban housing to sheltering these people. The table assumes that inner-city poverty areas in the two cities contained 15 percent of their 1980 populations (slightly less than the 16.3 percent average for rapidly declin-

TABLE 6-1. *Effects of Subsidized Suburban Housing on Distribution of Households in Atlanta and Chicago Metropolitan Areas, under Various Quantity Assumptions, 1980–90*

Added units subsidized		Equivalent of city units (percent)			Percent of all suburban households, 1990
Percent	Number	Inner-city poverty area	Low income	All	
		Atlanta[a]			
1	3,698	16.5	5.3	2.5	0.4
2	7,397	32.9	10.5	4.9	0.8
5	18,492	82.3	26.3	12.3	2.0
7.5	27,737	123.4	39.4	18.5	3.0
10	36,983	164.6	52.5	24.7	4.0
15	55,475	246.9	78.8	37.0	6.0
20	73,967	329.2	105.1	49.4	8.0
25	92,458	411.4	131.3	61.7	10.0
		Chicago[b]			
1	2,376	1.5	0.5	0.2	0.1
2	4,752	3.0	1.0	0.4	0.3
5	11,880	7.5	2.4	1.1	0.7
7.5	17,821	11.2	3.6	1.7	1.0
10	23,761	15.0	4.8	2.2	1.4
15	35,641	22.4	7.2	3.4	2.1
20	47,522	29.9	9.6	4.5	2.7
25	59,402	37.4	11.9	5.6	3.4

Households in central cities	*Chicago*	*Atlanta*
Number of households, 1990	1,058,555	149,810
Low-income households, 1990	497,521	70,411
Households in inner-city poverty areas	158,783	22,471
Very low income (percent)	50.0	50.0
Low income (percent)	31.9	31.9
Poor households in inner-city poverty areas	52,928	7,490
Very low income (percent)	16.7	16.7
Low income (percent)	10.6	10.6

Source: Author's calculations using data from Bureau of the Census, *Construction Reports, Building Permits* (Department of Commerce, annual). Table shows distribution of city and suburban households between 1980 and 1990 if governments had subsidized new units in new-growth areas for low-income households moving out of central cities.

a. Metropolitan area includes the eighteen Georgia counties in the Atlanta MSA.

b. Metropolitan area includes Illinois counties of Cook, Dupage, Will, Lake, McHenry, Kane, Grundy, and Kendall.

ing cities in 1990). If only a small percentage of new housing built during the 1980s in the suburbs of these cities had consisted of subsidized units occupied by inner-city households, the out-movement would have made a notable dent in reducing inner-city populations.

In the greater Chicago area, if 5 percent of the suburban housing added from 1980 to 1990 had been subsidized and occupied by inner-city residents, 7.5 percent of Chicago inner-city households could have moved out of the inner city. This is a low-impact percentage for two reasons. The city of Chicago has a very large population in relation to that of the greater Chicago area, and the area's slow growth has limited the number of new housing units built. In the Atlanta metropolitan area, if 5 percent of added suburban housing had been similarly subsidized and occupied by inner-city residents, 82 percent of these people would have moved to the suburbs. This impact is much greater because Atlanta has a small population compared with its suburbs, and rapid suburban growth added a lot of new housing from 1980 to 1990.

Similar calculations were carried out for forty-four of the nation's largest cities, using estimates of the number of households, new suburban housing units built, and inner-city households. For the forty-four areas combined, setting aside 5 percent of suburban housing units built in the 1980s would have permitted 12.7 percent of the 1980 inner-city households to move to the suburbs. In thirteen of these areas the share would have exceeded 30 percent.

This analysis implies two important conclusions. Suburbs would not have to be overwhelmed by out-migrants from central cities to achieve significant reductions in the poor populations of many central cities. But unless the household mobility strategy is carried out on a much larger scale (in terms of the percentage of new suburban units subsidized for inner-city occupants) than seems likely, it would take a long time to come close to emptying out the inner-city portions of most big cities.

What would happen to inner-city neighborhoods emptied by such a strategy? If Atlanta lost 82 percent of the residents of its poorest census tracts, it would lose one out of eight residents unless others replaced them. Many inner-city tracts in Detroit, Chicago, and New York have already lost comparable shares of their populations in the past few decades. In most cases the areas have remained vacant and derelict. A few have been substantially redeveloped through urban renewal or gentrification or programs that introduced new construction and nonpoor households and enterprises. Much of Chicago's near south, near west, and near northwest sides are in this category.

Nevertheless, how to treat such emptying-out neighborhoods over the long run must be considered in applying this strategy in any particular metropolitan area. Preventing inner-city neighborhoods from becoming permanently derelict would undoubtedly require substantial resources. The cost should be taken into account in computing the total cost of the strategy. This is another reason why household mobility and area development strategies cannot be considered entirely apart from each other; they would inevitably become heavily intertwined.

The Worker Mobility Strategy

In the past few years Mark Alan Hughes has been promoting a strategy of improving inner-city life by making it easier for workers living there to obtain and hold jobs in the suburbs without changing residences.[27] He contends that the other two main strategies for inner-city improvement—area development and household out-migration—are either impractical or politically blocked by suburban resistance. Both inner-city and general city development fly in the face of decentralizing trends that have been operating for seventy years. These trends have been accelerated by computers, fax machines, and other technical innovations. And although large-scale out-migration from the inner city seems fine in theory, suburban resistance is too strongly entrenched to permit it to be tried anywhere on a reasonable scale. He claims that neither strategy can become effective very soon.

Yet high levels of unemployment among inner-city residents need to be reduced as quickly as possible. That leaves a policy of trying to make it easier for inner-city workers to obtain and hold jobs being created in new-growth suburbs. Hughes's strategy involves job training, job information systems linking city workers and suburban firms, restructured transportation systems serving suburban job sites and city neighborhoods, improved inner-city day care facilities and support, an increased earned income credit supplementing wages from low-level entry jobs, and improved policing in inner-city neighborhoods. Several of these elements are actually forms of inner-city development. In fact only two, new regional job information centers and transportation links, deal directly with worker mobility.

Worker mobility has some advantages over other strategies. It does not further empty out declining areas, at least not in the short run. (However, workers might move out as soon as they became established in new suburban jobs.) It would not initially alienate politicians or community development organizations, which do not want to lose constituents. It does not antagonize suburban residents who want to benefit from low-income workers but are opposed to having more low-income residents in their communities. It would also presumably be strongly supported by suburban employers. Most of its elements are easy to carry out, at least in theory. Finally, the strategy would not be nearly as expensive as the others.

But Hughes's version of the worker mobility strategy includes elements of inner-city development subject to his own criticism that such development is impractical. More important, this strategy would not break up segregated concentrations of low-income minority households. If successful, it would introduce more income and more family stability into poor areas, thus enabling them to support some spontaneous development. But it would still leave them as separate and unequal enclaves.

In addition, the worker mobility strategy can only succeed if suburbs have acute shortages of low-wage workers. This is most likely during periods of strong general prosperity and low unemployment. It is also more applicable to northeastern and midwestern metropolitan areas that have high concentrations of poor residents in central cities rather than in western cities, which have more scattered enclaves.

A final drawback is that all the transportation arrangements Hughes cites as models have operated on only a very small scale. There is no evidence that they can be successfully expanded to the scale needed to provide significant improvement in the quality of inner-city life. The strategy may, then, really amount only to a minor tactic or set of tactics that should be incorporated into some more comprehensive strategy.

The Necessity for a Mixed Strategy

None of the six strategies I have described represents by itself the best way for society to respond to urban deterioration. Rather, a mixture of elements from five strategies (all except the continuation of present policies) is necessary.

Some elements of the adjustment strategy are necessary to help city governments compensate for the loss of revenues from falling populations and economic activities. Some elements of both forms of the area development strategy are necessary because of the nature of big-city politics and the need to improve the environment in inner cities for those who will have to remain living there. Such local improvement is especially critical to make lives and property more secure. Some elements of the personal development strategy are essential because inner-city neighborhoods badly need investments in education, job skills, health care, and changes in personal behavior. Some elements of the household mobility strategy are necessary because it is impossible in the long run to create truly separate but equal conditions in racially and economically segregated neighborhoods. More people in inner cities must have access to the same chances to move to better neighborhoods that so many nonpoor households have had. Some elements of the worker mobility strategy seem prudent because it will take so long to implement key portions of the other strategies.

Such a combination of elements presupposes a big enough response to urban decline by American society to finance the necessary action. The more financial resources available for conducting this mixed strategy, the more elements can be included. However, it is prudent to assume that there will be a shortage of resources, so priorities must be established. I have done this rather crudely by describing the tactics that seem most critical and then presenting a policy matrix containing them and other possible tactics.

Overcoming Obstacles to Setting Priorities

The very idea of setting priorities among possible tactics implies that some agency exists that can make such decisions. To do so, the agency must have a consistent set of preferences, the ability to predict the likely outcomes of various actions, the capacity to assign priorities, and a powerful influence on what actions are in fact carried out. No such entity exists in U.S. metropolitan areas, or in the federal government, or even within individual city governments. Nevertheless, it is useful to conceive of setting priorities from some overall perspective in order to make judgments about the efficacy of possible policy mixes, whoever controls them. Therefore this analysis assumes priorities are being assigned by a hypothetical agency with both a national perspective and a metropolitan area perspective.

Another difficulty is a common mental block caused by the complexity of these issues. Many observers have concluded that no effective remedies to particular inner-city problems can be launched until the entire structure of cities and society in general is reformed. This attitude reflects the view that every problem is rooted in general social conditions, which is surely true. However, such an attitude also makes progress seem hopeless. To avoid this impasse, I assume that remedial actions launched in one or a few areas can have at least some beneficial effects.

Assigning priorities among possible actions also requires making value judgments that cannot be scientifically verified. I have therefore used my own judgments. However, the general approach to assigning priorities has been structured so that other persons could use it while substituting their own value judgments.

Remedial Tactics

Any strategy for tackling urban decline and inner-city problems would have to contain the following elements to be effective.

—Federal and other government efforts to attack basic social problems must be conceived of and publicized as nationwide campaigns. These efforts should not be presented as primarily urban or inner-city programs, or as short-term remedies to immediate crises. Otherwise the efforts will not receive broad enough political support to obtain the resources needed.

—Significant economic resources must be transferred to city governments that have disproportionately high concentrations of low-income residents. This may seem to contradict the first element, but it does not. Such cities have more intensive incidences of basic social problems than other parts of the nation. Moreover, voluntary payments will certainly not accomplish a sufficient redistribution of resources. The money must come from state and federal taxes that collect revenues from suburbanites and others and spend them on aids to residents and local governments in declining cities. This policy must be accompanied by requirements that prevent the added resources from being used to raise the salaries of municipal workers without increasing benefits to city residents.

—Certain direct forms of assistance must be increased for low-income households and workers. This assistance should not require that recipients reside in any particular jurisdiction, including the one administering the aid. Thus all types of vouchers should be usable throughout a metropolitan area.[28] Such aids could include providing some direct financial or training assistance to low-income and un-skilled workers. The assistance should include helping inner-city residents learn about, and travel to, jobs located in the suburbs. Another form of aid would increase the resources directed toward improving the nurturing, health, and education of children growing up in poverty. A children's allowance like that used in nearly all other developed nations could help achieve this goal.

The quality of public schooling offered to all children must be improved, but especially for those living in concentrated-poverty areas and therefore attending schools where nearly all students come from impoverished homes. Vouchers that permit poor people to send their children to school anywhere in the metropolitan area should be publicly funded but usable in both public and private schools.[29] Finally, housing vouchers should be provided to at least some low-income households in inner cities that could be used to pay rent on units in the suburbs.

If these forms of aid were extended to a great many of the people eligible for them, they would disproportionately benefit concentrated-poverty neighborhoods.

—Antidiscrimination policies of all types concerning housing and job markets and the allocation of resources to public schools must be vigorously enforced.[30] A crucial remedy would be to establish non-profit agencies covering an entire metropolitan area that can test realtor and lender behavior, help minority households locate suitable homes in mainly white areas, find financing to purchase them, and initiate punitive lawsuits when necessary. Severe penalties should be levied against persons and firms found guilty of illegal discrimination. And gross inequities in the allocation of resources that handicap primarily black schools should be eliminated.[31]

—Extensive federal resources now being ineffectively expended in inner cities must be redeployed.

—Inner-city residents must be encouraged to change their self-destructive and socially negative behavior. A few public policies aimed at helping them do so can be adopted by society at large. For example, stronger legal pressure could be exerted on fathers of children born

TABLE 6-2. *Strategies and Tactics for Helping Inner Cities*

	Strategy			
Nationwide problem	Area development	Personal development	Household mobility	Worker mobility
Crime and insecurity	Federally fund more community policing[a] Shift drug control funding from interdiction to rehabilitation[a] Expand minority membership of police forces[a] Improve community relations training of big-city police forces Permit resident managers to expel disruptive and criminal households from public housing projects[a]	Expand programs working with young men in sports, mentoring[a] Decriminalize use of some drugs[a] Reduce constant violence on television and in movies Launch more antidrug publicity campaigns by prominent figures	Dismantle worst high-rise public housing projects and provide vouchers to former residents[a]	
Children raised in poverty	Fully fund local Head Start centers[a] Expand mother and child health centers[a]	Fully fund Head Start program[a] Expand mother and child health centers[a]	Provide more housing vouchers for use in suburban areas, plus counseling[a]	Provide more day care facilities serving inner cities

Poor education

Expand funding for public schools in inner-city neighborhoods[a]

Provide incentives for the best teachers to work in inner-city schools[a]

Increase training of inner-city teachers in child development skills

Fully fund the WIC program[a]

Immunize all young children[a]

Launch Head Start for 3-year-olds[a]

Create national Child Support Assurance program to replace AFDC, aiding all poor children[a]

Collect more child support from fathers

Expand contraceptive supply programs

Fully fund Head Start program[a]

Expand federal funding for schools participating in Choice programs[a]

Head Start for 3-year-olds[a]

Permit private groups to start own schools with public money[a]

Expand low-income tax credit and mortgage revenue programs to fund low-cost suburban rental housing

Tie funding of above two programs to state-mandated reduction of local regulatory barriers to affordable housing

Create housing availability information centers with metrowide jurisdiction[a]

Expand suburban school access programs serving inner-city children

Ease regulations concerning use of informal and family day care centers

Provide job training linked directly to suburban job opportunities[a]

TABLE 6-2. *Continued*

		Strategy		
Nationwide problem	*Area development*	*Personal development*	*Household mobility*	*Worker mobility*
	Create special education facilities for disturbed and disruptive children	Permit public schools to expel seriously disruptive students[a]		
		Provide strong rewards for good students and non-dropouts[a]		
Poor worker integration into mainstream labor force	Develop investment insurance program for poverty areas with federal and state funding[a]	Expand the Job Corps[a]		Create job information centers with metrowide territory[a]
		Provide job training programs for unemployed and low-skilled workers		Create transport and auto subsidies for inner-city workers with suburban jobs[a]
	Fund job location incentives for inner cities	Expand the earned income tax credit		Provide job training linked directly to suburban job opportunities[a]
	Create job program aimed at residents of high-unemployment areas			Encourage suburban firms to provide van pool programs with tax breaks
	Expand "City Year" volunteer program for inner-city and suburban youths			

a. Priority action. Some tactics are shown more than once because they relate to more than one strategy.

out of wedlock to contribute to their children's financial support. But most changes in such behavior can only come from the residents. Leaders of minority groups inside and outside these neighborhoods thus have a particular responsibility to help change the mores of persons living there.

—Regulatory and legal barriers to creating and maintaining lower-cost housing in suburbs and central cities themselves must be reduced. This would require extensive changes in state and local government policies. The changes needed are outlined in the report of the Advisory Commission on Regulatory Barriers to Affordable Housing, *"Not In My Back Yard."*[32]

—The many obstacles within city governments themselves to the efficient performance of business activities, including high local business taxes and bureaucratic barriers, must also be reduced. This is a responsibility that local governments must undertake themselves. Creating one-stop centers to handle all the permits necessary for businesses to carry out improvements or additions to their existing facilities is one of the most effective tactics of this type. The federal government should develop a central information source about effective ways to improve local government services to city businesses and publicize success stories widely.

Setting Priorities

A set of specific actions that might be carried out as remedies to all basic nationwide social problems is presented in table 6–2. It shows the four strategies for combating deterioration and the four main national problems found in inner cities. The tactics included by no means constitute a comprehensive list of possible remedial actions. Rather they represent actions with which I have become familiar in the course of this analysis that seem most likely to be effective.

The highest priority should be to reduce personal insecurity in inner cities. Insecurity paralyzes local initiatives and poisons the quality of life. Insecurity in inner-city neighborhoods also makes suburban residents unwilling to accept inner-city households as neighbors. If resources are extremely limited, therefore, they should first be focused on this matter. Admittedly, it is difficult to know just what approaches would be most effective in increasing personal security. Much more community policing is the change most commonly suggested, but others should also be tried.

The second priority should be to improve the care of poor children. Failing to do this will generate enormous future social costs. This emphasis should encounter little resistance from inner-city residents, since it provides unalloyed benefits. And it will appeal to sensible people throughout the nation.

The third priority should be to improve job opportunities for inner-city residents. However, attempts to attract jobs from suburban and other outlying locations into inner cities are not likely to work well. Instead, efforts should focus on retaining and expanding businesses and activities already there. City governments should make special efforts to discover what such firms need and meet those needs with a minimum of bureaucratic delay and red tape. Because businesses do not usually base location decisions on property tax or other local tax considerations, the best way for local governments to meet their needs would be to perform their normal functions in a more responsive manner. This could include taking a survey of major employers in the city, especially those located near inner-city neighborhoods, to see what problems they have and what can be done to solve them.

High priority should also be given to the worker mobility strategy. Especially important are creating a job information network throughout the metropolitan area with information centers in inner-city areas and providing job training closely linked to the needs of suburban and other metropolitan area employers.

Lower priority should be given to improving public schools and increasing household mobility. Both are important, but they involve long-run efforts. And they are closely related because one of the best ways to improve the education of inner-city children is to help them attend suburban public schools. Because suburban resistance to large-scale creation of subsidized housing is likely to be intense, it would be most prudent to begin the household mobility strategy through something like Chicago's Gautreaux program. It could begin in a limited way, then gradually expand.

Part 3
New Visions

7

Alternative Visions of Growth

A MERICANS' pursuit of the five elements in the dominant vision of low-density growth described in chapter 1 ultimately generates the growth-related problems identified there. It is beneficial for society to create other visions of how metropolitan areas ought to develop that would, if carried out, be less plagued by those problems or others equally undesirable.

Elements of the Visions

Each element in the dominant vision concerns an area of activity or structure within the overall pattern of metropolitan area growth. Ownership of detached, single-family homes concerns residential density and form. Use of private automobiles concerns transportation. Scattered, low-density, landscaped workplaces concern commercial and industrial location and density. Living in small, self-governed communities is in the field of governance, including infrastructure finance. Providing housing for the poor through the trickle-down process concerns sheltering low-income households.

Each field constitutes one broad aspect of life in metropolitan areas that might be organized in several different ways. The particular element within a field set forth in the dominant vision represents just one possible form of organization. Other elements could be defined to represent other ways of organizing that same aspect of life. For example, concerning commercial and industrial location and density, an alternative to scattering jobs in low-density structures would be to concentrate them in a few high-density clusters throughout the metropolitan area. Another would be to concentrate most jobs in one dominant node—the downtown area—and in a few large outlying nodes built around regional shopping centers.

The five fields of the dominant vision certainly do not encompass every important aspect of metropolitan life. They do not address the arts and culture, education, the justice system, religion, or health care, and they say little about recreation (although open space is important). Also, the way I have defined the key elements of the dominant vision and alternatives to it is subjective. Other observers of metropolitan life might define its main fields differently.

Yet these five fields cover the most important aspects of metropolitan life that directly affect and vary with the spatial development and extent of population and economic growth there. Therefore, using these five fields as a foundation for erecting alternative models of how metropolitan growth might occur is appropriate. Moreover, this approach treats an immensely complex subject in a relatively simple, comprehensible way.

This chapter describes elements in each field that are different from those in the dominant vision. These elements are then combined in various ways to create alternative visions of growth.

Criteria for Alternative Elements

Formulating alternatives for any set of elements is an art, not a science. A great many possibilities could be imagined, but only a handful are relevant to each real situation. The range of possibilities can be narrowed through use of a few broad criteria of desirability. These are traits that each alternative ought to have to be useful. This analysis uses three criteria applicable both to individual elements and to overall visions and two others applicable only to overall visions.

The first criterion is improved effectiveness. It applies to both individual elements and overall visions. Successful pursuit of an alternative to one of the five existing elements or to an alternative vision should notably reduce the severity of existing growth-related problems.

Another criterion is the appeal to self-interest. An alternative element or vision must appeal strongly enough to the self-interest of important political, social, and economic groups and leaders that they will support its adoption.

A similar but somewhat different criterion is cultural acceptability.

No alternative element or vision should call for behavior very different from that consistent with existing economic, political, and social values. For example, any vision that would require most people to give up driving their cars would be unacceptable to the vast majority of Americans.

Two other criteria apply only to overall visions. The first is internal consistency. Achieving any one element should not require behavior that would block realization of any of the other four elements in that vision. A goal of tightly bounded high residential density, for instance, is probably inconsistent with a system of governance that distributes powers over land use among many small, nearly autonomous localities. Citizens in each locality would object to the necessary increases in residential density.

The last criterion is compatibility with existing patterns of settlement. The pattern described by any new vision must be capable of being added to existing parts of metropolitan areas without either unduly disrupting an area or requiring extremely expensive adaptive processes.

Alternatives to Low-Density Residential Settlements

The first element in the low-density vision is nearly universal ownership of single-family detached houses. It generates two key settlement dimensions: relatively low average residential densities and unlimited expansion of metropolitan area growth. Two alternatives to low residential densities can be formulated.

—Very high average residential densities in all new-growth areas. For reasons discussed later, very high densities refers to more than 12.5 dwelling units for each net residential acre. At 2.5 residents in each unit, there would be 10,000 persons in a gross square mile if 50 percent of the land is residential (as in suburbs) and 5,000 persons a gross square mile if 25 percent of all land is residential (as in big cities). The resulting settlement pattern would resemble that found in London, Stockholm, and other European cities with high proportions of mid-rise multifamily dwellings.

—Low density as the dominant pattern, but interspersed with higher density housing, both single-family and multifamily. This pattern would permit average densities in new-growth areas substantially higher than those prevailing in most U.S. metropolitan areas without abandoning the dominance of single-family dwellings. For example, if 20 percent of new residential areas were developed at 30 units an acre and 80 percent at 4 units an acre, the average residential density would be 9.2 units a net acre. If 50 percent of the land is residential, there would be a gross density of 7,360 persons a square mile, much higher than in most suburbs.

The first alternative, uniform high density, is attractive to some urban planners, partly because it might make greater use of public transit economically feasible. But many observers would argue that this lifestyle would be so different from that prized by current American values that it does not meet the criterion of cultural acceptability. Nevertheless, it will be retained in the analysis.

Alternatives to unlimited outward expansion of settled areas must involve some constraint on peripheral growth. One mechanism for imposing such constraint is an urban growth boundary (UGB). It is a line drawn around the periphery of densely settled areas designed to keep most growth within the boundary.[1] The suitability of the boundary's location is usually reexamined at preestablished intervals as growth proceeds, perhaps every ten years. The boundary can then be extended if it does not include enough vacant land to accommodate likely expansion. Minor adjustments can also be made between major reevaluations. However, the extent to which growth is confined inside the boundary can vary greatly from place to place or over time in any one place. There are several alternatives.

—Confinement of all growth to the area within the boundary. This is the policy recommended for southern California by the Sierra Club.[2] This plan would permanently preserve undeveloped zones as green belts. If population growth becomes substantial, the policy would require greatly increasing residential densities inside the boundary.

—Confinement of most but not all growth within the boundary and allowing broad scattering of growth outside. This policy would slow the expansion of existing settlements but not halt it altogether.

—Confinement of most but not all growth inside the boundary, with growth permitted outside in only a few nodes. Most external territory would be left undeveloped. This policy amounts to preserving most undeveloped zones as permanent green belts but allowing compact new communities at intervals in the open spaces.

Certain terms in these definitions, such as *most but not all future growth*, are not clearly defined. Therefore these three alternatives permit variations that could be defined as many more alternatives. However, to keep the analysis manageable, only these three will be considered.

Which alternatives would be most appropriate for any given metropolitan area depends on the area's characteristics. One characteristic is the rate at which population is likely to grow. Rigid urban growth boundaries are probably not feasible in southern California or other areas of rapid population growth. If the boundary is drawn close to built-up parts of a metropolitan area, it will not take long before all developable land within the boundary is occupied. Any additional residents would have to be piled into existing residential neighborhoods. In fast-growing areas, sizable increases in existing density would be required, which would arouse strong resistance from people living in those neighborhoods.

If, however, the boundary is drawn far enough outside built-up areas to include sufficient vacant land to accommodate added growth for many years, it will not meaningfully constrain development for a long time. In Oregon the UGB is supposed to be large enough to encompass a twenty-year supply of developable land. The median compound annual population growth rate from 1980 to 1990 among the fifty-eight largest U.S. metropolitan areas was 1.21 percent; the highest rate was 5.21 percent, and only six areas grew faster than 3 percent.[3] If a metropolitan area is growing 2 percent a year, it will gain 22 percent in ten years and 49 percent in twenty. Including enough land to accommodate a 49 percent increase in population would locate the UGB very far from existing built-up areas. It would probably not act as the strong constraint on expansion that proponents of such boundaries desire.

Projections for six southern California counties indicate that their population might grow 43 percent from 1985 to 2010.[4] That is a compound annual growth rate of 1.44 percent. An urban growth boundary that truly constrains near-future expansion is not likely to encompass enough vacant land to permit a 43 percent increase in population within the boundary. Putting most newcomers into existing neighborhoods, however, would require an increase in average densities of 33 to 50 percent. Yet most of those neighborhoods would prefer downzoning to achieve lower densities. So the required increases are not likely to be approved by local governments.

Another important trait is the amount of development now located outside the boundary. If a great deal of scattered development already exists there, it would be difficult to adopt a loose boundary accompanied by concentration of development in a few nodes, such as around existing small towns. People seeking to live in low-density residences would build more single-family units near the existing ones scattered outside the UGB and the external nodes. It would be hard legally or politically to stop them. Yet in most metropolitan areas, a great deal of scattered urban development has already taken place outside the solidly built-up territory.

A third trait is the amount of developable land within the boundary. There must be enough to permit competition among landowners seeking to capture urban development. Otherwise the few owners of developable land would enjoy a monopoly. They would raise land prices so high as to make new housing on it unaffordable for most families. The more developable land within the boundary, relative to the amount needed each year to accommodate the area's growth, the more feasible a rigid boundary with strong prohibitions against external development. Also, localities with relatively high densities, such as New York City, are likely to be willing to accept higher density new development within the boundary than those such as Austin that have very low densities.

Another consideration is the possible use of transferable development rights. Many owners of vacant land outside the boundary are essentially deprived of the right to develop that land for urban uses. Some planners argue this does not violate principles of due process. After all, the possibility of the owners' developing their land for urban uses only arises because of society's previous investments in roads, water systems, and sewer systems and nearby development by other private investors. So society has the right to regulate the potential benefit that its actions bestow without paying landowners for doing so. Just how far such regulation can go without violating due process has been grappled with but not settled by the Supreme Court in recent cases.

This deprivation can be mitigated through transferable development rights. Owners of land outside the boundary could be allowed to sell development rights (the quota that they would not be allowed to develop on their own land) to owners of land inside the boundary. That would permit the owners inside to develop land inside at higher dens-

TABLE 7-1. *Alternatives to Low-Density Development and Unlimited Growth*

	Development pattern		
Density	Rigid urban growth border	Flexible border, dispersed outside	Flexible border, nodes outside
All new growth at high density	European urban settlement pattern	Not consistent with very high density	European pattern with outside new towns
Low density with high-density nodes	Not consistent with this density pattern	Slowed suburban sprawl with dense nodes	Not consistent with this density pattern

ities than if they had not bought those rights. Such a policy has been in effect in Montgomery County, Maryland, for many years as a means of preserving agricultural land. To make transferable development rights work, at least some land within the boundary must be zoned with relatively flexible density.

The foregoing analysis offers two alternatives to low-density development and three growth alternatives to unlimited extendability. This creates six combinations (table 7–1). But three of the combinations are not feasible. In each, the residential density pattern is not consistent with the urban growth boundary pattern. For example, very high density in all new residential settlements is not consistent with considerable dispersed growth outside the urban growth boundary. Eliminating these inconsistent alternatives leaves three combinations.

—A European-style settlement pattern of very-high-density new development entirely confined within the boundary.

—Further American-style suburban sprawl modified by keeping a greater percentage of growth within the boundary and mixing high-density nodes in the predominant low-density pattern both inside and outside the boundary.

—A second European-style pattern combining a strong boundary with some external growth clustered in high-density new towns surrounded by green belts.

Adopting one of these alternatives to low-density development could mitigate three growth-related problems. It could reduce traffic congestion and air pollution by cutting average trip lengths, make housing more affordable by increasing average residential densities, and preserve more open space.

Alternatives to Relying on Private Vehicles

The second element in the dominant vision is nearly universal ownership and use of automobiles or light trucks. In practice this means most auto travelers, especially commuters, drive alone. At least three alternative movement patterns could be adopted.

Use of public transit and bicycles and walking could become much more widespread. This alternative is successful in much of Europe and Japan. In Western Europe the proportion of all trips made on public transit in the late 1970s and early 1980s ranged from 4.8 percent in the Netherlands (where 29 percent of trips were made on bicycles) to 26 percent in Italy. The unweighted average among nine European nations was 14.4 percent.[5] Walking accounted for 18.4 percent of all trips in the Netherlands and 39 percent in Sweden, with an unweighted average of 28.5 percent among eight of the nations. In none did auto trips constitute half the total.

This alternative is favored by many urban planners, but it would require radical changes in American behavior. In 1978 only 3.4 percent of all U.S. trips were on public transit and 10.7 percent were by walking. More than 82 percent were by private autos and trucks, double the unweighted average of 41.1 percent for nine Western European countries.[6] Shifting a major proportion of travelers from cars to public transit would also require massive expansions of transit facilities. Yet almost all public transit systems fail to cover either their capital or operating costs from the fares they charge. Large and continuing subsidies would be required.

Ride sharing could also be encouraged as an alternative to solo driving. If 25 percent of U.S. commuters shared rides, that would more than double the present U.S. percentage. But more frequent ride sharing would require radical changes in existing behavior. And it would require intensive organization of employers in transportation management associations to pressure workers to share commuting trips, extensive construction of additional high-occupancy vehicle lanes on expressways, and some means of greatly increasing the costs of driving to work alone, such as peak-hour road pricing or high peak-hour parking fees. But this alternative could be achieved without huge public investment in additional transit facilities.

There could also be more widespread use of both public transit and ride sharing. This alternative simply combines the two preceding ones.

And some significant but still marginal increases in the use of both public transit and private ride sharing could be encouraged. This alternative could change existing travel patterns without requiring the radical alterations of behavior called for by the other alternatives. It would not require massive new public spending on transit facilities.

Adopting any of these alternatives could reduce traffic congestion and air pollution. It would also decrease national energy consumption.

Alternatives to the Scattering of Jobs

The third element of the dominant vision is scattering nearly all additional jobs among many low-density workplaces. There are a number of alternative locational patterns for future jobs.[7]

Most new jobs could be restricted to large employment clusters. The clusters could be either existing concentrations in built-up parts of a metropolitan area or new ones added on its periphery. They could be linked by public transit. The main purpose of the policy would be to make commuting by public transit or ride sharing more feasible. Every company wanting to open a new establishment or add many employees would have to obtain a permit from a central authority, which would grant permits only if the jobs were to be located within an approved job cluster.

This alternative might confer quasi-monopoly advantages on the owners of land within the approved clusters, causing price escalation. That outcome could be avoided by designating enough clusters to create competition among them. But designating many clusters might offset the basic purpose of the policy. And concentration of jobs would also deprive owners of land outside the clusters of the possibility of developing their parcels with commercial uses. Thus the policy would arouse considerable opposition because outsiders would greatly outnumber those who owned land inside the designated areas.

New jobs could continue to be widely dispersed, but job densities of existing employment nodes could be intensified by attracting more jobs there with market-based incentives. Incentives might include special property or income tax breaks for locating jobs at the nodes and density bonuses to owners of land within them for intensifying development there. This policy would have the same goal as restricting new employment to a few high-density centers, but would rely on purely voluntary decisions. Thus it would probably have only a marginal effect on the location of new jobs. Still, it might lead to at least some greater use of public transit and ride sharing.

Both alternatives would generate opposition from local governments. The localities that did not have designated job centers would be deprived of most increases in nonresidential property values and expansion of their tax base. And they would probably outnumber the localities that increased their tax base. Both policies could be made politically acceptable only through some system for sharing the commercial property tax base throughout a metropolitan area. Additions to the nonresidential tax base would be divided between the localities where jobs were located and an areawide pool. This arrangement has prevailed for more than a decade in Minneapolis–St. Paul. The assessed values in the pool would be distributed on a population-based formula somewhat favoring localities with high proportions of low-income residents. Some similar type of system for sharing retail sales tax receipts should also be included. It would permit localities that did not have major retail facilities to share in the tax receipts from them.

Shifting from the prevailing low-density workplace pattern to one of the alternatives could reduce total traffic congestion and air pollution.[8] It could also make infrastructure finance more rational and efficient than at present by more equitably sharing property tax bases and sales tax revenues.

Alternatives to Dispersed Control of Land Use

The fourth element of the dominant vision is the fragmentation of government power over land use decisions among many relatively small jurisdictions. There are a number of alternatives to this pattern.

A full-functioned elected metropolitan area government could be created, possibly by merging the governments of the central city and one or more major counties. Fewer than a dozen of the more than 330 U.S. metropolitan areas have such regional governance. Nevertheless, this is the most complete response to the regional nature of contemporary urban problems. But in most areas, there is little political support for true metropolitan government because it runs contrary to the perceived self-interest of most citizens. Therefore, I will not give it further consideration.

Another alternative is some form of regionally chosen body empowered by state law to carry out land use planning and infrastructure planning and management within an entire metropolitan area. This mechanism would not involve a full-functioned metropolitan government. But it would put control of at least the most important infrastructure components that shape metropolitan growth—major highways, airports, mass transit, sewer and water systems, waste disposal systems—in the hands of a public body with a truly regional perspective and the legal authority to implement it. This more limited approach now exists in Minneapolis–St. Paul and Portland, Oregon. However, in Portland it also operates within a statewide system like that in the following alternative.

A third alternative is that some state-mandated mechanism could coordinate land use plans that would be drawn up locally but would have to conform to state-formulated goals and procedures. This mechanism would involve review, possible alteration, and final approval of local plans by a statewide agency or state-supported regional agency. This approach now exists in Florida, New Jersey, and most of Oregon.

Fourth, control over land use planning and policies could be invested in a regional body operating throughout a metropolitan area under the authority of the federal Clean Air Act as modified by state agencies authorized to carry it out. This approach uses the geographically unrestricted power of federal law to overcome the fragmentation of authority typical in most metropolitan areas. However, the authority of the air quality management districts created by the act is limited to those aspects of land use that directly affect air pollution.

Finally, a single regional body could be created that would be responsible for coordinating the administration of all funds flowing into metropolitan area localities from federal sources. Such a body could be created only by a congressional mandate. It would devise and manage regional plans for the use of the funds within each field of specialized functioning, such as health care or education. However, federal funds are not directly involved in most land use planning. Such a body could not directly control development policies unless its overall authority were augmented by the relevant state government.

These approaches are discussed in detail in chapter 9. A regional body to carry out land use planning under the authority of the Clean Air Act is now implemented to some extent in southern California. But only limited regional governance over land use can be based on the act because not all such matters affect air quality. The state government would have to authorize added powers for such a body to make its authority comprehensive. Moreover, this approach is applicable only in areas threatened by air pollution levels exceeding federally permissible standards. Similarly, a regional agency administering federal funds would not have much authority over land use unless the relevant state government also augmented the agency's powers.

That leaves the second and third regional options as the only feasible alternatives to the decentralized governance of the dominant vision. Shifting from the dominant vision to one of these alternatives could affect all the growth-related problems described in chapter 1.

Alternatives to Trickle-Down Housing

The fifth element in the dominant vision is providing shelter for low-income households mainly through the trickle-down process. But there are alternatives based on three tactics.

First, the size and quality standards required for new housing could be modified so that low-income households could afford to occupy the housing without direct subsidies. This could be done by changing local zoning and building code regulations, especially by permitting smaller and higher-density units, including more multifamily units. This policy could also allow owners of large single-family dwellings to convert parts of them into accessory apartments they could rent to small households.

Another alternative is providing direct federal housing subsidies for all low-income households so they could occupy decent shelter at a cost of no more than 30 percent of their incomes. This would make housing subsidies an entitlement program for low-income renters, since every household with a qualifying income would be able to receive assistance. The subsidies would enable the more than 11 million low-income renter households who paid more than 30 percent of their incomes for housing in 1989 to cease doing so without having to accept substandard shelter.

This alternative provides an income subsidy that directly attacks the poverty of low-income people, including those living in inner-city, concentrated-poverty areas.[9] It would supplement their incomes by paying all their present housing costs greater than 30 percent of their total incomes. It would permit many low-income households to move to better neighborhoods and encourage dispersion. However, experience with housing voucher programs shows that only limited dispersion would occur. But this alternative would require massive federal funding. State and local governments could not raise the funds needed without causing many taxpayers to move somewhere else. The high total cost makes it unlikely that the federal government would adopt such a policy.

Finally, some low-income households could be provided with housing subsidies that would permit them to occupy new housing in new-growth areas. This program would not require making federal housing subsidies a full entitlement program. Instead, it would enable only part of all eligible households to enjoy subsidized units.

This approach could be carried out by building subsidized housing in new-growth areas, requiring developers to include low-cost units in every subdivision they build (inclusionary zoning), providing low-income households with vouchers large enough to permit them to occupy new units there, or using some combination of these tactics. Pursuing this alternative would require much less public funding than a low-income renter entitlement program. In some metropolitan areas this approach could be financed by a state government without large-scale funding.

Lowering regulatory barriers that increase housing costs could help many low-income households without using subsidies, but millions have such low incomes that they could not afford unsubsidized new units built to the lowest quality standards consistent with health and safety.[10] This problem could only be resolved by increasing their incomes. Such housing subsidies can be paid to the occupants, the owners, or the producers of the units involved.

Funding a low-income entitlement program in housing would use massive federal subsidies to eliminate the gap between 30 percent of the incomes of low-income households and the cost of decent rental shelter. Its adoption would largely solve the problem of affordable low-income housing. But it would not end the shortage of housing units for low-income households in new-growth areas. To hold down costs, the federal government would no doubt keep the maximum subsidy for each household too low to permit poor households to occupy new units. Yet most of the housing in new-growth areas is not old enough so that it could be rented with restricted subsidies. There would still be great geographic separation of low-income households from middle- and upper-income ones.

The third tactic addresses this separation by providing many low-income households with the subsidies necessary to occupy units in new-growth areas and permitting them to use the subsidies only in those areas. This would not solve the overall housing affordability problem; thus it would be much less costly than the entitlement alternative. But experience in Chicago's Gautreaux housing program shows that this approach can improve the lives of very-low-income people.[11] These three tactics are not mutually exclusive; some combination of them could be adopted. Table 7–2 summarizes the elements from which alternative visions can be constructed.

Formulating Alternative Overall Visions

To be congruent with the dominant vision, every alternative vision should contain specific goals in each of the five fields I have described. Each field has from two to six alternative elements. To avoid internal inconsistency, only one goal from each field of activity should be incorporated in any one vision.[12] Even so, the number of possible combinations is more than 1,000.[13]

Experts using computers might be able to analyze and compare all these alternatives. But this book is written for real-world citizens and policymakers. Therefore, the set of alternative visions it proposes must be small enough so that people can easily understand each, clearly perceive differences among them, and readily compare them.

Winnowing 1,000 alternatives down to some usably small set requires arbitrary judgments. My first step was to apply the criteria of desirability described earlier. I then made further judgments that eliminated all but four visions, including unlimited low-density development.

Unlimited Low-Density Growth

Unlimited low-density growth permits unlimited expansion of low-density settlements and workplaces served primarily by automobiles. No urban growth boundaries would be drawn to inhibit growth. Developers would not be legally constrained from building new residential, commercial, or mixed-use subdivisions beyond existing built-up areas. Developers might, however, be compelled to pay for the extension of infrastructure trunklines there.

The pattern in which many autonomous local governments encourage mainly low-density housing would be extended through stringent limitation on the construction of new multifamily units. Jobs could be scattered almost anywhere; no efforts would be made to concentrate them within designated centers. Shelter for low- and moderate-income households would be provided almost entirely through the trickle-down process. They would remain concentrated in older neighborhoods in the central city and close-in suburbs.

Limited-Spread, Mixed-Density Growth

Limited-spread, mixed-density growth imposes an urban growth boundary around existing settlements within which most growth during the next twenty years would be located. Public financing of most additional infrastructures would be restricted to subdivisions within the boundary. However, some growth—perhaps 25 to 30 percent—could occur outside the boundary, especially if developers financed the required infrastructure. Inside and outside the boundary, residential settlements would consist of clusters of relatively high-density housing surrounded by much larger areas of low-density housing. This pattern would cause higher overall average densities than now prevail. Both housing and workplaces could spread widely; no green large belts would be created.

Jobs could be scattered almost anywhere, but public policies would encourage voluntary concentration within a few designated employment nodes. These policies would rely entirely on market-oriented incentives. Policies would also encourage ride sharing and public transit, other than fixed-rail transit, more than the low-density vision but much less than bounded high-density growth. Governance could continue the current fragmented autonomous arrangements or could emphasize local land use planning within a state-mandated framework. Housing for the poor could be achieved by some reduction of regulatory barriers to less expensive housing and some subsidized units for moderate-income households in new-growth areas.

New Communities and Green Belts

The new communities and green belts pattern of growth also limits most expansion to the territory within an urban growth boundary. But it seeks greater clustering of residential and job growth in higher-density settlements, especially outside the boundary. Again 25 to 30 percent of growth might be in external territory, but it would be concentrated in new communities. Each new community would be sepa-

TABLE 7-2. *Alternative Elements in Five Fields of Development Activity*

Housing type, density, and spatial extension

Continued low-density sprawl

Single-family housing for all new construction in a very-low-density settlement pattern with unlimited outward spatial extension.

High-density bounded growth

High-density housing for all new construction, including a large proportion of multifamily units, confined almost entirely within a tightly drawn urban growth boundary.

Slowed sprawl with dense nodes

New construction, predominantly single-family housing but containing many nodes of high-density (not necessarily high-rise) multifamily units, mostly confined within an urban growth boundary, but with some dispersed extension outside that boundary.

High- or mixed-density bounded growth with outlying new communities

High- or mixed-density housing for all new construction, including a large proportion of multifamily units, confined within a tightly drawn urban growth boundary except for planned new communities outside the boundary, surrounded by open green belts.

Transportation and movement

Nearly total auto dependence

Widespread ownership of private vehicles, with almost all present and future commuting done by solo drivers.

Heavy dependence on public transit

A major shift from travel by automotive vehicles to travel by buses or fixed-rail transit or both within existing settlements and in new-growth areas.

Heavy dependence on private ride sharing

A major shift from solo driving to ride sharing within existing settlements and in new-growth areas.

Heavy dependence on public transit and private ride sharing

A combination of the two preceding alternatives.

Marginally greater use of transit and ride sharing

Reliance on automotive transportation by solo drivers but with notable gains in public transit and private ride sharing.

Location of future job growth

Wide scattering of jobs

Continued dispersal of new jobs across all suburbs in mainly low-density workplaces.

Concentration of added jobs in major clusters

Location of new jobs in large employment nodes, existing or new, as a result of government regulatory requirements. Examples are clusers in and around downtowns, major regional shopping centers, and large office parks.

TABLE 7-2. *Continued*

Continued scattering of added jobs but with higher job density in major clusters
    Continued dispersal of new jobs, but concentration within major clusters as a result
    of market-oriented incentives attracting businesses to put the jobs there voluntarily.

Forms of governance within metropolitan areas
Fragmented and autonomous local governments
    Continued fragmentation of powers among local communities, with no legally
    binding mechanisms for coordinating policies and actions concerning infrastructure
    and land use development.
General regional government
    Shifting of all local government powers to a single elected regional government.
Limited regional government
    Shifting of control over infrastructure planning and development to one or more
    regional bodies empowered by state law to exercise those functions. Such bodies
    might be elected by citizens throughout the metropolitan area.
Local comprehensive land use planning within a state-mandated framework
    State comprehensive land use planning goals and procedures that local government
    must follow. A state agency would be responsible for approving all locally
    originated plans so they meet state requirements and are consistent with the plans
    of other communities within a metropolitan area.
Local land use planning within an air-quality management framework
    Functional control over local government decisions that strongly affect air quality
    invested in a regional air-quality management agency under the federal Clean Air
    Act.
Creation of an agency at the metropolitan area level to plan and manage all federal aid
    entering the area (except aid paid directly to individuals)
    This agency would require regional plans for all uses of federal funds.

Housing for low-income households
Almost total reliance on trickle-down housing
    Shelter for low-income households provided mainly through occupancy of older
    housing. No direct housing subsidies.
Limited reduction of existing regulatory barriers to affordable housing
    Encouraging construction of smaller new housing units, in higher densities, built
    with less costly materials.
Making direct federal housing subsidies a low-income entitlement program
    Federal funds for direct housing subsidies to all renter households with low incomes
    so they will not have to pay more than 30 percent of their incomes for shelter.
Limited direct housing subsidies for use in new-growth areas
    Providing direct housing subsidies, federal or state, to limited numbers of low-
    income households so they can locate in new or relatively new units in new-growth
    areas.

rated from the others and from the older settled area by large permanent green belts.

Most new communities would be new settlements extending from existing small towns or cities on the periphery of the metropolitan area. They would consist of high-density clusters in the midst of larger areas of low-density housing, with a higher average density than in outlying portions of limited-spread growth. Local comprehensive land use planning would exist within a state-mandated framework.

Strong market-based incentives, and perhaps some compulsory regulations, would be adopted to encourage location of jobs in designated centers. These would include the new communities outside the main urban growth boundary and relatively high-density employment nodes inside the boundary.

This plan would emphasize mass transit, including fixed-rail or bus systems linking the new communities with nodes inside the boundary. It would also incorporate some reduction of regulatory barriers and more direct subsidies for low- and moderate-income housing within its high-density growth clusters to promote more complete economic integration there.

Bounded High-Density Growth

Bounded high-density growth would be the opposite of unlimited low-density sprawl. It would resemble the growth patterns of many Western European metropolitan areas. Expansion would be limited by a strongly enforced urban growth boundary within which nearly all growth would occur. The boundary would be drawn relatively tightly around built-up areas to pressure new development to occur at high densities.[14] This would also encourage increases in density in built-up neighborhoods.

Regulations would require that most new jobs be located in designated concentrations inside the urban growth boundary. The higher job and residential densities would permit greater reliance on public transit, especially for commuting. In fast-growing metropolitan areas, turning future growth inward might push housing costs inside the boundary notably higher. Extensive federal housing subsidies would become a low-income entitlement program. Centralized areawide governance or limited-function regional governance would virtually be required.

A Spectrum of Visions

The growth models just described are only four among many possible blueprints for metropolitan area growth. At one extreme is the unlimited low-density vision. Its elements emphasize self-interested action by most people and local governments, without much regard for the consequences for society as a whole. This individualistic behavior is especially prevalent among middle- and upper-income groups, not because they are any more self-centered than the poor but because their actions are not as constrained by lack of purchasing power and political strength. The fact that poor people cannot afford to own detached houses, travel almost exclusively by private car, and similar behavior is disregarded by this growth model.

At the other extreme the bounded high-density vision is what might be called the communitarian approach. Its elements emphasize community-focused action by everyone and considerable regard for the consequences for society. The elements include living in higher-density housing, including many multifamily clusters, using public transit or ride sharing or walking, working in establishments clustered together in high-density nodes, living under the authority of some type of regional governance controlling land use patterns, and providing housing for low-income people throughout the metropolitan area, including many subsidized units.

Between these extremes lie the other two plans. The limited-spread, mixed-density model is closer to the unlimited low-density end of the spectrum; the new communities and green belts vision is closer to the bounded high-density end.

The spectrum is broad enough so that other visions could be defined along it. However, I believe that serious consideration of just these four would force society to confront most of the major planning issues connected with metropolitan area growth.

8

Elements in the Alternative Visions

*I*MPORTANT elements of any vision of metropolitan area growth are the density patterns it proposes, the limits, if any, it places on growth, the transportation patterns it advocates, the governance it would require, and how it would house low-income people.

Defining Levels of Residential Density

Certain terms used in chapter 7 need more specific definitions if they are to serve as guides to policy. *High residential density* means considerably greater suburban density than the average under the dominant model of unlimited low density. How high are existing residential densities in U.S. metropolitan areas? Table 8-1 shows the percentage distribution of gross residential densities (residents per total square mile, including all other land uses) in counties or suburbs in some major metropolitan areas. Thus 13.6 percent of the total population of all suburbs of Chicago inside Illinois live in localities that have average densities of less than 2,500 people a square mile; 6.5 percent live where average densities are more than 10,000 a square mile. The average density of these Chicago suburbs combined (their total population divided by their total area) was 3,483 people a square mile in 1989.

Suburban densities vary greatly among metropolitan areas and within each. The highest suburban density shown in table 8-1 is 5,884 persons a square mile in Los Angeles County; the lowest is 1,422 in the Orlando area. The proportion of residents living in suburbs with densities of more than 7,500 a square mile varied from zero in the Orlando area to 54 percent in Los Angeles County.

TABLE 8-1. *Distribution of Suburban Residents, by Population Density, Ten Suburban Areas, 1989*
Percent unless otherwise specified

Residents per square mile	Illinois suburbs of Chicago	California							Florida		New York suburbs of New York City
		Los Angeles County suburbs	Cities in Orange County	Cities in Riverside County	Cities in San Bernardino County	Alameda County suburbs	Cities in Contra Costa County		Dade County suburbs	Orlando area suburbs	
2,500 or fewer	13.6	4.9	9.2	60.0	28.7	22.0	29.1		7.4	36.9	24.6
2,500–3,999	37.7	6.6	10.8	37.9	47.5	35.8	49.7		19.1	48.4	15.3
4,000–4,999	17.7	4.4	8.6	2.1	18.3	7.4	4.9		10.2	12.5	12.3
5,000–5,999	13.9	16.0	20.3	0	5.6	9.9	9.5		12.6	2.1	8.2
6,000–7,499	6.7	13.8	30.2	0	0	0	3.6		20.4	0	12.3
7,500–9,999	3.9	22.4	19.7	0	0	25.0	3.3		19.9	0	16.7
10,000 or more	6.5	31.9	1.3	0	0	0	0		10.3	0	10.5
Average density	3,482.6	5,883.6	5,129.4	2,003.3	1,934.2	3,526.9	3,344.4		4,844.0	1,422.1	2,557.7

Source: Author's calculations using unpublished 1989 population density data from Aetna.

TABLE 8-2. *Sample Conversions from Gross Residential Density to Net Residential Density*

	Dwelling units per net residential acre[a]	
Residents per gross square mile	Low density (50 percent of land residential)	High density (25 percent of land residential)
1,500	1.875	3.750
2,500	3.125	6.250
3,200	4.000	8.000
3,500	4.375	8.750
3,750	4.688	9.375
5,000	6.250	12.500
7,500	9.375	18.750
8,000	10.000	20.000
10,000	12.500	25.000
12,000	15.000	30.000
15,000	18.750	37.500
20,000	25.000	50.000
25,000	31.250	62.500

Source: Author's calculations.

a. Assumes 2.5 persons per dwelling unit.

In the United States, developers, city planners, and residents are more accustomed to thinking about dwelling units per acre (net residential density) than about persons per square mile (gross residential density). Gross residential density (of all land) can be translated into net residential density (of only the land used for housing) by making two assumptions: the average number of people in each dwelling unit and the percentage of land devoted to housing, exclusive of streets, parks, commercial uses, open space, government uses, and so forth. A convenient assumption is 2.5 persons in each dwelling unit, slightly less than the national average household size of 2.63 in 1990. Within suburbs, a reasonable assumption is also that 50 percent of the land is residential; in large cities, this estimate drops to 25 percent (see table 8-2 for density conversions).

Many suburban communities have single-family zoning requirements that call for no more than four dwelling units on a net residential acre, or 3,200 persons a square mile. But multifamily projects can be built with up to twenty-five units an acre and still be aesthetically attractive and not overcrowded, even when restricted to structures of no more than three

TABLE 8-3. *Gross Residential Densities of Selected Cities, 1990*

City	Persons per square mile	City	Persons per square mile
New York City	23,699	Detroit	7,412
East Los Angeles	16,800	Minneapolis	6,703
San Francisco	15,503	Pittsburgh	6,655
Jersey City	15,369	Seattle	6,150
Chicago	12,254	San Jose	4,565
Boston	11,860	Portland, Ore.	3,504
Philadelphia	11,739	Houston	3,021
Newark	11,555	Dallas	2,941
Miami	10,084	Phoenix	2,341
Los Angeles	7,426	Tulsa	2,000

Source: Bureau of the Census, *Statistical Abstract of the United States: 1991* (Department of Commerce, 1991), pp. 34–36.

stories. That net density is equivalent to 20,000 people a square mile in the suburbs or 10,000 a square mile in big cities.

For comparison, gross 1990 densities for twenty large American cities are shown in table 8-3. Nine have densities of 10,000 people a square mile or more, the city equivalent of twenty-five units a net residential acre. All except East Los Angeles, which attains its high density through overcrowding, are older cities mainly built before the advent of the automobile.

In view of these data, it is reasonable to define *relatively high density* in new-growth areas as any average net residential density of 9.375 units or more. That is the equivalent of 7,500 persons a square mile in the suburbs or 3,750 in big cities. It implies multifamily housing or townhouses rather than single-family homes. No suburban counties shown in table 8-1 come close to an average density that high. In all but Los Angeles County less than 30 percent of residents live where gross densities are that high. *Very high density* for suburban areas is defined as average net residential density of 12.5 units an acre or more, the equivalent of 10,000 persons a square mile.

The limited-spread mixed-density model uses the term *density* but does not imply a definite numerical target. Rather it envisions densities in new-growth areas significantly higher than those in areas built in the recent past within the particular metropolitan area concerned.

An important residential density goal is to avoid very low average densities in any large part of a metropolitan area because they generate

long average commuting trips. Increasing average gross densities from
1,000 to 5,000 people a square mile reduces average commuting distances much more than increasing densities from 5,000 to 10,000 people a square mile. Therefore limited-spread growth involves establishing minimum acceptable residential densities for any large part of a
metropolitan area. One acceptable minimum might be 2,500 people a
square mile, which is equivalent to 3.1 dwelling units a net residential
acre in suburban areas.

Accepting this minimum would still permit some parts of a metropolitan area to have net densities of less than 3.1 units an acre. Sizable
areas could even have five-acre minimum zoning, which is 0.2 units a
net residential acre. But such subregions should not occupy huge contiguous territories. And they should be located close to other subregions with much higher densities. Then the average net residential
density for any large part of the metropolitan area would not fall below
3.1 units an acre. Exactly how to divide a metropolitan area into subregions can only be determined by officials and residents of each area.

Relatively High Densities in New-Growth Areas

There are two ways to attain relatively high gross densities in new-
growth areas. One is for nearly all new housing to have densities of
9.38 units an acre or higher. That would mean that new housing units
would mostly be multifamily units, townhouses, or very small single-
family detached units. The other way is to mix a few areas of high-
density housing with larger areas of low-density housing. For example, if 32.1 percent of the net residential land in an area contained
multifamily housing with a net residential density of 25 units an acre,
the other 67.9 percent could contain single-family units at only 2 units
an acre. The average would be 9.38 units an acre, which would qualify
as relatively high density. Thus relatively high average residential
densities can be attained in new-growth areas even if most residential
land there is developed with low-density, single-family units. And this
would not require constructing high-rise housing.

Relatively High Densities in Built-Up Areas

The really difficult issue connected with residential density in the
bounded high-density vision and the new communities and green
belts vision is whether public policies could significantly increase residential densities in built-up areas. Both models would increase den-

TABLE 8-4. *Projected Increases of Densities in Built-up Areas as Housing Is Built on Vacant Sites*

Units built per acre of in-fill land	Percent of all land that must be vacant and then developed to achieve a final gross density (persons per square mile) of:		
	5,000	7,500	10,000
9.375	37.5	100.0	Impossible
15	17.7	47.1	76.5
25	9.1	24.2	39.4
30	7.3	19.5	31.7
40	5.3	14.0	22.8
100	2.0	5.2	8.5

Source: Author's calculations. Assumes initial overall density of 3,500 people per square mile.

sities to accommodate nearly all future growth within close-in urban growth boundaries. A tightly drawn boundary will not encompass much vacant land. Thus much of the area's growth would have to be accommodated within built-up areas. How could that be done? For example, how could gross density in a built-up locality containing 3,500 persons a square mile be raised to 7,500 a square mile?[1] Two tactics are possible.

Vacant sites zoned for housing could be developed with very high density residential projects. If vacant land constituted 19.5 percent of all suburban residential land in such an area, and all in-fill land was developed at an average net density of thirty units an acre (24,000 persons a square mile), the average gross density would rise from 3,500 to 7,500 persons a square mile.[2] Thirty units an acre on in-fill sites is easily feasible. But it is not likely that any built-up area would still have 19.5 percent of its residential land vacant and available for such development.

Table 8-4 shows the percentage of all residentially zoned land, both vacant and already built-up, that would have to be available as vacant in-fill sites and then developed at six average densities to achieve overall gross densities of 5,000, 7,500, and 10,000 persons a square mile. Thus to increase an area's overall density from 3,500 to 5,000 persons a square mile would require building new housing at one hundred units an acre if only 2 percent of the land were vacant or at forty an acre if 5.3 percent were vacant. Under most circumstances overall densities could be increased from 3,500 persons a square mile to any of the three levels shown only if a considerable part of the area were still vacant at the outset.[3]

A second tactic would be to tear down existing housing and replace it with higher-density structures. Another table could be drawn up showing the percentage of built-up residential land in a suburban area with an initial gross density of 3,500 that would have to be redeveloped to achieve specified overall gross densities after redevelopment. Every cell in such a table would contain the same numbers as the analogous cell in table 8-4. But the percentages in the other table would indicate how much initially built-up land would have to be redeveloped through demolition and new construction; the percentages in table 8-4 refer to the portion of all land in the area that would have to be vacant and available for initial development. Thus table 8-4 can be used to analyze both means of increasing densities in built-up areas.[4]

To raise overall density from 3,500 to 7,500 persons a square mile, 47.1 percent of all housing land would have to be redeveloped with new housing at fifteen units an acre, 24.2 percent at twenty-five units an acre, or 14.0 percent at forty units an acre. Clearly, any substantial increase in the residential density of built-up areas that is to be achieved through redevelopment would require major clearance and rebuilding. This would be extremely disruptive to existing neighborhoods.

Such extensive redevelopment would be necessary in fast-growing metropolitan areas if rigid growth boundaries were drawn tightly around present settlements and all growth was confined within those boundaries. This policy is what the Sierra Club has recommended for southern California. It is hard to believe that residents where such up-zoning is planned would permit it, considering the pressures they have exerted in the past to down-zone residential land there.

Effects of Higher Densities

Directing growth pressures inward under the bounded high-density vision or the new communities and green belts vision would raise both land and housing prices inside the urban growth boundary. That would benefit owners but harm renters and potential purchasers. It would be especially hard on low-income renters in neighborhoods where pressures for redevelopment steeply escalated land prices. That is one reason why a crucial policy for bounded high-density development would be to provide rental subsidies as entitlements for low-income households. Rising land and housing prices would benefit local governments by increasing property tax bases.

Under limited-spread mixed-density development, prices of land inside the boundary would rise less and prices outside fall less than under bounded high-density growth.[5] Limited-spread mixed-density growth would allow enough development outside the boundary to constrain land prices inside. Because bounded high-density development seeks to accommodate nearly all growth within the boundary, tighter public control over land development would be needed than under limited-spread mixed-density development.

One purpose of higher residential densities is to reduce daily travel. If more people lived in each square mile, the area required to accommodate any given population would be much smaller. This would decrease total miles traveled in private vehicles, even if there were no increase in the use of public transit. I have analyzed this problem in a previous book, *Stuck in Traffic*.[6]

Increasing density in new-growth areas alone has little effect on overall metropolitan commuting distances. Unless an area is growing rapidly, most of whatever development will be there in twenty years is already there. So reducing the density of new areas will mainly affect traffic patterns within those areas. In the bounded high-density model, public policies would try to increase densities in built-up areas too. But resistance from residents would probably limit the possibility of increasing densities enough to cut average travel distances significantly.

Commuting distances are longer in new-growth areas built at very low densities than in those built at medium or high densities. This is true even though low-density areas, which are spread out, would contain more scattered job sites than would higher-density areas. A simulation model in *Stuck in Traffic* shows that a large new-growth area with 886 residents a square mile generates an average one-way commuting distance for its residents significantly longer than that generated by a similar settlement at 9,075 persons a square mile. The exact percentage increase in the distance is not important; but the conclusion has serious implications for energy consumption. And the average commuting distance of all U.S. workers increased 24 percent between 1983 and 1990, partly because of rapid growth in the suburbs of large cities.[7]

The percentage reduction in commuting distances achieved by increasing residential densities is much smaller than the percentage increases in densities needed to achieve it. In one model, a 924 percent increase in residential density produced only a 21 percent decrease in suburban commuting distance. Tripling suburban densities would cut average commuting distance less than 4 percent. Low-density settlement patterns generate more dispersed job locations, so that cutting commuting distances significantly in new-growth areas requires extremely large density increases.

Moving from very low to medium densities has a much greater effect than moving from medium to very high densities. If 1 million persons resided in a perfectly circular metropolitan area, its radius would be 17.84 miles at a gross density of 1,000 persons a square mile, 7.98 miles at 5,000, and 5.64 miles at 10,000. The radial difference between the lowest density and the highest is 12.20 miles. But 81 percent of that difference lies in going from a density of 1,000 to a density of 5,000; only 19 percent lies in making the larger leap from 5,000 to 10,000.[8] Thus to conserve energy and reduce total travel, it is much more important to avoid having new growth occur at very low densities than to make sure it occurs at very high densities.

Reducing commuting distances does not always decrease traffic congestion. Long average commutes will not generate intensive traffic congestion if they occur in low-density areas well served with expressways and other roads, if employment sites in those areas are widely dispersed, and if the number of daily commuters does not greatly exceed the road system's capacity to handle them. Furthermore, commuting accounts for no more than half of all peak-hour trips in the morning and less than half in the evening. What happens to commuting, then, is only part of what causes peak-hour traffic congestion.

In summary, bounded high-density growth could notably reduce travel distances in new-growth areas better than unlimited low-density growth. But the ability of bounded high-density growth to reduce average overall metropolitan travel distances is much more limited, except in very fast-growing areas.

The new communities and green belts model would have effects on commuting distances in new-growth areas similar to those of bounded high-density growth. It would create higher densities in new-growth areas within the main urban growth boundary. New communities and green belts development would also reduce commuting distances for people living in new-growth areas outside the boundary if most were persuaded to live and work in the same new community.

Limited-spread mixed-density growth would reduce average commuting distances less than the bounded growth or green belts alternatives but more than the continuation of unlimited low-density growth. Thus it would only moderately reduce commuting distances in new-growth areas, and do so very little within the entire metropolitan area compared with the continuation of unlimited low-density growth.

Whether gross residential densities of 7,500 persons a square mile or higher in new suburbs would absorb less open space and reduce infrastructure trunk line costs depends heavily on the specific lower density levels with which they are compared. Most U.S. suburbs have densities of 3,500 persons a square mile or less. I will use that density as representing typical suburbs developed under unlimited low-density growth.

Among the 335 U.S. metropolitan areas in 1990, 22 had population increases of 250,000 or more from 1980 to 1990. One was New York City and environs, but I will exclude it from this analysis because its huge size distorts average statistics. The average 1980 population of the other 21 areas was 1.866 million, and their average population gain from 1980 to 1990 was 534,000.[9] If their average gross density in 1980, including central cities, was 5,000 persons a square mile, the average settled area they covered was 373 square miles. A gain of 534,000 people would have required an additional 152.6 square miles, or 41 percent, if it occurred at an average gross density of 3,500 people a square mile.

At a density of 7,500 people a square mile, the same population gain would have required 71.2 square miles. So moving from low density to relatively high density for this growth, as in the bounded high-density vision, would have cut the open space absorbed by 50 percent. It would also have reduced the costs of adding infrastructure by 50 percent, if those costs were proportional to the radial distances involved.[10]

Thus considerable open space could be preserved and infrastructure costs saved by increasing marginal growth from 3,500 persons a square mile to 7,500, as in the bounded high-density vision. At 5,000 persons a square mile a gain of 534,000 persons would have required 106.8 additional square miles. Thus shifting from low density to moderately higher density, as in the limited-spread mixed-density vision, would have cut the open space absorbed and the required infrastructure by 30 percent.

Whether savings in housing costs would be achieved depends on many factors other than a change in average density. Savings could be achieved from the construction of units with net densities of fifteen to forty units an acre. Not all units with those densities would necessarily feature low-cost construction. Nor would the builders of all lower-cost units pass on the savings to the occupants. But the more units built at higher densities, the more likely that at least some would have relatively low costs passed through.

In any community the average density results from a mixture of some high-density developments and some low-density ones. But the percentage of all new housing units built at densities of fifteen to forty units an acre would be much greater in places with overall average densities of 7,500 persons a square mile than it would in those with 3,500.[11] Compared with conditions under unlimited low-density growth, the chance of having some higher-density units made available at low cost would be vastly greater under the bounded high-density model and somewhat greater under limited-spread mixed-density development and new communities and green belts development.

The effects of growth on inner cities under the alternative visions would depend heavily on the following factors. First, how strong are the pressures for growth? Second, how powerfully do local policies deflect growth from expanding outward and raise average densities within the growth boundary? This deflection would be most likely under bounded high-density growth, somewhat less likely under new communities and green belts, even less likely under limited-spread mixed-density, and unlikely under unlimited low-density growth. Metropolitan areas experiencing very strong pressures for growth and significant constraints on expansion might deflect enough demand inward to affect otherwise undesirable inner-city neighborhoods. However, cities in which growth pressures are weak would not have enough demand for redevelopment to overcome the antipathy of non-poor households and businesses toward locating in or even close to such neighborhoods. That would probably be the case even under bounded high-density growth.

Finally, the effects of growth would depend on the national policies that were adopted toward the social problems discussed in chapter 5. This factor would not be inherently related to the form of future growth adopted in each metropolitan area.

Another potential benefit of higher densities is an intangible gain from a more intensive community spirit. There is no way to make reasonably objective judgments about whether higher densities would produce such a change.

Using Urban Growth Boundaries to Limit Expansion

A central feature of the alternatives to unlimited low-density growth is use of an urban growth boundary to limit expansion. Authorities would finance normal infrastructure only inside the boundary and would give priority to private developers creating projects there. Projects outside the boundary might be prohibited altogether. Leapfrog development far from built-up areas would be banned in the bounded high-density and the new communities and green belts visions and discouraged under limited-spread mixed-density growth.

Urban growth boundaries are designed to achieve certain benefits. One is the preservation of farmland and other open space outside the boundary. To accomplish this, all land outside the boundary must be specifically reserved for farming, grazing, or timber production; recreation; wetlands; or rural housing development. Only a very small part would be in the last category under bounded high-density growth. Under limited-spread mixed-density growth a much larger share would be so designated. And the type of development permitted would not be limited to rural housing—that is, units on very large lots—but would include normal suburban housing and commercial developments. In the new communities and green belts vision, an even higher percentage of growth might occur outside the main boundary, but only within boundaries around designated new communities.

Another benefit of growth boundaries is that average residential densities in new-growth areas would increase. Those areas would presumably be more concentrated within the boundary than they would be otherwise. Growth boundaries would also reduce public infrastructure costs by confining new roads, sewer systems, water systems, and other utilities to areas contiguous to existing systems. A final gain is that development would speed up and be more predictable. This is because planning procedures would more clearly designate what uses are permissible on each parcel, and local officials would have less discretion in imposing standards on new projects. This would cut public and private costs associated with new development.[12]

Workplace Location

Unlimited low-density growth would continue to scatter jobs throughout new-growth areas. Although a few large edge cities containing clusters of jobs would appear, most employment would be spread almost at random. Most commuters could not use public transit or share rides. At the other extreme, bounded high-density growth would require concentrating new jobs in major employment centers. The centers would include the region's downtown and yet-to-be-built outlying concentrations of retail, office, and service space. They would also include older outlying downtowns such as Evanston outside Chicago and Beverly Hills near Los Angeles, and the edge cities that have appeared around such outlying regional shopping centers as South Coast Plaza in Orange County, California, and King of Prussia Center outside Philadelphia. These centers would be linked together by improved public transit, possibly including fixed-rail systems but at least more frequent bus service.[13]

The main purpose of this pattern is to switch more commuting to public transit and private ride sharing. In theory, locating many jobs in one relatively small zone makes the switch economically, technically, and socially more feasible.[14]

However, it would be difficult to persuade very many American workers, especially those living in suburbs, to commute by public transit or ride sharing. It therefore seems improbable that concentrating new jobs together would achieve its main purpose to any great degree.

Concentrating jobs would also require powerful and repugnant regulatory pressures on employers and might require regulations for the owners of land in the employment centers. Those who owned land outside the centers would be angered by the policy's weakening or precluding their ability to locate commercial and industrial activities on their land.

Given all these problems, trying to achieve a compulsory concentration of jobs is not worth the costs and efforts required. But voluntary concentration of jobs might be encouraged through market-oriented incentives. This is the approach to job location embodied in the limited-spread mixed-density model. Incentives could include reduced property taxes, subsidies paying for employer memberships in transportation management associations, lower state tax rates for businesses located in the centers, and permission to provide more parking spaces for ride-sharing employees.

But to make even voluntary job concentration more acceptable to local governments, there must be two other key changes. One is tax-base sharing among all the local governments in a metropolitan area (see chapter 7). The second is sharing sales tax receipts. Both would permit localities that did not contain major job centers to share in their fiscal benefits. Those localities would therefore be less likely to oppose a job concentration policy. Tax-base sharing has been adopted in the Minneapolis–St. Paul area. But the failure of any other areas to try the policy indicates that getting it adopted as part of a limited-spread mixed-density plan would not be easy.

Even compelling the clustering of new jobs would probably not increase use of public transit or private ride sharing much. A policy of limited-spread mixed-density growth is even less likely to attain this outcome. Nevertheless, the methods the limited-spread plan would use to pursue this goal are far less objectionable than those that would be used by a bounded high-density plan. It might be worthwhile therefore to employ those methods to attain even small increases in public transit use or ride sharing. So this element is retained as part of the limited-spread mixed-density vision.

The reduced emphasis on job concentration also implies that a limited-spread mixed-density plan would not try to create new fixed rail systems connecting employment centers. Any more intensive linkage of these centers would be accomplished through improved bus service and exclusive HOV lanes.

A new communities and green belts policy would seek to cluster jobs in new communities through a combination of market-oriented incentives and a few regulations. Its prohibition of locating jobs in designated green belt areas would almost compel employers outside the major urban growth boundary to choose sites within new communities. Inside the boundary this policy would have to rely more on voluntary measures.

Achieving Transportation Goals

All three alternative visions seek to reduce automobile travel and achieve greater use of public transit and ride sharing. The bounded high-density approach would make the most radical changes. It would use all possible means to discourage people from driving alone during peak hours. It would also expand public transit facilities, including fixed-rail systems, and facilities that encourage ride sharing. It would even try compulsory concentration of new jobs in a few large nodes to encourage more use of these facilities.

A new communities and green belts plan would apply similar but more moderate policies. Public transit systems would mainly aim at linking outlying new communities with the regional downtown and other major job concentrations within the urban growth boundary around the largest built-up area. The plan would also use only one or two means of directly raising the cost of solo driving during peak hours.

A limited-spread mixed-density policy would use only one tactic that directly raises peak-hour solo driving costs, focus much more on encouraging ride sharing than on expanding public transit, and avoid added fixed-rail transit services.

Aside from those living in a few large older cities, especially New York City, Americans overwhelmingly choose private automobiles for daily trips. About 87 percent of all travel in the United States in 1990 was by automobile; only 2 percent was by public transit. Among suburban dwellers, the share of all travel on public transit is 1.25 percent. Dependence on cars has been increasing. From 1983 to 1990 total vehicle miles of travel soared 40 percent, whereas the number of people age five years or older rose only 4.3 percent.[15] In contrast, use of public transit has been declining absolutely and relatively since 1945.

Barriers to Success

The most important cause of rush hour traffic is that so many people choose to drive alone at the same times. In 1989, 75 percent of all commuters drove alone.[16] Any strategy for reducing peak-hour traffic congestion—an important element of each alternative vision—must therefore reduce the percentage of peak-hour travelers who drive alone. But people drive alone for what seem to them extremely good reasons. It is usually faster, more convenient, more comfortable, more private, and often less costly than using public transit. The cost advantage is especially significant for drivers who have free parking. Unless these advantages are greatly reduced or traffic congestion becomes unbearable, it will be difficult to lure people from solo driving.

Because of the principle of triple convergence, peak-hour congestion might not decrease much even if a significant proportion of commuters started taking public transportation or sharing rides.[17] Commuters using main expressways are in "travel time equilibrium" with others using regular city streets and arterials. If congestion on a commuter expressway would suddenly decrease because the road has been widened or more drivers begin to use public transit, the drivers remaining would at first experience much faster rush hour travel. But drivers on still-crowded local routes would soon hear about this improvement and begin to use the expressway. Similarly, some commuters who had been driving before or after the rush hour to avoid congestion would start traveling during it because that is a more convenient time. Finally, some users of public transit who were barely tolerating its longer trip times and crowding would begin driving.

As a result of this triple convergence, the expressway would soon become so crowded again that driving on it would no longer offer any advantage over alternative routes, times, and modes. True, the initial improvement would not have been wholly in vain. More commuters than before would be traveling during the most convenient hours, and the period of maximum congestion would be shorter. But maximum congestion would not have disappeared altogether.

The impact of triple convergence is evident from what has happened in metropolitan areas that have introduced new rapid transit systems. In San Francisco 3 percent of all workers commute on the Bay Area Rapid Transit system; in Washington about 20 percent commute on Metro rail and buses. Yet peak-hour highway congestion in both areas remains high.

In fast-growth areas this problem is compounded. Even if highway improvements increased peak-hour road capacity by 10 percent, population growth and greater vehicle use would soon expand travel by much more than 10 percent. Even a new or expanded public transit system would be swamped by growth within a few years.

Curbing Peak-Hour Auto Use

In most large metropolitan areas the only way to reduce traffic congestion directly is to make solo driving during rush hours so much more expensive than it is now that fewer people would be willing to do it. The main methods of accomplishing this objective are

—to charge peak-hour tolls on major commuter routes;

—to charge sizable parking taxes in addition to normal fees for anyone parking a vehicle between 6:00 A.M. and 9:30 A.M.;

—to prohibit employers from providing free parking except to workers who use car pools;

—to raise the federal sales tax on gasoline from its 1992 level of 14 cents to perhaps $1.00 a gallon.

The bounded high-density plan would employ all four tactics. The limited-spread mixed-density model would use either peak-hour tolls or higher parking charges but not both, since these are likely to be the most effective approaches. The new communities and green belts model would adopt a strategy somewhere in between.

The limited-spread model assumes that trying to convince commuters to give up their cars is not worth either massive public investment in expanding transit facilities or using all the unpopular pressures that would have to be exerted on solo drivers. Instead this policy would use only some of those measures to encourage ride sharing. One tactic would be to build additional lanes on commuter roadways and designate them as exclusively for high occupancy vehicles. Transportation management associations could be sponsored among major employers to persuade them to pressure their workers to share rides and use public transit. Finally, employer tax deductions for providing free employee parking could be abolished. But deductions could be retained if the employers offered commuting allowances that could be used for public transit or ride sharing.

Unfortunately, experience with these ideas suggests that they are not likely to be very effective unless accompanied by at least one of the draconian measures that raise the costs of driving solo.[18] That implies a strong centralized body with authority throughout a metropolitan area over roads, public transit, parking, traffic flows, and transportation investments.

Residential Densities and Public Transit

All three alternatives to unlimited low-density growth would create higher residential densities to reduce the total amount of movement required by daily living and to transfer more of this movement to public transit. However, only a revolution in American behavior could increase use of public transit to anywhere near the levels in Western Europe or Japan. In 1989 among U.S. commuters who lived in suburbs, thirty-six times as many drove to work as took public transportation. And on average, drivers spent less than half the time commuting that transit commuters did.[19] Even if twice as many commuters used public transportation, commuting by automobile would at most be reduced by only 2.8 percent.

In a 1977 study Boris Pushkarev and Jeffrey Zupan concluded that residential densities do affect public transit use.[20] At net residential densities less than seven units an acre, use is minimal. But it increases sharply at higher densities. Densities of seven to fifteen dwellings an acre can support moderately convenient service by trains, buses, and taxis. These net densities are equivalent to gross densities of 5,600 to 12,000 persons a square mile, assuming 50 percent of all land is used for housing. However, most American suburbs have gross densities much lower than 5,000 persons a square mile.

The authors also concluded that for transit use, residential density is less significant than location. Residential areas near major downtowns generate much higher proportions of transit trips than those with the same densities farther out. And areas within 2,000 feet of transit stops show much greater use than those farther away. Therefore clustering high-density housing near downtowns or rapid transit stops is more effective at increasing the use of public transportation than raising average residential densities over large areas.

My 1992 book, *Stuck in Traffic*, presents a detailed analysis of the potential effects of clustering high-density housing around transit stops.[21] It shows that even extensive suburban rapid transit systems serving many high-density housing clusters near their stops would carry relatively few suburban commuters.

According to Pushkarev and Zupan, the density of nonresidential clusters such as shopping centers or business districts is much more important than residential density in generating public transportation use. Clustering nonresidential land uses close together would be more effective at promoting the use of public transportation than would raising residential densities but keeping commercial space dispersed. However, commercial nodes need 10 million square feet or more of nonresidential space to generate much public transportation use. And the space must be concentrated within not much more than a single square mile to make bus service effective.

Stuck in Traffic also contains a detailed analysis of clustering suburban jobs. The proportion of suburbanites who commuted by private vehicles was 90.8 percent in 1977, 89.1 percent in 1983, and 91.1 percent in 1989.[22] The proportion using public transit fell from 4.6 percent in 1977 to 3.3 percent in 1983 and 2.5 percent in 1989. There is no evidence that concentrating jobs in suburban clusters would produce any notable changes in commuting behavior. Surveys in Walnut Creek, California, and Bethesda, Maryland, concerning how workers commute to large job clusters next to fixed-rail stops indicate that less than 5 percent use mass transit.[23] Moreover, trying to get employers to locate new jobs in large clusters would require administrative controls repugnant to Americans.

Pushkarev and Zupan also concluded that major outlying shopping centers can support intermediate-quality bus service if surrounding residential areas have net densities of seven units an acre or higher. Intermediate-quality service means half-mile route spacing and about forty buses a day, one at least every half hour. If 50 percent of the land (excluding streets) is used for housing and the average household size is 2.5 persons, seven an acre is equivalent to 5,600 people a square mile.[24]

It would be extremely difficult to reduce peak-hour automobile use solely by improving public transit service and capacity. Pushkarev and Zupan estimated that cutting transit fares (including bus fares) by 50 percent could increase ridership between 7 and 43 percent, with the biggest increases in nonwork trips. Cutting running time by 50 percent could increase ridership only 14 to 20 percent. Cutting the time people wait for transit by 50 percent by doubling service frequency could increase ridership 24 to 77 percent under various circumstances. But these tactics would greatly increase transit operating losses.

None of the tactics would come close to doubling ridership, especially for work trips. Therefore, Pushkarev and Zupan concluded that "from the transit viewpoint, it is much more 'profitable' to gain riders either from restraints on automobile use or from increased density of urban development."[25]

At least two changes in public policy could improve the prospects for increasing commuters' use of public transportation. One is a legal prohibition against spreading potentially transit-supporting development—such as office buildings and multifamily housing—through low-density areas. However, this policy has the administrative and bureaucratic drawbacks already noted. The second change would make property taxes put more emphasis on taxing land and less on taxing improvements to encourage higher-density development.

Increasing suburban residential densities either overall or in a small number of clusters is therefore not likely to increase commuters' use of public transit much. In all, it would be difficult to cajole or command enough Americans out of their cars to achieve the transportation goals of any of the alternative visions. To most Americans the cures for traffic congestion are worse than the congestion itself. This does not mean that no changes in travel behavior can be accomplished. Undoubtedly marginal changes could be made if elected officials were willing to adopt the required tactics. But the tactics likely to be most effective would impose heavy costs on millions of Americans. Only if rush hour congestion becomes unbearable will they be willing to support them. That is likely to occur in only a few parts of the nation experiencing extremely rapid population and job growth.

More Unified Governance

Realization of the bounded high-density vision would require radical changes in Americans' personal behavior and institutions. Even trying to accomplish such changes would require centralized metropolitan governance that could affect land use, transportation, housing, and employment location. For example, managing the urban growth boundary in a growing metropolitan area would be extremely difficult if various local governments controlled land uses both inside and outside the boundary on land lying within their legal jurisdictions. Some outside agency, like the Land Conservation and Development Commission in Oregon, could be given strong powers over the boundary. But in spite of its powers over local governments, even the Oregon commission has complained about insufficient coordination of urban development inside and outside growth boundaries.

Even more daunting is the challenge of changing commuting habits. Only very strong and unpopular measures applied throughout a metropolitan area could make solo driving so costly as to cut its incidence. Similarly, the administrative controls required to concentrate new jobs in a few employment centers have no more than a remote chance of working even if the agency responsible for them has strong powers throughout the metropolitan area. Such powers would be critical in setting up and administering the programs for sharing tax bases and sales tax revenues. Moreover, coordinating the growth of job centers with the creation of a public transit network connecting them would require centralized planning and control of both land use and public transportation facilities in the metropolitan area. This is also true of the policies necessary to provide housing to the poor.

The most powerful form of metropolitan area governance would be the "pure" metropolitan government described in chapter 7. However, fewer than a dozen metropolitan areas have such governments and few more are ever likely to adopt that form. A second possible form of governance in the bounded high-density model would be a regional government with limited functions. It would have control only over those government functions that most influence land use patterns.

In theory, two other strongly centralized forms of government could be used as well. Both are based on the powers of the federal government over various aspects of metropolitan life. One would use the authority of the Clean Air Act to impose controls on behavior that affects air quality, including the use of automobiles. The second would be possible only if Congress required every metropolitan area to have a single regional body to administer all federal funds flowing into its constituent communities and public and private agencies (except direct federal aid to individuals). However, neither approach provides very direct regional controls over land use decisions, which lie outside the normal purview of federal policies. So they would be effective in dealing with growth-related problems only if state governments augmented the powers such agencies derived from federal laws. They might then be strong enough to support implementation of the bounded high-density policy.

Realization of the new communities and green belts vision would also require concentrating strong authority over land use and transportation in some regional agency. Local governments would be unlikely to divide up a metropolitan area's potentially developable land between open space and urban uses in a manner either satisfactory to existing communities or rationally related to regional planning goals. And the existing division of tax bases and services would be too haphazard for the goals of such a policy. Localities containing mainly permanent open space would be unable to raise much revenue. Localities dominated by intensive development, either within the major urban growth boundary or in new communities, could raise tax revenues but would also have to finance infrastructures and services. The vision of new communities and green belts would work only if some regional agency had at least strong coordinative authority over localities' land use and taxing powers.

A limited-spread mixed-density policy would not require either a centralized metropolitan government or a governing body that wielded powers directly affecting transportation and land use. Instead, it could depend on local land use planning within a framework controlled by state government. The framework would ideally involve the seven elements discussed in chapter 9. This complex form has been successfully employed in Oregon and Florida for many years and is now being tried in Georgia and New Jersey.

It is not clear how well this degree of decentralization would work in a large metropolitan area. In Portland, Oregon, a single regional agency has been established to manage public transportation and major infrastructure construction and operation. The agency's top officials are elected by the entire population of the metropolitan area. Portland's experience suggests that more centralization of major land use and transportation functions may be necessary than is incorporated in the decentralized state-managed system described in chapter 9. In any case, a limited-spread mixed-density policy would still require what many Americans would consider radical changes in the existing division of governmental authority among individual localities.

Housing Low-Income People

The alternative visions would use varying combinations of three tactics to provide more low-income housing in new-growth parts of metropolitan areas. The bounded high-density vision would employ all three; the others would employ one or two.

The first tactic would relax regulations that preclude multifamily housing or require excessively costly new residential units. This would permit builders to construct housing much more inexpensively than they now can.[26] All three alternative visions would incorporate this tactic.[27]

A second tactic would provide direct federal housing subsidies to large numbers of low-income households so they could occupy decent units without spending more than 30 percent of their incomes. Under a bounded high-density policy, making an entitlement out of low-income housing assistance would be especially important in fast-growing metropolitan areas. That policy would deflect growth inward, raising land and housing prices and rents throughout the areas. A universal low-income renter subsidy program would offset the effects of higher prices and rents on such households. The bounded high-density vision needs this tactic more than the other visions. But the new communities and green belts vision might employ it too if enough federal funds were available.

The third tactic would make some housing subsidies large enough to enable low-income people to occupy new units scattered throughout new-growth areas. Only through such subsidies can newly built sub-divisions be economically integrated. Because all three visions seek greater housing opportunities for low-income households, all would use this tactic.

This tactic differs from the second in both the depth of the subsidies and the breadth of households that would be eligible. The second tactic would turn low-income housing subsidies into entitlements available to all eligible households.[28] However, the federal government would be unlikely to permit such widely distributed subsidies to reach high enough amounts for each household aided to allow occupancy of new units, the only kind available in new-growth areas. It would simply cost too much.

The third tactic would require higher subsidies per household than the second. Yet it would be far less costly overall because the subsidies would be extended only to enough low-income households to achieve significant economic integration in new-growth areas. It would, however, favor units in relatively high-income neighborhoods and would be politically difficult to implement. It could probably be supported only as part of a larger effort that included some housing subsidies for those remaining in poor central city neighborhoods. The cost of the third tactic would thus be larger than the cost that would be necessary solely to achieve economic integration in new-growth areas. Still, the cost might be far lower than the cost of a complete entitlement subsidy program for low-income renters.

Achieving decent housing in new-growth areas would require every community in a metropolitan area to establish how much affordable housing it should contain. The target would have to be defined through a method devised by the state government or by a metropolitan agency.

Each community would be required to develop specific plans for meeting its target within a reasonable period. Progress in carrying out the plans would be monitored by a metropolitan agency. The agency would apply the same approach in every community to be free from charges of favoritism. Merely describing this approach demonstrates that it could only be pursued effectively by a single agency with legal authority throughout the metropolitan area over at least some residential zoning decisions. Otherwise, many local governments would refuse to accept housing for low- and moderate-income households.

This centralized agency could function in either of two ways. It could review all local housing plans as they are drawn up, or it could review only cases in which individual developers have appealed adverse decisions made by local governments, as in Massachusetts. The housing agency would need the power to override local decisions if it deemed the underlying grounds unreasonable or inconsistent with statewide planning goals. The second approach is less intrusive on local planning sovereignty. It also leaves the initiative in the private sector. But some regional public body with ultimate authority would have to be created to carry out the plan.

Part 4
Turning Visions into Realities

9

Offsetting Fragmented Land Use Powers

SOLVING growth-related problems requires somehow off-setting the ill effects of the fragmentation of land use powers among U.S. metropolitan area governments. But that decentralization is deeply embedded in American institutional structures. In theory, the simplest way to counteract the adverse effects of fragmentation is to adopt regionwide government structures, so-called metropolitan government. But in practice metropolitan government is rare.

Metropolitan government is strongly advocated by David Rusk, former mayor of Albuquerque.[1] That city has the legal power to annex surrounding subdivisions and has done so aggressively. Rusk's experience as mayor convinced him that this power helped solve a lot of urban problems. He divides American cities into categories according to their "elasticity." Elastic cities can expand their boundaries almost indefinitely to encompass growing areas. Inelastic cities cannot expand because they are surrounded by autonomous suburbs. Thus most metropolitan area growth occurs *inside* elastic cities but *outside* inelastic ones.

Rusk presents impressive evidence that elastic cities are economically healthier and less plagued by racial segregation in housing and schools. They are therefore better able to attract investment and maintain vigorous economies. Some of these benefits probably result from causes other than a city's elasticity, such as when it became established (cities maturing in the automobile era are generally more prosperous than older ones) or the economic health of the region. However, it does seem logical that cities which can annex growing areas will do better than those that must watch growth move beyond their boundaries. Rusk therefore recommends policies that would encourage states to permit central cities to expand.

The weakness in Rusk's approach is not the logic of his argument but the difficulty of persuading people that adopting metropolitan government is truly in their interest. Metropolitan government has almost no political support. Officials of central cities do not want to risk competing for the votes of suburban residents. Suburban residents are likely to have higher incomes, and therefore be politically more conservative, than the constituents who have elected city officials. Those officials are especially reluctant if the central city contains a majority or near majority of blacks, Hispanics, or members of a combination of minority groups. Many of these citizens and their elected leaders do not want their political power diluted.

Suburban officials and residents are even more strongly opposed to metropolitan government. Most suburban officials would lose their jobs as duplicate positions were abolished. And suburban residents fear loss of control over land use, schools, and use of tax revenues. Nor do they want to pay higher taxes to help grapple with the difficult problems of central cities.

Both city and suburban residents believe that transferring all local government powers to a metropolitan government would make officials more remote from any influence individual citizens might hope to exert. In fact, stronger individual influence is why decentralized government has long been one of the mainstays of the dominant vision of metropolitan growth.

In short, almost no one favors metropolitan area government except a few political scientists and intellectuals. Proposals to replace suburban governments completely are therefore doomed. That is why fewer than a dozen or so metropolitan areas have regional governments.

Alternatives to Metropolitan Area Government

If full metropolitan government is not feasible, what other means might be used to achieve the regional powers necessary to cope with growth-related problems? I have chosen seven possibilities; they are explored in the rest of this chapter.

Voluntary Cooperation among Local Governments

Voluntary cooperation is the least satisfactory response to decentralization and has the fewest applications to growth-related problems.

Under this arrangement nothing can compel local governments to co-ordinate their behavior or monitor and adjust it. Yet voluntary coop-eration could coordinate some policies. Cooperation could, for exam-ple, reduce traffic congestion by easing the process of upgrading intersecting local streets, timing traffic signals, converting streets to one-way flows, and creating roving regional teams to clear traffic ac-cidents quickly. But when growth-related policies require allocating benefits and costs among jurisdictions, sacrifices on the part of one locality or another, or other controversial decisions, this approach does not work.

State Government Departments

In some matters, state government departments are already respon-sible for planning policies and facilities, and for financing, construct-ing, and operating them throughout metropolitan areas. In most states they are responsible for the construction and maintenance of major highways; in some they also control public transit. Some states have established housing departments or housing finance agencies that could take on regional roles.

State government departments have three significant advantages in carrying out regional policies. First, their jurisdiction encompasses the entire metropolitan area, unless it includes parts of more than one state. Second, they already have established capabilities and channels of finance, information, and political influence. Finally, for some func-tions, such as improving transportation, monitoring air quality, and sometimes overseeing housing, these agencies have access to contin-uing flows of money to finance activities and investments. State agen-cies could, then, carry out many policies in response to growth-related problems.

State agencies could also help create cooperative arrangements for uniform zoning and building codes, for instance, among local govern-ments. However, even where a state agency provides a technically competent vehicle for achieving some policy, that policy will not be carried out unless there is strong and broad political support for it. Thus state agencies are poor vehicles for instituting policies that re-quire people and their elected officials to change long-established be-havior. In a democracy, leadership in instituting such change rarely comes from public officials; they are essentially followers of public opinion. Such followership is one of democracy's greatest strengths, but it means that adopting new methods, especially controversial ones, requires some other source of change.[2]

Public-Private Coordination

Americans have long been noted for forming associations.[3] One type especially important in changing public policy has been the public-private organization that transcends the boundaries of individual communities: for example, the United Way organizations that raise and distribute charitable contributions throughout a metropolitan area.

This type of organization has some major advantages in creating a regional basis for growth-related policies. First, it can recruit members from both private and public organizations, including business firms, labor unions, nonprofit associations, universities, government agencies, and legislatures. It can thus provide a forum in which these people come together to discuss concerns outside their organizations. Second, it can establish any geographic jurisdiction its members desire, including entire metropolitan areas. Finally such an agency can take controversial stands without making individual members publicly commit themselves to those stands. Such an organization would seem an ideal vehicle for changing public opinion to support some controversial new policy.

But public-private organizations usually have little money, and they have no governmental powers. So they have no ability to carry out the public policies they support. This means they are confined to influencing public opinion and persuading those who do have money and power to adopt the policies they favor. Still, they can become vehicles for persuading the public and its leaders that some problem is serious enough to demand concerted action. And they can formulate and analyze possible means of remedying the problem.

These functions are all vital in securing adoption of regional approaches to growth management. I believe it is crucial for some type of public-private regional association to strongly support such strategies if they are to be adopted anywhere. The membership should consist of executives of major employers, citizens' groups in the metropolitan area, and government leaders who can influence crucial transportation and land use policies. The deliberative process they share of jointly analyzing growth problems, examining possible solutions, and arriving at final recommendations creates a unifying common experience among them. That experience is vital to securing their emotional commitment to carrying out their final recommendations in the face of the strong resistance sure to arise. Then the organization should launch a concerted and sustained information and political pressure campaign urging adoption of the regional approaches it has recommended. Examples of such organizations are the Bay Area Council in the San Francisco Bay region, the Regional Planning Association in greater New York City, and Los Angeles 2000.

Unfortunately, no privately sponsored campaigns favoring regional growth management have yet been successfully carried out anywhere in the United States, insofar as I know.

Functionally Specialized Regional Agencies

In some U.S. metropolitan areas, most activities concerning a specific urban function have been turned over to special regional agencies. Regional public transit agencies run bus lines and fixed-rail mass transit systems. Some are responsible for bridges, tunnels, and other highway facilities. In the New York City area the regional Port Authority runs bridges, tunnels, bus terminals and bus lines, port facilities, and major airports. Sometimes a single agency is responsible for operating an area's water or sewer system. Where such specialized agencies exist, they could under some circumstances be used to carry out regional growth management policies. For example, agencies that run rapid transit and bus systems could improve the service and facilities of those systems to divert traffic from highways.

Where a regional highway agency exists, its scope for carrying out tactics to reduce congestion is even greater. For example, the agency that operates the Golden Gate and Bay Bridges leading into San Francisco could charge rush hour tolls on both. However, this assumes the agency has sufficient political courage to raise the tolls high enough to keep many auto commuters off the bridges during peak periods. Once again, widespread support for regional growth management policies must be created among citizens and their political leaders before such policies can be implemented.

In most metropolitan areas no such specialized agencies exist. However, it is certainly easier to create them than to create a full regional government. For one thing, the regional nature of congestion, air pollution, and other growth-related problems is so obvious that hardly

anyone can dispute it. And local governments feel much less threatened by specialized agencies than by more general regional governments.

Therefore people promoting regional growth management should
seriously consider setting up one or more regional agencies to handle
specific functions related to growth. Ideally the jurisdiction of each
agency should include the planning, construction, and operation of
major public facilities related to the specific problem it is supposed to
cope with and the regulation of private facilities related to that problem. Such an agency is easiest to create when the entire metropolitan
area lies within a single state.

Federally Rooted Regional Agencies

The federal Clean Air Act and Intermodal Surface Transportation
Efficiency Act (ISTEA) have created potentially powerful regional
forces that might affect growth management. The Clean Air Act establishes air quality standards for all metropolitan areas. The Environmental Protection Agency requires state governments to create plans
for cleaning up the air in nonattainment areas where air pollution
exceeds acceptable levels (nonattainment areas have boundaries identical with those of metropolitan areas and consolidated metropolitan
areas). A state can thus set up a regional organization to coordinate
air quality improvement throughout an entire metropolitan area. And
acting through these agencies, the federal government can override or
preempt certain local ordinances related to air quality.

Similarly, ISTEA requires every urban area with more than 50,000
inhabitants to establish a metropolitan organization to handle transportation planning.[4] These organizations are supposed to pursue fifteen objectives, including relieving congestion and taking into account
impacts on land uses. Each organization must prepare a long-range
transportation plan and a transportation improvement program with
a three-year list of specific projects. These plans are to be coordinated
with counterparts at the state level. The programs must be especially
sensitive to likely effects on air quality.

This connection arises, of course, because vehicle emissions are a
major cause of air pollution. Long average commuting trips and traffic
congestion increase pollution. So regional agencies for air quality improvement have become concerned with traffic flows, especially in
California. The Southern California Air Quality Management District

has proposed regulations that would require major changes in driving and commuting behavior over large territories. For example, it has proposed that a significant percentage of all automotive vehicles must use fuels other than gasoline by 2010.

Such federally backed agencies could potentially implement growth management tactics at regional levels. They could, for instance, impose peak-hour road pricing and parking charges throughout a metropolitan area. However, very few of these agencies have been established.

Such agencies could adopt and carry out regional growth management tactics effectively only if three conditions prevail. First, agency control based on provisions of the Clean Air Act can only be applied in metropolitan areas that are not in compliance with federal air quality standards. Second, an agency's leaders must be convinced that specific actions are absolutely necessary to reduce their region's air pollution to acceptable levels or to achieve regional transportation goals. This is not a forgone conclusion. There has been so little experience with the application of such steps that no one can be sure just how they would work. Moreover, there is always a lot of resistance to regional approaches. The third condition is that people must voluntarily follow the regulations. Widespread rejection of laws that require major behavioral changes may destroy their effectiveness, as happened during Prohibition in the 1920s and is happening now with various antidrug laws.

In spite of inherent resistance, however, the legally established powers of agencies to act across an entire metropolitan area provide a potentially effective means of carrying out action to manage regional growth.

Creating a Federal Incentive for Regional Institutions

The federal government transfers funding to metropolitan areas through many federal, state, and local agencies. But this flow is not coordinated by any one plan dealing with each metropolitan area as a whole. Rather, many separate federal agencies provide transfers to many separate state, local, and regional agencies operating in different jurisdictions.

This situation provides an opportunity for the federal government to create powerful incentives for all the recipients in a metropolitan area to support a centralized distribution of federal and other resources.[5] The federal government could put all the funds for a metro-politan area into a single pot of money. The money would still be divided programmatically into the same funding categories as now, but it would be pooled geographically or jurisdictionally within each category. Thus all the money allocated for transportation to different localities in a metropolitan area would be combined into a unified federal transportation fund for that area. The Intermodal Surface Transportation Efficiency Act already does something similar for fed-eral surface transportation funding. The federal government could re-quire that funds for each program category then be allocated within the metropolitan area by a regional agency created by area residents or by the state government in accordance with a few basic principles.

A primary assumption underlying this idea is that federal funds are critical to most governments in a metropolitan area, and those juris-dictions include most of an area's residents. Being required to form a regional agency in order to obtain federal funds would therefore strongly motivate the local governments or the relevant state govern-ment to do so, even though some local governments, mainly in wealthy suburbs, would not want to participate. (They would prefer receiving no federal funds to being part of any regional resource-allocation agency.)

CREATING A REGIONAL ALLOCATION AGENCY. The principles and procedures to create a regional agency might include the following, although different regulations could be developed.

—The governing members of the regional agency could be chosen in a number of ways. They could be periodically elected by the resi-dents of the entire metropolitan area, as in Portland, Oregon. They could be appointed by the governor (or governors) of the state (or states) in which the metropolitan area is located, as in the Twin Cities area in Minnesota. Or they could be appointed by the local govern-ments in the metropolitan area. The number of members representing each such government should have some relationship to the total pop-ulation of the localities concerned so that big cities are not under-represented.

—Once chosen, the members of this agency could delegate some of their powers to existing organizations or appointed subagencies to handle funds within each program category, or use any other admin-istrative methods they chose.

—The regional agency could allocate the federal funds within each program area either to local governments or directly to households, service delivery agencies, or other recipients.

—Within each categorical program, the regional agency would have to develop a plan for the way it allocated funds among the recipients and make the plan public. It would also be required to hold public hearings before a plan was put into effect. Every such plan would have to address the needs and capacities of all potential recipients on an areawide basis and show how it was meeting those needs for persons living in all parts of the metropolitan area.

—Every allocation plan would have to take at least some account of resources from local government taxation, fees, private sector funds, and other nonfederal sources. Doing this would help coordinate federally funded activities with other activities within a program category. However, taking account would not have to involve detailed overall planning of all funds in a program category. Each plan for a particular category (such as transportation) would be subject to the same federal regulations and reviews that now apply to such planning by individual states or localities receiving federal funds in that category.

—The federal government would provide some basic funding for administering each regional agency and for some initial training of the agency's personnel.

—Any metropolitan area that failed to use this method of allocating federal funds would not be eligible to receive such funds at all.

To make this regional approach work, it would be necessary to place certain federal fund flows under the control of the regional allocation agency. At the outset, these should at least include

—all federal funding for highways, bridges, mass transit, and airports;

—all federal funding for combating air pollution, controlling water flows and purification, managing sewage flows and purification, managing solid waste, and building any other physical infrastructures;

—all federal funding for public housing, housing vouchers, and all other housing subsidies, including Federal Housing Administration mortgage insurance; and

—all federal funding for urban planning assistance (other types of federal funds that might be included are those for education, welfare, and health care).

To ensure nearly universal participation in this regional allocation process, Congress might consider linking eligibility of metropolitan homeowners' mortgage interest and property tax deductions to residence in a locality that was part of a regional agency. Or at least homeowners in localities that were not participating might have their deductions cut in half. With modern computers, making such distinctions is technically feasible. That would provide a strong grass-roots incentive for such participation without adding any costs to the federal budget.

THE IMPORTANCE OF GRADUAL PHASE-IN. The transition from present methods of allocating federal funds among localities and states to using regional coordination agencies should not occur abruptly. A phase-in period of three to five years would permit gradual adjustment to the new requirements, especially trial-and-error testing of new procedures and training of personnel.

OTHER ASPECTS OF THIS APPROACH. A regional allocation body would not replace or eliminate existing local governments or their constituent agencies; in fact, it would mostly work through them. Neither would it control nonfederal funds raised and spent by each local jurisdiction or by the state government. These funds would comprise most public spending in education, police and fire protection, land use zoning and planning, and most other program categories. The nonfederal funds would, however, be taken account of by the overall planning required of the agency in each program category.

Because local agencies would retain many powers, planning and coordination resulting from a regional federal allocation agency would not resolve all the growth-related problems in a metropolitan area. But once the regional agency had been created and was operating, its presence might lead to far more coordination of nonfederally funded activities than now exists.

WINNING POLITICAL SUPPORT. The greatest flaw in trying to create a regional allocation agency is that Congress has no significant political incentives to adopt it, and many not to. The present committee structure motivates members of each committee to keep the spending of each federal agency separate from that of agencies under the jurisdiction of other committees. This fragmentation permits members of each committee to develop considerable power and authority as well as expertise in their specialized areas. If control over the allocation of federal funds for metropolitan areas were given to a regional allocation agency, members of Congress would lose much of their power and influence. And it is well to remember that members of Congress are elected from geographic districts, and many have come up through local and state governments. They may very well believe that the authority of local governments should be as strong as possible—certainly not subject to review or modification by any regional body.

The only incentive for Congress to adopt a regional approach to federal spending is to increase the effectiveness of public policies in dealing with growth-related problems. Up to now, Congress has paid little attention to that incentive. However, widespread public support for Ross Perot's harsh criticisms of federal waste and mismanagement has inspired more interest in improving the efficiency with which federal money is allocated. The failure of federal agencies to coordinate their activities in metropolitan areas is an obvious source of waste and inefficiency. A regional approach to federal spending would directly attack such lack of coordination and create a strong incentive for greater coordination of state and local funds, too. In essence it would merely extend the precedent already established for transportation funding in the ISTEA.

A Broader Framework for Local Land Use Powers

A final institutional arrangement for achieving a more regional focus in growth-related policies is to embed the independent land use powers of local governments in a broader framework established by state government. Rather than trying to take powers over land use away from local governments, this framework would leave most in their hands. But it would greatly increase the coordination of land use plans. I think this is likely to be the most promising approach in most U.S. metropolitan areas experiencing serious growth-related problems.

People favor independent local governments for what they think are good reasons. They believe—correctly—that merging their local government into some monolithic metropolitan structure would reduce their ability to influence conditions in their own neighborhoods. Strong local governments are better able to adapt local policies to the desires of residents of each neighborhood because they are closer to knowing those desires than larger governments would be.[6]

Yet many people recognize that greater coordination of local government decisions within a metropolitan area is necessary to cope with the problems of growth. Coordination permits each locality to draft its own land use plans but requires that the plans serve goals sanctioned by the state legislature. It also requires each locality to follow certain standardized procedures in preparing its plans. Such a framework has been created in Oregon, Florida, and New Jersey.

The constitutional base for the framework is that of state governments. They have fundamental authority over all aspects of local governments, which are legally creatures of the state. A state government can require local governments to exercise their existing powers within a broader framework. For maximum effectiveness, such a framework should contain the following major elements.

—The state legislature should create a statement of planning goals applicable to all communities throughout the state. Local plans and policies inconsistent with these goals should be challengeable by local residents in court or in special forums created for such adjudication.

—Every local government should be required to develop a comprehensive land use plan that addresses common elements (such as transportation and housing) and follows common procedures and methods of presentation. Significant citizen participation should be required in formulating these plans. Planning and revising must remain in the hands of local governments, which will help preserve local sovereignty, but within a broader state framework.

—A single government agency at either the state or regional level (for example, a county agency) should be empowered to review all local land use plans, check their consistency with the state's goals and their consistency with each other, and suggest revisions where inconsistencies of either type are found. This agency must have the power to withhold approval of local plans, and withholding should carry significant penalties in the form of ineligibility for various types of state financial assistance. In some cases the agency should have the power to override local government decisions, such as zoning decisions that prevent creation of low-cost housing. Most often, however, the agency would simply request the local government to revise its plans and repeat the process until final approval is obtained.

—The same agency that coordinates the plans of local governments should also coordinate state transportation departments, utility regulation departments, environmental protection departments, and other agencies. The purpose is to be sure that the functional plans of the state agencies are consistent with local government plans and with each other.

—An adjudication process should be set up to settle disputes between local governments and the state coordinating agency and between developers and local governments. A special court could be created to settle the disputes without resorting to state or federal courts. Or a quasi-judicial administration agency could be designed. A special process such as this would permit development of relevant expertise by the officials of the adjudication body. It could also provide much speedier and less costly remedial processes than those provided by normal courts.

—Finally, formal reports should periodically evaluate the effectiveness of the entire system. The evaluation should be carried out by an agency other than the coordinating agency or the adjudicative body.

The most controversial of these elements is the coordinating agency. To be effective, it must have the legal power to compel local governments to revise their comprehensive land use plans, and it must have powers to coordinate the activities of state functional agencies. This arrangement would be controversial because it would weaken the absolute authority of local governments over land use planning. It would also create another layer of government in land use planning, although this layer would not directly participate in approving plans for individual developments. This additional layer would add to overall planning costs, add time for final approval of local plans, and generally make planning more complicated.

Nevertheless, without a coordinating agency, local governments could not be pressured to make their land use policies consistent with either state goals or each other. The separate adjudicatory agency is not quite as vital and could be eliminated. The evaluative and reporting agency is also dispensable.

The great advantage of this approach is that it retains the existing structure of local governments and permits them to exercise most of their present powers. It does, however, significantly limit how local sovereignty can be exercised. This limitation will surely be interpreted by many local officials as a grave weakening of their sovereignty. But in truth they do not have much control over the conditions that generate the growth-related problems they have; those conditions are regionwide. In fact, this approach would empower them to attack the problems more effectively with tactics coordinated throughout the whole metropolitan area.

This basic structure can be used within specific functional areas, such as housing, as well as in relation to comprehensive land use planning.

The Potential of Multiple Regional Institutions

My analysis of how to organize regional growth management policies does not imply that such policies can best be created through a single agency acting as a regional policy czar. Instead, it might be desirable to have different growth management policies run by different local and regional agencies that organized themselves in ways best suited to their individual tasks. But if several growth management agencies are created at the regional level, they should certainly be linked through both formal and informal coordination.

Conclusions

Overcoming the deeply entrenched resistance of local governments to sharing any of their authority over land use is the biggest obstacle to carrying out cohesive strategies for metropolitan area growth. Among the alternatives I have considered, the two with the greatest potential are regional agencies to coordinate federal funding in each metropolitan area and state requirements for local governments to engage in comprehensive planning within a state-established framework. The coordination of federal agency funding has the added advantage of requiring only a single political action by Congress.

Some may complain that both ideas should be rejected because they add another layer of government to our already overregulated society. But the major shortcoming of local governments in metropolitan areas is that their failure to take account of the welfare of each area as a whole is undermining the long-run viability of American society. Unless Americans confront this reality by creating institutions that operate at the same scale as their major problems, their problems will only get worse.

10

The Politics of Choosing among Visions

*T*HE PRECEDING CHAPTERS have described four growth patterns that American metropolitan areas might pursue. How can residents of an area decide which one to follow? Both asking and trying to answer this question pose conceptual, analytic, and practical difficulties. Asking it presupposes three conditions missing from most U.S. metropolitan areas. The first is that most residents must be willing to have society make a deliberate choice about what growth strategy ought to be followed, rather than leaving development to market forces and other seemingly unplanned influences. The second condition is that government mechanisms must exist for determining and adopting growth-related policies that would be enforceable throughout the metropolitan area. The third is that a sufficient consensus must be generated from diverse viewpoints to support a coherent and effective growth strategy.

Creating widespread willingness to develop a growth strategy would require a major change in the perspectives of most metropolitan area citizens. Creating mechanisms for determining growth policies would require equally radical changes in institutional structures. So just considering the question of which pattern is appropriate involves describing the political and other forces necessary to bring about such radical changes.

Even if those radical changes were made, which growth pattern should be chosen by each area? Theoretically, making a rational choice involves defining goals, formulating means of attaining them, and evaluating those means against the goals. But that process presupposes a shared unity of purpose and perspective. In particular, the interests of the middle- and upper-income majority of people—mainly white— concerning growth are not the same as the interests of most low-

183

income people, who are a relatively small minority of each area's total population. Moreover, most citizens and their public officials do not really understand what growth patterns are possible or all the adverse consequences of continuing the low-density pattern that now predominates.

The Politics of Adopting a Regional Perspective

People will support adopting a new vision of how metropolitan area growth ought to occur only if they believe doing so will benefit them personally as much as it will benefit society. A crucial step in persuading them to embrace a new pattern is to show them the potential gains. These are of two types: ones that would flow directly from changing the dominant pattern of metropolitan growth and ones that would flow from effectively attacking the four national social problems described in chapter 1. Effective attacks on those national problems would require adopting many policies other than those that directly bear on growth. The attacks would probably not succeed, however, unless the vision of how growth should proceed were also changed.

These two types of major potential benefits are presented in table 10-1. The first type contains at least partial solutions to the growth-related problems described in chapter 1. The second type presents at least partial solutions to the basic social problems also discussed in chapter 1. No doubt some additional gains might be identified or these might be defined differently, but this list is sufficient for this analysis.

The list of potential benefits assumes that growth in a given metropolitan area occurs through one of the three alternatives to the dominant model, and that this alternative achieves its major objectives. Not every alternative would provide each benefit to the same extent as every other, but all three would produce gains. The list of benefits also assumes that the United States adopts nationwide policies attacking all four basic social problems and that those policies are also effective within the metropolitan area concerned. These are admittedly heroic assumptions. Yet they are necessary to identify the *potential* benefits from adopting a different vision of growth and its associated policies. In reality, it is unlikely that such a change in models would produce all these results. Nevertheless, their potential realization can be used to elicit support from groups that could gain.

Each benefit would vary in both nature and intensity from place to place, time to time, and group to group. More particular definitions, therefore, or attempts to quantify any definitions, cannot be reliably provided at this point. They can be arrived at only when one applies a specific alternative to a particular metropolitan area.

Potential Beneficiaries of Changing Visions

In the long run the vast majority of Americans would benefit from adopting a new vision, insofar as the change would help remedy basic social problems. But a long-range benefit is hard for many people to see. And whether it would appear at all and how large it would be are by no means certain. For many people, then, the chance of receiving the benefit would not outweigh the immediate losses of welfare they believe they would suffer. To generate near-future political support for such a change, it will be necessary to appeal to particular groups likely to benefit sooner and more directly from it.

Analyzing these potential sources of support requires identifying potential benefits, defining groups that might gain from them, and estimating the importance of each benefit for each group. Table 10-1 shows thirteen groups of potential beneficiaries at the heads of the columns: six are governments or business groups and seven are mainly types of households. Undoubtedly, other groups could be defined or these could be divided up differently. However, this table is offered to show how a benefit analysis might be conducted in each metropolitan area.

The potential gains are listed in the stub of the table. Each cell in the chart represents the extent to which one potential benefit would affect one group of beneficiaries. There are three benefit levels: very important, somewhat important, and unimportant. No attempt has been made to identify which groups might suffer losses of welfare from the outcomes because the usefulness of the table is to reveal potential sources of support for adopting an alternative vision of growth.

To compare the overall benefits that the thirteen groups might receive, a benefit has been awarded two points if it is very important, one if it is somewhat important, and zero if it is unimportant or nonexistent. Overall scores for each beneficiary group have been computed by adding the column entries without further weighting. This is admittedly a very crude estimate because the relative importance of each benefit to different groups could vary tremendously.

Central city governments would appear to benefit most and inner-

TABLE 10-1. *Benefits of Alternative Visions for Thirteen Population Groups*[a]

Potential benefits	Suburban govern-ments	Central city govern-ments	Nondevelopment business — Suburbs	Nondevelopment business — Central city	Real estate developers and builders
Direct benefits of alternative visions					
Less energy consumption for transportation	1	1	2	2	1
Less peak-hour congestion	2	2	1	1	1
Shorter average commutes in growth areas	0	0	0	0	0
Less air pollution	1	0	0	0	0
Low-wage suburban jobs closer to workers' homes	1	0	2	0	1
More affordable housing in suburbs	2	1	1	0	2
Better schooling for suburban low-income residents	2	2	2	2	0
Greater certainty of planning parameters	1	1	0	0	2
Shorter delays in planning	0	0	0	0	2
Greater uniformity of development rules	0	0	0	0	2
Greater demand for higher-density living	0	2	0	0	1
Less competition among cities for ratables	2	2	1	0	0
Better coordination of suburban land use plans	1	0	1	0	2
Easier access to open space	0	0	0	0	0
Less conversion of open space	1	0	0	0	1
Easier location of LULUs	2	2	1	1	1
Reduced concentration of poor in inner cities	0	2	0	2	0
Better financing of new infrastructure	2	1	1	1	2
Greater recognition of need to aid central cities	0	2	0	2	0
Benefits of attacking basic social problems					
More opportunities to move out of cities	1	0	0	0	1
Greater security and lower security costs from less crime	1	2	1	2	0
Better quality public schooling	2	2	2	2	2
Higher incomes stimulating consumer demand	0	2	1	2	1
Improved travel links from cities to suburban jobs	2	2	2	0	0
Better access to suburban jobs	2	2	2	0	1
Improved training links with suburban jobs	2	2	2	0	0
Improved quality of area labor force	1	2	2	2	2
Easier recruiting and retention of skilled workers	1	2	2	2	0
More jobs in central cities	0	2	0	1	0
Unweighted total score	30	36	26	22	25

a. 2 = benefit very important. 1 = benefit somewhat important. 0 = benefit not important.

Suburban employers of low-wage workers	First-time home buyers	Low- and moderate-income renters	Suburban elderly and young households	Inner-city residents	Auto-motive com-muters	People with respira-tory diseases	Environ-mental advocacy groups
1	0	0	0	0	2	0	0
1	1	0	0	1	2	1	1
2	1	0	1	0	2	0	1
0	0	0	0	1	1	2	2
2	2	2	2	2	1	0	0
1	2	2	2	2	1	0	0
2	2	2	2	2	0	0	0
0	0	0	0	0	0	0	0
0	0	0	0	0	0	0	0
0	0	0	0	0	0	0	1
0	0	0	0	0	0	0	1
0	0	0	0	0	0	0	0
0	0	0	0	0	0	0	2
1	1	1	1	1	0	1	2
0	0	0	0	0	0	0	2
1	0	0	0	0	0	0	1
0	0	1	1	2	0	0	0
0	1	1	0	0	2	1	2
0	0	0	0	2	0	0	0
1	2	2	0	2	1	0	0
0	1	1	1	2	0	0	0
2	2	2	0	2	0	0	0
1	1	0	0	2	0	0	0
2	2	1	0	2	1	0	0
2	2	2	0	2	1	0	0
2	1	0	0	2	0	0	0
2	0	0	0	1	0	0	0
2	0	0	0	1	0	0	0
0	1	2	0	2	0	0	0
25	22	19	10	31	14	5	15

city residents next. But suburban governments are not far behind. Next are suburban employers of various types, including real estate developers and builders (because most of their activities are suburban). However, this relative ranking should not be given much significance. The actual importance of each potential gain to each group is subjective and will vary immensely from place to place and among businesses and households within each place. Still, this analysis shows that a considerable number of governments, enterprises, or households in each metropolitan area could benefit significantly. Some similar analysis could be used by advocates of new-growth policies to identify potential allies.

Yet it is difficult to persuade these groups that they would indeed gain and that the gains would more than offset any losses they would also experience. One reason for the difficulty is that the institutional changes required to adopt alternative strategies would have to be made well before the benefits would begin appearing. Motivating people to make what they perceive as radical changes to obtain distant potential gains is especially difficult in a commercialized democratic culture that is routinely self-indulgent and promotes expectations of instant gratification.

The best approach would simultaneously emphasize two reasons for making institutional changes. One is avoiding the imminent threat to American society if basic social problems are not resolved. The second is the potential for resolving growth-related problems within each particular metropolitan area. Those problems are less threatening to American society in the long run than are its basic social problems. But to residents of many metropolitan areas, the problems of growth pose more immediate threats or costs. The possibility of simultaneously attacking basic social problems and alleviating immediate local costs of growth makes the most powerful case for action.

Sources of Resistance to Structural Change

New ideas and alternative visions of growth would certainly be resisted, and not only on the local level. State and federal resistance also would be all too stiff.

LOCAL RESISTANCE. Powerful people and institutions have vested interests in continuing to allow unlimited low-density development. Local officials fear that major structural changes, especially stronger regional decisionmaking powers, might weaken their control or take away their offices entirely. Suburban homeowners fear that these changes might harm property values or introduce undesirable people into their neighborhoods. These two groups alone constitute a majority of residents in nearly every U.S. metropolitan area. Unless current policies produce completely unacceptable results, they will oppose any significant alteration of present structures.

Other groups also benefit from strong local controls over land use. Real estate developers can play one community off against another to get the best possible concessions for new projects that promise to pay significant local taxes. Realtors who have established quasi-monopolistic positions and multiple listing services in their communities do not want the arrangements disrupted.

STATE GOVERNMENT RESISTANCE. State governments have the constitutional power to create strong regional institutions at any time. Because their jurisdictions include entire metropolitan areas or large parts of them, they should not be subject to the same narrow parochialism as local governments. Besides, in most metropolitan areas the territory of regional agencies would lie entirely within a single state. Creating such agencies would therefore not involve complex interstate compacts. But very few states have regional agencies with significant land use powers. Why not?

One reason is that a regional agency would most likely be given powers now exercised in part by state highway departments and housing finance, environmental, public works, and other state agencies. Officials in those agencies do not want to give up any of their present powers. In addition, no state legislature is willing to incur the wrath of local governments unless the legislators have very strong incentives to do so. State legislators are elected from local districts. They are often linked personally and politically to local governments. And they are rarely elected from districts large enough to encompass an entire metropolitan area. So their viewpoints are also parochial.

What potential benefits might motivate legislators to establish regional growth management agencies over the objections of local governments? The main one would be reductions in the severity of growth-related problems in the long run. That gain would be spread over residents and businesses in all parts of the metropolitan area. For each it would be only a small part of the total benefits received from all state government actions. Very few beneficiaries would vote for or against a state legislative candidate on the basis of growth management alone.

In contrast, local officials would consider the potential loss of sovereignty caused by the creation of a regional agency as a major threat to their welfare. So how each state legislator voted on this issue would heavily influence the amount of support he or she received from local officials at the next election. For most legislators the potential loss of such support caused by their favoring creation of strong regional agencies would outweigh the gains from reducing growth-related problems.

FEDERAL GOVERNMENT RESISTANCE. Strong resistance to major structural changes would also arise at the federal level. Many members of Congress would oppose losing authority to regional agencies because the members represent suburban constituents fearful of being saddled with urban problems. Others represent central city constituents fearful of having their power over local affairs diluted by a suburban majority in their metropolitan areas.

The federal administration should be more amenable to making such changes. Unlike members of Congress, administrative officials are supposed to represent the entire nation, which is being threatened by serious social problems. And the effects of the problems are clearest to observers with a national perspective. Some federal bureaucrats might, of course, oppose creation of strong regional governance mechanisms that would take over some powers they now exercise directly. Nevertheless, an ethically responsible federal administration would be more likely to support the need for widespread regional governance mechanisms than any other organ of government. Therefore attempts to generate political support for creating such mechanisms should certainly seek to enlist the aid of the federal administration.

Social Crises and Institutional Change

Creating effective growth management institutions would require changes that many local and state officials, households, and businesses would regard as sacrificing their present interests. But political leaders in a democracy are not normally willing to ask citizens to make significant sacrifices except in times of crises. Otherwise they would be blamed for the sacrifices and would likely be defeated at the next election. Only if the need for sacrifice is overwhelmingly clear and strongly affects almost everyone can officials impose sacrifice without being personally stigmatized. For example, the fear of requiring sacrifices that do not have overwhelming popular support is what has kept the nation from reducing its burgeoning federal deficit. Significant pressure for major changes in land use institutions or powers will therefore appear only in metropolitan areas where growth-related or other problems have become so costly to so many that they have generated a social crisis.

A social crisis in this sense is usually conceived as a sudden, drastic, and widely perceived deterioration in vital conditions that requires rapid and unusual responses to avoid imminent disaster. It normally involves a sharp discontinuity in some important variable, such as one's health, or the level of a major river system, or the available supply of electricity. But both growth-related problems and basic national social problems mainly involve continuous variables. These variables change gradually; they do not normally exhibit drastic discontinuities. This is true of traffic congestion, air pollution, the financing of infrastructure, the amount of open space, the availability of suburban housing for low-income households, the availability of low-wage workers in the suburbs, the quality of life in inner-city concentrated-poverty neighborhoods, the increase in crime rates, the percentage of children growing up in poverty, the quality of public schools, and the integration of workers into the mainstream work force. The only problems that might involve obvious discontinuities are the location of vital facilities serving a region and the violence in inner-city neighborhoods, as when Los Angeles exploded in rioting in 1992. Even substantial worsening of the problems involving most of these conditions will not galvanize public opinion into demanding drastic changes.

Indeed, even widespread agreement that a social crisis has erupted may not evoke truly effective responses from elected officials or other social leaders. If only one condition generates a crisis in a metropolitan area, officials will focus on that condition. They will ignore broader institutional changes, such as more regional powers over land use, that might affect other problems as well. Yet because growth-related problems spring from several causes, attacking only one would do little to achieve effective growth management.

Also, democratic political leaders prefer quick fixes to fundamental institutional and procedural reforms. For example, California's 1992 state government fiscal crisis ultimately sprang from voters' passage in the 1970s and 1980s of Proposition 13 and other referendums affecting the state's fiscal policies. Proposition 13 drastically limited local property taxing powers, stripping local governments of their ability to pay for necessary local services. Another amendment to the state constitution that was passed by referendum forced the state to spend heavily on education, regardless of all other circumstances or needs. California cannot effectively reform its fiscal system without nullifying Proposition 13 and modifying other amendments adopted by referendum. But no major political leaders have even proposed such a strategy, in spite of the near collapse of state government financing.

Social crises limited to relatively small areas may also not evoke effective responses. The rioting in Los Angeles in 1992, for example, directly threatened only those neighborhoods near where the violence erupted, though it may have increased feelings of personal insecurity much more widely. Thus residents distant from an inner city will not be strongly motivated to attack the problems that plague it. In fact, distant residents may feel thankful for having successfully isolated themselves from such violence. So some social crises reinforce the psychological separation of suburbanites from central-city residents.

Only one of the problems associated with growth, the concentration of very poor households in inner-city neighborhoods, is likely to generate a social crisis by itself. And none is likely to cause a crisis that will motivate politicians to make wholesale changes in the institutional status quo. However, if several problems became extremely serious simultaneously in a metropolitan area, and they were clearly interrelated, diverse interest groups might form a coalition strong enough to change the decentralization of government control of land use.

This has not happened anywhere in the United States, although attempts have been made in several metropolitan areas. People simply do not believe the problems associated with growth are bad enough to energize them to demand the necessary reforms. And neither leaders nor citizens connect the recent increase in the severity of social problems with unlimited low-density growth, even when they believe crime or other social problems are at a critical stage.

Poorly Understood Creeping Crises

Instead of occurring in a discontinuous way, a dangerous condition can arise so slowly that people do not realize just how dangerous it has become, even if it is happening under their noses. America is currently experiencing such creeping crises in its lack of personal security, so many children growing up in poverty and without hope, the dismal quality of public education, and inadequate integration of too much of the work force into the mainstream economy. These problems, of course, have hardly gone unnoticed. In fact, the inadequacies of American education have received an immense amount of attention over the past fifteen years. But most parents do not regard the deterioration as being as critical as it is. They have no easily visible examples of good education—such as that offered in certain other nations—to compare with the education their children are receiving. Nor do they realize that so many children in poor neighborhoods are being so badly educated that the quality of the entire U.S. labor force is endangered.

The other basic social problems have also received some attention in the press. But their most intensive forms are concentrated in a few inner-city neighborhoods that contain a small percentage of the entire population, mostly minority groups. For most people these problems are remote. Yet the future quality of their daily lives is endangered. Meanwhile, traffic congestion, air pollution, failure to finance adequate infrastructures, shortages of decent housing available to low-income households, and other growth-related crises are slowly spreading. And although the worst forms of these problems are concentrated in just a few very large metropolitan areas, those areas account for a sizable part of the nation's population.

The seeming invisibility of the threats these crises pose is aggravated by society's increasing tolerance of deviant and undesirable behavior. As Daniel Patrick Moynihan has pointed out, no society likes to admit the existence of more than certain levels of deviance from what it considers acceptable norms of behavior.[1] When deviant behavior begins greatly to exceed those levels, society may react by redefining what is considered deviant so as to reduce the perceived level.

Moynihan argues that Americans redefined acceptable behavior when they supported the deinstitutionalization of mentally ill persons, accepted the breakdown of the traditional family, and adjusted to the escalation of violent crime. This redefinition underlies the increase of homelessness, the broadening of what types of family structures are considered merely alternative life styles in spite of their devastating effects on the children raised in them, and the unwillingness of society to devote sufficient resources to reduce crime rates and maintain minimal civic order in all neighborhoods. Moreover, the acceptance of single-parent families, especially those living in poverty, as normal and the refusal to provide adequate resources to help single parents cope with their problems has contributed directly to the rise of violent crime. As Moynihan has written,

> from the wild Irish slums of the 19th century Eastern seaboard to the riot-torn suburbs of Los Angeles, there is one unmistakable lesson in American history: a community that allows a large number of young men to grow up in broken families, dominated by women, never acquiring any stable relationship to male authority, never acquiring any set of rational expectations about the future—that community asks for and gets chaos. Crime, violence, unrest, unrestrained lashing out at the whole social structure—that is not only to be expected; it is very near to inevitable.[2]

Violent crime in American society has now risen to levels that would formerly have been considered intolerable. According to Judge Edwin Torres of the New York State Supreme Court, "the slaughter of the innocent marches unabated: subway riders, bodega owners, cab drivers, babies; in laundromats, at cash machines, on elevators, in hallways . . . [our] numbness [to violence], the near narcoleptic state can diminish the human condition. . . . A society that loses its sense of outrage is doomed to extinction."[3]

A society is in deep trouble when it cannot see that certain fundamental problems in its midst have exceeded the intensity that will permit its continued prosperity and stability. Therefore it must act decisively to change the status quo. Americans look about them and see many problems, yet most do not believe any are bad enough to demand more intensive and effective responses. And fewer still connect such deterioration with the continued dominance of the unlimited low-density vision.

Sounding the Alarm

A crucial function of leadership in a democracy is for perceptive people such as Senator Moynihan who realize that creeping crises are as yet undetected by most citizens to call for responsive action, even if that action requires significant sacrifices from a complacent majority.

A central purpose of this book is to help perform this function and to provide potential leaders with the factual and logical ammunition they need to alert others to the necessity of acting soon.

In particular, American metropolitan growth patterns are intensifying the isolation of the very poorest households in concentrated-poverty neighborhoods that breed crime, broken families, drug abuse, and other social ills. But these conditions are not confined to inner-city neighborhoods. In fact, some of the most serious problems found there simply represent worse-than-average manifestations of nation-wide conditions that threaten the welfare of all of American society.

The same dominant metropolitan area growth patterns that are making inner-city conditions worse are attenuating the links most suburbanites perceive between their own welfare and that of their central cities. This weakens the willingness of the suburban majority to support attacks on central-city problems that are crucial to the welfare of the nation as a whole.

Certainly metropolitan growth patterns are not the only factor causing these problems. So adopting some different vision of how metropolitan areas ought to grow would definitely not in itself cure America's basic social ills. Other remedial policies would have to be adopted at the same time, and some of them are even harder to carry out than weaning Americans from their attachment to unlimited low-density growth. But without any changes in that vision, it may be impossible to carry out those other policies effectively over the long run.

The Chances for Change

Will enough American public and private sector leaders and other citizens accept the arguments and adopt the changes called for in this book in at least some metropolitan areas? The odds are against it. Too many people will try to protect vested interests; too many others genuinely fear that change will mean the deterioration of their neighborhoods and danger to their families. The sense that they are faced with a major social crisis has not yet become strong enough. Still, which alternative vision has the best chance of being adopted?

The changes involved in implementing bounded high-density growth would be much greater and more radical than those involved in realizing the other two alternatives. Bounded high-density growth is the polar opposite of the dominant vision. The other alternatives lie somewhere between these extremes. This implies that much larger or more visible crises would have to erupt to motivate the adoption of bounded high-density growth.

One aspect of the bounded high-density model especially weakens its chances of being adopted. Serious growth-related crises are most likely to arise in metropolitan areas that have two traits simultaneously: they are very large (more than 2 million inhabitants) and their populations are growing rapidly. But these same traits would make it extremely difficult to maintain rigid urban growth boundaries drawn tightly around the periphery of built-up areas. Where rapid growth is occurring, such tight boundaries would soon require significant increases in residential densities in built-up neighborhoods. But attempts to increase residential densities there would provoke hostile political reactions from residents. Thus the very conditions most likely to cause political acceptance of this vision would also generate intense resistance to it.

It is unlikely therefore that any metropolitan area will adopt the bounded high-density vision in its entirety, although a few areas might adopt selected elements. But this situation does not mean that all my previous analysis of the model has been useless. In fact, only by thoroughly understanding this extreme alternative can planners and public officials realize why its seemingly most alluring elements will not be adopted. Such an understanding is especially important because so many professional planners espouse such elements. Recognizing the serious failings of unlimited low-density growth, they leap to the conclusion that adopting nearly opposite policies would be the best way to remedy those failings. That conclusion is false.

Thus limited-spread mixed-density growth or new communities and green belts growth are left as the major alternatives.[4] The new communities and green belts vision would require keeping growth out of designated green belts. Growth would be confined within the urban growth boundaries drawn around existing built-up suburbs and designated outlying new communities (which would mostly be clustered around existing settlements rather than wholly new ones). This model would require more rigid controls over land use and the location of economic activities of all types than the more ambiguously defined limited-spread mixed-density vision. Embracing the new communities and green belts model would also require more radical changes in both institutional controls over land use and their day-to-day applications. For that reason, adoption of a limited-spread mixed-density plan is likely to arouse less political resistance, so it is more likely to occur.

A few metropolitan areas are better suited than others to new communities and green belts patterns because of their particular traits. Lexington, Kentucky, for example, has many close-in suburbs bordered on their outer edges by rolling bluegrass hills occupied by extensive horse farms. These farms embody the life style that made the area famous. They are also a major tourist attraction. Preserving them from urban development is a primary goal of the entire community. Thus this metropolitan area is ideally suited to a new communities and green belts plan. Its implementation would involve clustering almost all urban development around towns that lie beyond the main horse farm zones.

But most U.S. metropolitan areas already contain urban developments that gradually decline in density as they extend outward from the areas' central cores, which include many close-in suburbs. These developments include scattered subdivisions, shopping centers, occasional office parks and industrial plants, and other urban uses. Too many of them already exist to make fully open green belts possible anywhere near each area's central core. A more feasible growth strategy would contain two key elements. One would be to draw an urban growth boundary near the outer edges of the central core but inside many of the scattered developments. The second would be to confine most, but not all, urban expansion within the boundary, mainly by providing public infrastructure financing within it. This approach might achieve many of the goals of limited-spread mixed-density growth. The objectives could include raising average residential densities, reducing total travel distances, reducing the costs of providing future infrastructure, and making more housing in the suburbs available to low- and moderate-income households.

Thus if any significant movement away from the unlimited low-density model occurs in planning and controlling metropolitan area growth, it is most likely to involve the limited-spread mixed-density vision or some variant.

Choosing among Alternatives

Assuming a metropolitan area has created the political decision-making machinery that will enable it to choose among alternative growth patterns, how should it decide which specific vision is best for it?[5]

The first step is to use regional decisionmaking machinery to set up a broad participatory process of determining a very general growth strategy for the metropolitan area. Residents of a metropolitan area will not accept a growth strategy handed to them without significant prior consultation. So there must be some means of enlisting both initial and later inputs from many different groups. These should include subgroups defined in terms of geography, socioeconomic status, occupation, ethnicity, and political perspective. Just how this should be done cannot be described here. For one thing, there are too many different means of accomplishing such participation to discuss all of them in detail.

The second step is to designate a small group of community leaders or representatives to devise a growth plan suitable to their metropolitan area. This would involve detailed analyses of existing conditions, desired goals, and alternative courses of action. It would also require evaluating the results and selecting the final elements of an ultimate vision of desired growth. These actions demand intensive and time-consuming briefings and deliberations that cannot be carried out effectively by large groups. How this group should be selected and how it should operate depend on the nature of the regional political decisionmaking machinery in each metropolitan area.

The third step is to conduct empirical studies to identify and analyze the area's most serious growth-related problems. Problem identification is often done by polling a random sample of citizens concerning the issues they consider most critical.[6] This step may already have been carried out as part of building the consensus for adopting regional decisionmaking machinery. The citizens and officials in a metropolitan area would probably not even consider adopting such machinery unless they believed one or more growth-related problems were extremely serious.

These studies should analyze the nature and extent of each problem and possible remedies. Although defining a vision for growth does not require preparation of detailed plans, the quality of the vision will be greatly improved if those involved have accurate information about current conditions.

In many metropolitan areas, no problem related directly to growth will appear serious enough to warrant major changes in institutional structures and government procedures. But such an implicit endorsement of the status quo is less likely concerning basic social problems. However, at least some leadership groups will decide their area is encountering serious growth-related or basic social problems that are likely to become much worse. Their thinking should then focus on which alternative vision or elements of different visions would most effectively respond to the particular problems plaguing their metropolitan area.

The fourth step is to analyze relationships between each severe problem in the area and the five elements—residential density, transportation, the density of commercial and industrial activities, governance (including infrastructure finance), and the provision of low-income housing—in the alternative visions of future growth. The purpose is to determine which elements are most likely to help solve the area's most pressing problems. They constitute the specific parts of each vision that would be directly responsive to the major problems discussed in chapter 1. Therefore, it is sensible to focus on these elements first rather than focusing first on which vision seems preferable.

The fifth step is to select at least five elements, one for each of the goals or fields of activity in the unlimited low-density growth vision. Perhaps more than one element will be chosen for a single field of activity because different elements affecting that field were considered best in dealing with different problems. For example, a tightly drawn urban growth boundary may have been selected as the best way to limit future losses of open space, but a more loosely drawn one may have been selected as the best way to permit more suburban housing to be developed for low- and moderate-income households.

The sixth step is to mold this set of elements into a coherent strategy that has policies reasonably consistent with each other. Conflicting choices within a single field of activity must be reconciled to achieve the most promising overall improvement in the area's problems. Possible inconsistencies among elements in different fields of activity must also be reconciled or at least limited. For example, a tightly drawn urban growth boundary would be inconsistent with spreading out jobs to reduce average travel times for workers who live in the suburbs. Adjustments in both elements would be necessary.

The seventh step is to define one or two basic themes that express the essence of the final vision. People can much more easily understand overall themes than the detailed elements shaping them. In a previous book I argued that most people make voting decisions in response to symbols and postures rather than to candidates' detailed policy positions.[7] Voters and candidates alike have learned that concentrating on a few themes is the only effective way to make decisions in view of the flood of information available. If they tried to understand every important policy, they would have to spend their whole lives reading newspapers and journal articles.

Clearly, leaders formulating visions of metropolitan growth need widespread support to get them adopted. To obtain support, they must describe the visions in terms of a few easily understood themes. Each set of themes should embody the underlying concepts built into the policies constituting that vision.

The eighth step is to communicate the proposed growth strategy to the citizens. Members of the small group that has formulated the plan must return to the broader groups they represent and from whom they got ideas. Their initial presentations should combine strong advocacy with a willingness to listen to critical responses.

The ninth step is to adjust the vision to take account of the responses and then to create a final version. This step may be more an on-going process starting with the preceding step than a single well-defined activity. It may occur over a considerable period as the small group repeatedly revises and tests the revisions against public opinion.

The tenth and last step is to disseminate the final plan widely and seek to get it adopted by the necessary legislative bodies. An intensive public relations campaign must begin to drum up public support. This is critical. The success of the campaign will determine whether the new vision will actually be adopted. Exactly how to do this cannot be described here because of the variety of decisionmaking processes in different areas. However, members of the small group that formulated the plan must spend as much time and energy—and perhaps more— carrying out this step as they did carrying out all the preceding steps.

Getting new visions of growth accepted will require two distinct processes. The first is to put into place regional decisionmaking machinery capable of adopting land use policies that cover an entire metropolitan area. No such machinery now exists in most metropolitan areas. The second process is to create and adopt a vision of how growth and development ought to occur. In theory the second process cannot be carried out unless the first has already taken place. But in reality the strongest motive for creating regional machinery will be widespread acceptance of the need for some alternative vision. The shortcomings of unlimited low-density growth will create the basis for this acceptance. Thus the need for an alternative vision, and perhaps even tentative definition of one, will precede the creation of regional institutions.

In most metropolitan areas the two processes will be carried out simultaneously, and each will influence how the other is done. Effective regional decisionmaking machinery will be created as part of the definition of some vision of growth. That makes it all the more important for potential participants to understand both processes before participating in either.

Creating a Spirit of Community

Development will not occur in accordance with strategic responses to growth-related problems as long as no strong bonds of community and social solidarity link the residents of a metropolitan area. But such bonds have often not been forged. What, then, can be done?

The Economic Impetus toward Interdependence

In large modern societies, economic efficiency requires huge numbers of persons to interact through both markets and nonmarket institutions. Technical changes have continually expanded the most efficient sizes of such interactions until they have reached global dimensions. This prohibits direct personal contacts among any significant number of people who are economically interdependent.

Unfortunately, the most efficient scale for economic activities is much larger than the most efficient scales for political and social interactions. As a result, people in different parts of a metropolitan area fail to perceive their underlying long-run coincidence of economic interests. Every metropolitan area contains thousands of different market and nonmarket relationships with myriad interlocking connections. People are interconnected indirectly through countless untraceable linkages among these relationships. Therefore, the welfare of every resident is at least indirectly connected to that of every other.

And the effective functioning of economic systems, including whole metropolitan areas, requires peaceful interactions among constituent parts and a willingness to observe the rules of the game that transcends pure market relationships. Maintenance of this framework cannot depend solely on relationships in which all participants clearly gain. It must also include activities that in the short run harm some participants. Market competition is an example. It increases overall social efficiency in the long run but causes short-run injuries to losers of each competitive encounter.

To sustain this vital institutional and psychological framework, people must be willing to accept short-run setbacks as a price for longer-run gains. They will be far more willing to do so if they have a strong sense of solidarity with the entire system. Then they will be both rationally and emotionally committed to pursuing the long-run good of the whole. Consequently, group identifications and loyalties must be created that transcend direct personal contacts among group members.

Developing strong personal and group attachments to very large groups—such as whole nations—among people who come from diverse smaller groups will probably be the major challenge to democracy and all other forms of governance in the twenty-first century. Failure to achieve such allegiance is already creating violent conflicts in the former Soviet Union, the former Yugoslavia, and many other societies. Thus the basic political problem in U.S. metropolitan areas is a small-scale example of a fundamental worldwide political and social issue.

This problem is especially crucial in the United States because of likely changes in the nation's ethnic and racial composition. Between 1995 and 2020 U.S. population will increase by about 60 million people, according to the Census Bureau's middle projection. But 79 percent of those people will be members of minority groups. So the proportion of all minorities in the nation will increase from 24 percent in 1990 to 36 percent in 2020.[8] The two largest minorities, African Americans and Hispanics, have average incomes and educational attainments far below those of non-Hispanic whites. Unless the economic and educational status of these minority groups compared to that of whites is markedly improved during the next twenty-five years, their rapid expansion will notably reduce the average income and educational level of the nation's population. That will compromise the prosperity and global competitiveness of the entire economy, including its suburban residents. So all members of the non-Hispanic white majority have an immense stake in improving the economic and educational lot of blacks and Hispanics, who are heavily concentrated in central cities. But the suburbs will be willing to help the cities only if a much stronger sense of community is developed among all residents in each metropolitan area.

The Social and Political Impetus toward Smaller Groups

In the social and political spheres, people's natural solidarity of interests focuses on much smaller and more homogeneous groups than in the economic sphere. In fact, proper initial development of every person's consciousness, personality, and basic humanity depends on intense relationships within a very small group—the family. Relationships governing social life in the neighborhood, the workplace, and schools also rely heavily on face-to-face interactions. The solidarity created among members of such groups is a key force shaping, enriching, and supporting their lives and personalities. Each group member must feel that he or she not only belongs to the same group as the other members but shares traits and beliefs that make their interests similar. Only where such social solidarity exists will people be willing to sacrifice some of their own resources and welfare to assist other group members. The more dissimilar people are and the less visible their interdependencies, the harder it is to generate such solidarity.

At a somewhat larger scale are relationships with local governments, which in democracies operate through representation. But it becomes more and more difficult to sustain each citizen's personal identification as groups become larger. That is why nations devote so much effort to inculcating patriotic sentiments in their young citizens.

Within each metropolitan area, an emotional and perceptual dissonance arises between the shared but not very visible economic interests of many citizens and their differing but clearly perceived social and political interests. They become more much intensively connected to members of the small political communities where they live and to other small social groups than to the entire metropolitan economy, even though that economy sustains them materially. Many suburbanites in particular do not recognize the actual coincidence of their interests with those of central-city residents.

This difficulty is aggravated by genuine conflicts of interest between the nonpoor and the poor. Nonpoor households, which are a large majority in most U.S. metropolitan areas, benefit from hiring low-wage workers and from minimizing the amount of their own resources they must shift to lower-income people through government transfers. Many similar adversarial relationships exist among members within each economic group. But conflicts between the nonpoor and the poor interfere with the forging of a strong sense of solidarity between them, particularly because they tend to live in different neighborhoods. Moreover, nonpoor people have what are to them cogent social, economic, and personal security reasons to remain physically and socially separated from poorer people. These motives are reinforced by the social and ethnic differentiation of suburbs from central cities, widespread racial discrimination and intolerance, and constant media reporting of adverse conditions in central cities. In contrast, many of the poor believe that they would benefit from being more geographically integrated with better-off groups. That would give them better access to jobs and schools and an escape from concentrated-poverty environments. But the nonpoor control the institutional processes that determine how income groups are geographically distributed.

This conflict of interests is not illusory; there are indeed differences in the goals of these two groups, especially in the short run. But in the long run, gains for the nonpoor majority obtained at the expense of the poor minority will be outweighed by mutual losses from the resulting weakening of the overall metropolitan and national economies. Many nonpoor, however, do not recognize this reality.

The failure of most nonpoor suburban residents to develop strong feelings of, or rational commitments to, social and political solidarity with central cities has severe consequences. It causes the nonpoor to resist any transfer of decisionmaking powers over land use, transportation, and local fiscal policies to a regional level. Yet without such transfers, metropolitan areas cannot cope effectively with growth-related problems, which are all basically regional.

Resolving Tensions

The ultimate solution to this dilemma involves convincing the members of each metropolitan locality, especially nonpoor suburban members, that the interests they share with all parts of their metropolitan area are more important to their long-run welfare than the conflicting interests they more easily perceive. Such solidarity is extremely difficult to establish. Metropolitan areas are far too large to permit direct relationships among all members, and they contain many subgroups with few traits in common.

Therefore, effective metropolitan area solidarity must be strengthened through two other means: mediating institutions and mass media. Mediating institutions interact with individuals on one hand and with labor unions, professional or trade organizations, and similar larger entities at regional and higher levels on the other. But it is hard to establish strong mediating institutions at the metropolitan level. In most of the United States there are no publicly funded bodies at that level to which mediating institutions might be attached. In some areas homebuilders' associations, church councils, and a few other organizations exist, but in most, new public-private organizations would have to be created.

Other rational and emotional relationships between individuals and large groups or society as a whole are developed and expressed symbolically through mass communications and participation in sports and other media-related activities. The resulting common experience helps generate some solidarity. But constant reporting on adverse conditions in central cities can undermine any such sense at the metropolitan level.

Conclusion

In the long run America must strengthen the bases for its continued unity as a society by placing much more emphasis on social solidarity and less on individualistic values. This must begin in early school years. And because the news media are just as important as schools in educating children, they should assist in changing this emphasis on individualism. But advertising themes vital to the commercial interests that own the media relentlessly stress the desirability of unlimited self-indulgence—the exact opposite of social solidarity.

There are no easy or fast ways to strengthen social solidarity among metropolitan area residents. I believe it will prove more effective to persuade residents of suburbs across the nation that their interests largely coincide with the interests of all central city residents than to try to persuade them this is the case in each separate metropolitan area. And this more general approach would lay a political foundation for major federal funding of nationwide programs that disproportionately aid central cities and their residents, which is vital to the long-run prosperity of the entire U.S. economy.

Appendix A

Paradigms for Metropolitan Growth

*T*HE SPRAWL dominating growth in large U.S. metropolitan areas was made possible by dramatic changes in transportation and communications in the twentieth century. These transformed traditional concepts of urban form that evolved from 400 years of city growth in Western societies. Specifically the view of urban life as center focused is giving way to the view of urban societies as low-density networks.

The Idea of a Paradigm Shift

A paradigm is a basic metaphor used to explain the operation of a complex system. For example, the Ptolemaic system theorized that the sun and other heavenly bodies revolved around the earth. A thousand years later Copernicus proposed that the earth and other planets revolved around the sun. Since then, other paradigms, such as Albert Einstein's theory of relativity, have provided other explanations of the same phenomena. When most of a society abandons one basic metaphor for another, a *paradigm shift* occurs. Many such shifts have taken place in the history of science.[1]

Metropolitan growth is now involved in exactly such a change. In 1990 Robert Fishman wrote "Megalopolis Unbound" about the physical and social form of large U.S. metropolitan areas. He pointed out that nearly every metropolitan area initially embodies a center-focused pattern.[2] The area's point of origin becomes more intensively developed than any other location. This initial center retains its dominance because, as the area expands, new transportation and communications arteries are built converging on it. At the same time, the center becomes more densely developed than any other point. These trends reinforce its dominant position.

But since 1950, U.S. metropolitan areas have grown outward in a low-density sprawl. As each suburb was built farther out from the city center, the whole area became less center focused. Facilities once found only in or near the center were replicated in outlying locations. Large-scale, more intensively developed outlying nodes contained shopping centers, office complexes, entertainment and hotel facilities, and hospitals. Industrial complexes sprang up along outlying freeways and around airports.[3]

More and more residents not only lived far from the initial center, but worked, shopped, and did everything else far from it, too. One factor behind this evolution was that central business districts became so large that no further economies of scale could be gained by concentrating more jobs there. In fact, higher rents and wages encouraged increasing decentralization of many types of economic activities.[4] Technological changes in transportation and communications reduced the costs of moving people, goods, documents, and ideas. Government policies favored extensive, low-density growth. These factors have been operating throughout the world, but they have gone furthest in the United States.

This evolution gradually transformed the physical and social structure of the largest metropolitan areas. As these areas became decentralized, each household developed its own unique pattern of relationships with jobs, shopping, schools, recreation, and other facilities. This pattern was measured by daily car trips from home to these other destinations and back. This evolution constituted a paradigm shift from the traditional center-focused pattern to a low-density network.[5] Such a network has no real center at all. Its aggregate form results from a complex overlay of the individual home-centered networks of thousands or millions of households. It is like a giant amoeba with no nucleus, or only a very small one that other parts of the amoeba ignore.

At first glance, there is little new about this idea. But urban planners, the people who write most about urban forms, prefer the center-focused pattern. Bemoaning the dominance of the automobile, the growth of ticky-tacky suburbs, and the deterioration of "culturally rich" downtowns, they have not examined the most important implications of this paradigm shift. This book seeks to do so.

However, three observations must be made at the outset.

—The strongly center-focused pattern and the centerless low-density network are two extreme points on a spectrum of possibilities. Most American metropolitan areas have evolved from the first extreme toward the second. In theory, there are an infinite number of intermediate positions combining elements of both patterns, and all U.S. metropolitan areas lie between these two extremes.

—The shift from a center focus to a low-density network has occurred mostly in very large metropolitan areas. They are a small minority of all metropolitan areas, but they contain a sizable part of the nation's entire population. "Very large" (4 million residents or more) applies to the greater Los Angeles (including Los Angeles, Ventura, Orange, Riverside, and San Bernardino counties), greater San Francisco (including San Jose and Oakland), greater Chicago (including Gary, Aurora-Elgin, Joliet, and Lake County), northern New Jersey (including Newark, Jersey City, Middlesex-Hunterdon, and Bergen-Passaic), and Washington-Baltimore, Boston-Lawrence-Salem, Detroit-Ann Arbor, and Philadelphia-Trenton areas as low-density networks. (New York has not been included because Manhattan still exerts a powerful influence throughout its metropolitan area.) "Fairly large" (from 2 million to 4 million residents) includes Dallas–Fort Worth, Houston, Miami–Ft. Lauderdale, Atlanta, Nassau-Suffolk, San Diego, Minneapolis–St. Paul, St. Louis, Phoenix, Tampa–St. Petersburg, and Pittsburgh. Combined, these areas contained 80 million residents in 1990, one-third of the total U.S. population. However, this third contains a large portion of the wealthiest and most influential people in American society.

Nevertheless, most U.S. metropolitan areas, containing a majority of urban residents, remain small enough so that people living on their fringes have retained a significant center focus and probably will continue to do so indefinitely.

—No metropolitan area has become so fully decentralized that its center cannot be readily distinguished from its outlying nodes. Even in greater Los Angeles, the quintessential low-density network, downtown Los Angeles is much larger than any other node and contains a significant portion of the area's jobs. Thus a completely centerless, low-density network remains only a theoretical construct, although a few areas with extremely weak downtowns—Phoenix, northern New Jersey, southeastern Florida, and Tampa–St. Petersberg—come close.

But almost all metropolitan areas embody elements of the low-density network pattern around their edges.

Characteristics of the Low-Density Network

The fully developed low-density network pattern has attributes very different from those of the center-focused pattern. Networklike areas are geographically much larger. "The basic unit of the new city is not the street measured in blocks but the 'growth corridor' stretching 50 to 100 miles. Where the leading metropolises of the early 20th century—New York, London, or Berlin—covered perhaps 100 square miles, the new city routinely encompasses two to three *thousand* square miles."[6]

The edges of low-density networks also no longer seem highly dependent on the area's original center. They are still physically linked to the center and to all other parts of the area by transportation and communication systems, but the network no longer contains any one nucleus. Instead, it has multiple nodes of different sizes linked by roadways. Some vital links still connect all parts of the network at least to the central city, though not necessarily to its downtown.

Another trait is that no single center plays a direct role in the lives of people in all parts of a low-density network. This is true of both daily activities and institutional processes. No single location is critical to all parts of the network because the social network is an accidental result of the overlapping of individual household networks, each of which is centered on a single household. Each household has a unique network of its own, though many paths in it are shared with other households. There is also no one institutional center.

Yet another difference is that the crucial dimension for travel and locational decisionmaking in low-density networks is the time required for movement rather than the distance covered. Outside of peak hours, movement has become faster, easier, and less costly than in the era before expressways. Using modern expressways, people routinely travel one hundred miles a day commuting or on single-purpose trips.

In addition, the low-density network pattern encourages—even requires—unlimited outward extension. Low-density networks are literally boundless. Their extension occurs through leapfrogging connections of new-growth areas to facilities already present in the networks. New residential subdivisions are typically the pioneers in previously vacant territory. At first, their residents rely for shopping, jobs, and recreation on driving to built-up portions of the network. Only gradually do these activities start locating near the new subdivisions. By then, still newer subdivisions have been started on land even farther from the original center.

From Center Focus to Low-Density Network

As a large metropolitan area evolves, its original center becomes harder to reach from its extremities, and movements flow more and more from one point to another around the area's periphery, without reference to the original center. This outward extension is accompanied by intensification or deepening urbanization in the outlying portions, which contain more and more of the full range of activities and services found in the area.

This intensification occurs through both the clustering of certain activities in sizable nodes (such as Tyson's Corner, Virginia, or Oakbrook, Illinois) and the scattering of industry, services, and small retail activities all over the landscape, especially along main transportation arteries. Intensification reduces the dependence of the outer edges on the original center, so that the center becomes weaker both relatively (which has happened in all U.S. metropolitan areas) and eventually absolutely (which has not yet happened in most of them).

How fast the center loses its original position depends on its initial size and dominance. Washington, D.C., has the federal government as an anchor, which keeps it more center focused for its size than are Orlando and Phoenix, which never had significant central dominance. The decline of the center also depends on when the metropolitan area as a whole experienced most of its growth. If it grew mainly after the automobile became dominant, the area probably has no radial fixed-rail system; highways are its main arterials. Thus newer U.S. metropolitan areas usually have a weaker center focus than older ones.

The area furthest advanced toward low-density network dominance is southern California, yet most urban Americans reside in metropolitan areas that are still center focused. This means that there is an enormous diversity of conditions regarding this evolution among U.S. metropolitan areas. Consequently, no single growth management policy or set of policies is appropriate to all.

Appendix B

Comment on "The Myth of America's Underfunded Cities"

*A*s I NOTED in chapter 5, a 1993 study by Stephen Moore and Dean Stansel of the Cato Institute claims that urban growth and decline are caused primarily by local government fiscal policies.[1] They reject the view that higher spending in declining or slowly growing cities results from the high proportions of low-income residents there or any other "objective" city characteristics. Instead they claim slow growth stems from high levels of state and local taxation that drive away businesses and households and from inefficient use of funds to hire too many workers, which creates the need for higher taxes. If city governments would raise and spend less money, they contend, the cities would be restored to economic health.

Undoubtedly, city governments differ greatly in the efficiency with which they use their resources. However, Moore and Stansel's methods of analysis are seriously flawed. They do not statistically test the relative contribution of the independent variables they discuss to their dependent variable of rates of growth or decline. They also omit from their analysis a number of variables that might be expected to influence growth rates. To understand this criticism, it is necessary to describe their approach in some detail.

Moore and Stansel's Methodology

Moore and Stansel created an index of relative growth (or decline) based on four variables: population change from 1965 to 1990, change in number of employed residents from 1960 to 1989, increase in per capita money income from 1969 to 1987, and percentage point increase in female-headed households from 1970 to 1990. Then they grouped seventy-six of the nation's eighty largest cities in 1990 into four cate-

211

gories of growth, based on their scores on the index. They computed average levels of six fiscal policy variables for these categories. The six variables were municipal expenditures per capita in 1990, excluding health, education, and welfare spending; municiple expenditures as a percent of per capita money income in 1990; the increase in municiple expenditures as a percentage of per capita money income in 1990; the increase in municipal expenditures per capita from 1965 to 1990; state and own-source revenue per capita in 1990; city tax revenue per capita as a percentage of money income per capita in 1990; and city employees per 10,000 residents (apparently *not* excluding employees engaged in health, education, and welfare activities). The results show that cities in the categories with the fastest growth have much lower average local tax and expenditure rates and fewer employees per 10,000 residents than cities in low-growth or declining categories.

An Alternative Method of Analyzing the Data

This rank-order comparison does not really test the contribution that each of their independent fiscal variables makes to their growth index. To remedy that deficiency, I conducted a multiple regression analysis of the same cities, using the same data set forth in their report. My dependent variable was not an index of growth or decline, but simple city population change, either from 1980 to 1990 or from 1970 to 1990. Moreover, I added a number of additional variables that might be expected to influence city growth rates. These included city population in 1980, metropolitan area population in 1990, mean January temperature, whether the cities coincided with counties and therefore had county-type responsibilities, how fast the suburbs of their metropolitan areas grew in the same periods, city poverty rates in 1979, city population density, the percentages of blacks and Hispanics in each city in 1980, and each city's unemployment rate in 1979. I also used all six fiscal variables in their report and their measure of female-headed households as independent variables.

The Results for City Population Change, 1980–90

The results show that their fiscal variables have some impact on city growth or decline, but nothing like the dominant influence they claim. For example, when percentage population growth from 1980 to 1990 is the dependent variable, a regression using nineteen of these independent variables (not shown) produces a multiple R^2 of .747 (.659 adjusted for degrees of freedom). Eliminating variables with t-statistics of less than 1.0 and running subsequent regressions eventually produced a regression with ten independent variables and a multiple R^2 of .740 (.700 adjusted). The results of this regression are shown in table B-1. Only one of their fiscal variables remains (increase in per capita city expenditures from 1965 to 1990). In contrast, four of the five independent variables with t-statistics higher than 2.0 are objective characteristics of city population not directly affected by local fiscal policies. They are the percentage-point increase in female-headed households, the percentage of poor persons in 1979, the percentage of total PMSA population formed by the central city's population, and the percentage growth rate of the city's suburbs from 1980 to 1990. Even more paring of the number of independent variables can be done without lowering the adjusted R^2 very much. A regression using just four independent variables (not shown) produces a multiple R^2 of .705 (.689 adjusted). They are the percentage-point increase in female-headed households, the percentage of poor persons in 1979, the percentage growth rate of the city's suburbs from 1980 to 1990, and the percentage increase in city per capita spending from 1965 to 1990. The last is the only fiscal variable, and it has a lower beta coefficient and a lower t-statistic than any of the others.

Thus city growth or decline appears to be more heavily influenced by each city's population traits than by its fiscal policies. High proportions of low-income and female-headed households are associated with population decline and low proportions with population gains.

Other Regressions

Similar results occur using population change from 1970 to 1990 as the dependent variable. Starting with twenty independent variables and eliminating those with t-statistics less than 1.0 then running repeated regressions results in eleven independent variables with a multiple R^2 of .601 (.532 adjusted). Further paring of this set reduces the adjusted R^2 notably. Results of this regression are shown in table B-2. Its independent variables include eight objective ones and three fiscal policy ones. Both types are among those with the highest beta coefficients and the highest t-statistics.

TABLE B-1. *Influence of Nine Variables on Percentage Change in City Population, 1980-90*[a]

Independent variables	β	Standard error of β	B	Standard error of B	t (64)	Significance of t
City population, 1980	0.30729	0.16188	0.00001	0.00000	1.89827	0.05895
Percentage Hispanic, 1980	0.16683	0.09300	0.22044	0.12288	1.79393	0.07396
Increase in per capita city expenditures, 1965-90	-0.22006	0.06884	-0.06538	0.02045	-3.19654	0.00250
City tax revenue as percent of per capita income, 1990	-0.19995	0.13499	-1.55902	1.05251	-1.48124	0.13968
Percentage point increase in female headed households, 1970-90	-0.31294	0.09945	-1.61640	0.51370	-3.14661	0.00285
Percentage of residents poor, 1979	-0.34044	0.08002	-1.23273	0.28976	-4.25432	0.00021
Metropolitan area population, 1990	-0.20073	0.13163	0.00000	0.00000	-1.52498	0.12834
City population as a percentage of metropolitan area population, 1990	-0.27963	0.10609	-0.25550	0.09694	-2.63571	0.01022
Suburban population change, 1980-90	0.30873	0.07309	0.29854	0.07067	4.22473	0.00022
City also a county (dummy)	0.11824	0.10004	5.39632	4.56583	1.18189	0.23993

Source: Author's calculations based on variables from Stephen Moore and Dean Stansel, "The Myth of America's Underfunded Cities," *Policy Analysis*, no. 188 (1993).

a. Multiple R: 0.860389. F (10, 64): 18.24093. Intercept: 77.193418. Adjusted R^2: 0.699687. Number of cases: 75. Multiple R^2: 0.740270.

TABLE B-2. *Influence of Eleven Variables on Percentage Change in City Population, 1970–90*[a]

Independent variables	β	Standard error of β	B	Standard error of B	t (64)	Significance of t
City area in square miles	−0.15769	0.10741	−0.0634	0.04320	−1.46818	0.14330
City population, 1980	0.31965	0.15865	0.0000	0.00001	2.01485	0.04546
Average January temperature	0.1591	0.10979	0.7259	0.50092	1.44914	0.14858
Per capita expenditures as percentage of per capita income, 1990	0.21987	0.17224	4.4258	3.46698	1.27657	0.20377
Increase in per capita city expenditures, 1965–90	−0.28872	0.10497	−0.2736	0.09946	−2.75046	0.00771
City tax revenue as percent of per capita income, 1990	−0.40563	0.17061	−10.0873	4.24280	−2.37751	0.01935
Percentage point increase in female headed households, 1970–90	−0.27479	0.11147	−4.5270	1.83634	;2.46524	0.01562
Percentage of residents poor, 1979	−0.34521	0.10901	−3.9869	1.25895	−3.16682	0.00273
Metropolitan area population, 1990	−0.19784	0.12933	0.0000	0.00000	−1.52979	0.12722
Suburban population change, 1980–90	0.24456	0.10277	0.7543	0.31696	2.37961	0.01925
City also a county (dummy)	0.17250	0.12293	25.1093	17.89382	1.40324	0.16196

Source: See table B-1.

a. Multiple R: 0.775538. F (10, 63): 8.64336. Multiple R^2: 0.601460. Adjusted R^2: 0.531874. Intercept: 179.167031. Number of cases: 75.

TABLE B-3. *Influence of Eight Variables on Number of City Workers per 10,000 Residents*[a]

Independent variables	β	Standard error of β	B	Standard error of B	t (64)	Significance of t
City population density	0.21587	0.09873	0.00589	0.00269	2.18642	0.03039
Average January temperature	-0.12521	0.08940	-1.07106	0.76476	-1.40052	0.16254
City tax revenue as percent of per capita income, 1990	0.38464	0.12255	17.93339	5.71391	3.13855	0.00289
Increase in per capita money income, 1969–87	0.17299	0.0823	2.01210	0.95723	2.10199	0.03704
Percentage point increase in female headed households, 1970–90	0.21296	0.09470	6.57766	2.92499	2.24878	0.02621
Percentage of residents poor, 1979	0.12301	0.0831	2.66346	1.79936	1.48023	0.13979
Suburban population change, 1980–90	0.1861	0.08614	1.07606	0.49811	2.16031	0.03232
City also a county (dummy)	0.29121	0.09884	79.47437	26.97533	2.94619	0.00467

Source: See table B-1.

a. Multiple R: 0.839057. F (10, 66): 19.62316. Multiple R^2: 0.704016. Intercept: -136.48471. Adjusted R^2: 0.668140. Number of cases: 75.

As an additional test of their approach, I used city expenditures per capita in 1990 as a dependent variable, and ran regressions (not shown) with all the other variables that might affect it as independent. Because city expenditures as a percentage of income are highly correlated with per capita city expenditures, I omitted the former. Repeated paring yielded a regression with eight independent variables, all with t-statistics over 1.5, and an R^2 of .789 (.764 adjusted). The highest beta coefficient and t-statistic belonged to per capita expenditure change from 1965 to 1990. But seven of the remaining eight influential variables were objective city characteristics, including the city's percentage of total PMSA population and whether it was also a county. Thus high per capita city spending is *not* simply a policy decision made by greedy city governments. It also reflects conditions that impose high burdens of coping with poverty on city governments.

Finally, I used the number of city workers per 10,000 residents as a dependent variable, employing all the other variables as independent. I eventually achieved a multiple R^2 of .704 (.668 adjusted) using eight independent variables. Only one, per capita taxes as a percentage of per capita income, was a fiscal variable; it also had the highest beta coefficient and t-statistic (table B-3). The other seven were all objective traits of each city or its population.

Conclusions

Altogether, these results reject the conclusion reached by Moore and Stansel that changing fiscal policies would be sufficient to revive declining cities, presumably by turning around their recent losses of population and jobs. Too many objective characteristics of cities themselves, which are difficult to change, influence both their growth or decline and their fiscal policies. The results further suggest that city fiscal policies are themselves strongly responsive to such local conditions as poverty rates and whether the city has responsibilities as a county government. Finally, it appears that people and businesses fleeing cities are trying to get away from poverty and adverse social conditions more than costly local fiscal policies.

Appendix C

Comment on *The Next American Metropolis*

A FTER MY BOOK was almost completed, Peter Calthorpe proposed another approach to creating new visions of metropolitan area growth in *The Next American Metropolis*.[1] He developed both general principles and specific building blocks out of which several models of growth might be constructed. His approach is somewhat different from my own but has many similarities and overlaps this book in many ways. This appendix briefly describes Calthorpe's approach and relates it to mine.

Calthorpe's Basic Concepts

Calthorpe calls his basic idea transit-oriented development (TOD). It involves creating additional urban development in ways that will motivate people to use both walking and public transit more intensively. According to Calthorpe, transit-oriented development must be

—mixed use: not segregating residential from retail and commercial and public spaces, but placing them close together and intermixed;

—transit-oriented: relying heavily on transit arterials and transit feeders to those arterials are bus lines or fixed-rail systems;

—walkable: street layouts, building designs, building layouts, and overall street planning designed to maximize the ease and pleasure of pedestrian movements rather than vehicular ones;

—diverse: containing multiple uses in relatively small and compact areas.

He summarizes the principles of TOD:

—Organize growth on a regional level to be compact and transit-supportive.

—Place commercial, housing, jobs, parks, and civic uses within walking distance of transit stops.

—Create pedestrian-friendly street networks that directly connect local destinations.

—Provide a mix of housing types, densities, and costs.

—Preserve sensitive habitat, riparian zones, and high-quality open space.

—Make public spaces the focus of building orientation and neighborhood activity.

—Encourage in-fill and redevelopment along transit corridors within existing neighborhoods.[2]

In many respects, these principles are similar to those in the bounded high-density vision proposed in this book. That vision is built on (1) regional government's covering most land use and transportation activities and policies, (2) strong orientation toward public transit rather than automotive transportation, (3) use of urban growth boundaries to constrain low-density peripheral development, (4) much higher average densities in new-growth and in-fill areas than now prevail, (5) clustering jobs and retail and commercial businesses in planned nodes rather than scattering them, except for certain types that are not suitable for pedestrian movements, and (6) sufficient inward pressure from marginal growth limits to increase population in already developed neighborhoods.

However, Calthorpe's approach could also be consistent with either the limited-spread mixed-density vision or the new communities and green belts vision. In essence Calthorpe proposes basing at least part of future urban growth on neighborhood building blocks that apply his basic principles with varying degrees of intensity. Each transit-oriented district is such a building block. His scheme incorporates three different types of TODs.

Urban TODs would include the areas near major transit stations or interchange points. They would contain retail and office space as well as relatively high-density residential structures, including walk-up apartments, garden apartments, townhomes, and small-lot single-family homes. The average residential density of urban TODs would be fifteen to eighteen units a net residential acre. However, residential land uses would normally comprise less than half an entire urban TOD. (The proportion of each type of TOD devoted to housing is discussed in detail later.)

TABLE C-1. *Residential Land Use in Transit-Oriented Development, by Type of Use and Development*

Type of unit	Units per net residential acre	Percent of residential land for each type of unit		
		Urban TOD	Neighborhood TOD	Secondary area
Standard single family	6	0	0	100
Small-lot single family	8	40	60	0
Townhouses	15	25	20	0
Garden apartments	20	15	20	0
Walk-up apartments	25	20	0	0
All types	. . .	100	100	100

Source: Author's calculations based on information from Peter Calthorpe.

Neighborhood TODs would be slightly farther from major transit stops and have less commercial space and lower residential densities, about twelve units a residential acre. They would typically contain high proportions of single-family homes on small lots and garden apartments, but no walk-up apartments. Residential uses would occupy two-thirds of the land in neighborhood TODs, so they would normally contain more residents a gross square mile than urban TODs.

Secondary areas would be still farther from major transit stops and would contain only standard single-family dwellings at an average density of six units a net residential acre. Three-fourths of the land in secondary areas would be devoted to housing. The approximate percentages of total residential land devoted to different housing types in each type of TOD and the average densities of each housing type are shown in table C-1.

Conversations with Peter Calthorpe suggest that the percentages could be varied substantially in each type of TOD, depending on local circumstances. In high-density large cities, both urban and neighborhood TODs might have higher proportions of apartments, which would increase residential densities well above fifteen units a net acre. In far-out suburbs, both types of TODs might have smaller proportions of apartments, decreasing residential densities well below fifteen units a net acre. Calthorpe clearly intends that TODs be flexible. That is why their use is compatible with the three alternative visions of growth described in this book.

The Feasibility of Calthorpe's Strategy

Could Calthorpe's approach be used to accommodate the growth likely to occur in major U.S. metropolitan areas? I applied two versions of his method to accommodating actual growth rates during the 1980s in the U.S. metropolitan statistical areas with 1990 populations of 1 million or more. If these applications of Calthorpe's strategy could have handled past growth well, they should be able to cope with future growth too, since that will be slower than the rate in the 1980s.

The average population of these MSAs was 2,103,744 in 1980, with 773,234 residents in the central city and 1,330,510 in the suburbs. By 1990 these averages had become 2,385,956 in the MSAs, with 817,362 in central cities and 1,567,594 in the suburbs. Thus the average MSA in this group experienced suburban growth of 237,084 persons in the 1980s, or 17.82 percent. Calthorpe's scheme therefore has to be able to handle the highest growth rates as well as the average rate.

To test his strategy's ability to handle high rates, I estimated the population that could be included within each type of TOD under various assumptions about the amount of land in it devoted to residential uses and its average residential density. These calculations were based on an example of his approach that Calthorpe sent to me in the form of a map and accompanying statistical data. I then determined whether different types or combinations of TODs could feasibly have accommodated the past metropolitan area growth described above.

Accommodating Past Growth in Urban TODs

Urban TODs can be of many different shapes and sizes. For purposes of analytic simplicity, I assumed that every urban TOD was a circle with a radius of 2,000 feet extending from a major public transit station at its center. This circle would have an area of 12.566 million square feet or 288.48 acres. This size was chosen because Calthorpe (and others) have estimated that Americans are typically willing to walk 2,000 feet from their homes to a transit station, but not much farther.[3] In fact, 288 acres is much larger than the minimum size TODs that his book declares (p. 66) are necessary for in-fill pedestrian pockets (10 acres) and new growth areas (40 acres). Using this larger size in the analysis thus greatly reduces the number urban TODs needed in theory to accommodate any given population growth.

A key variable is what percentage of the 288 acres would be devoted to residential use. In this book I have usually assumed 25 percent for large cities and 50 percent for suburbs. Calthorpe says housing should cover 20 percent to 60 percent of an urban TOD and 50 percent to 80 percent of a neighborhood TOD. The midpoints of these ranges are 40 and 65 percent respectively. In the example he sent me, housing appeared to occupy about 35 percent of the urban TOD and 63 percent of the neighborhood TOD. I have used the last two figures in this analysis.

A second variable is the net residential density of each acre of residential land. Calthorpe states that "average minimum densities should vary between 10 and 25 dwelling units per net residential acre" (p. 64). He also says that average densities of 10 units a net acre are necessary to support local bus service and higher densities are necessary for light rail. He states that an urban TOD should have an average density requirement of 18 dwelling units an acre (p. 59). In the example he sent me, he assumed an average net residential density for an urban TOD of 15 units an acre; so I have used that figure in this analysis. I further assumed that each dwelling unit contained 2.5 persons.

These variables can be used to estimate the total population of each urban TOD. If it contains 288.48 acres, 35 percent of which is occupied by housing at a net residential density of 15 units an acre, it would contain 1,515 dwelling units occupied by 2,787 persons (no allowance is made for vacancies). That is a gross residential density (persons a square mile of all land uses) of 8,400 persons a square mile. Therefore if urban TODs alone had been used to absorb the total suburban population growth of 237,083 persons in the average large U.S. metropolitan area in the 1980s, 63 would have been required.

I assume these urban TODs would have been built along the radial lines of a rapid transit system (either fixed-rail or bus lanes) running outward from the central city's business district. In metropolitan areas that are roughly circular in shape, such as Atlanta and Minneapolis, and that have no major bodies of water or other terrain obstacles impeding transit development in any direction, that would be sixteen urban TODs along each of four radial transit lines. If these stations were 1.5 miles apart, the average distance between outlying stations on the Washington Metro system, each line would have to be 24 miles long beyond the boundary of the central city or the edges of previously built-up suburbs. The system would have to be 96 miles long, plus whatever distance it covered within the central city and previously built-up suburbs. The Washington Metro system has a total length of about 90 miles, more than half of which are outside the District of Columbia. The Bay Area Rapid Transit System has a total length of more than 70 miles, of which at least half lie outside San Francisco and Oakland.[4]

However, in many metropolitan areas it is not possible to expand from the central city in all directions. Thus if one-half the territory around the central city consisted of water (as in many U.S. metropolitan areas on the Great Lakes, the Gulf of Mexico, or the Atlantic and Pacific Oceans) and only two radial transit lines could be used, the average length of each line outside previously built-up areas would have to be 48 miles. If three lines could be used, the average length could be 32 miles. These are much longer suburban lines that serve most U.S. cities that have rapid transit systems, though they are not longer than the suburban commuter railroad systems serving Chicago and New York City.

What about growth in areas expanding faster than average? If the suburbs in an average-size metropolitan area grew 40 percent from 1980 to 1990 (as happened in several areas), its suburban population would have expanded by 532,204 persons. Urban TODs of the type described earlier could have handled that growth only if 140 had been built, rather than 63 under average growth rates. That would have required 210 total suburban radial-line miles rather than 96 miles.

In summary, if the urban TODs needed to accommodate all the average growth of large U.S. metropolitan areas during the 1980s had been connected to each other with a fixed-rail rapid transit system, the system would have to have been much larger than the actual systems in either the Washington or San Francisco Bay metropolitan areas. Yet both those areas have much larger total populations than the average total population used to calculate the absolute amount of growth involved in this hypothetical case. If these urban TODs were connected by busways separated from the main highway network instead of a fixed-rail system, the busway network would have to have been vastly larger than any such network now extant in the United States. These conclusions indicate that accommodating *all* suburban growth of the 1980s in urban TODs would probably not have been feasible. It would have been particularly impractical in very rapidly growing large metropolitan areas.

It might be argued that placing all that growth inside urban TODs would have reduced the total investment in streets and highways required to handle the growth far below what was actually spent. The funds saved thus could have easily paid for whatever rapid transit network was necessary to link the TODs. But even in metropolitan areas served by extensive separated transit systems, such as Washington and San Francisco (with the possible exception of New York), the vast majority of daily movements are made in automotive vehicles, not on rapid transit or other public transit. Hence it is not clear how much savings in highway construction could have been made by shifting all growth to urban TODs.

It is not possible to evaluate this argument reliably within the scope of this appendix. However, the analysis I have provided at least throws substantial doubt on the feasibility of accommodating *all* future urban growth in urban TODs alone.

Accommodating Growth in Three Types of TODs

The analysis of Calthorpe's urban TODs is not really fair to his overall strategy for metropolitan growth because it does not take into account neighborhood TODs and secondary areas as he defined them. Yet they are integral parts of his strategy, so I also examined the feasibility of using all three types together to accommodate the growth of large U.S. metropolitan areas during the 1980s.

With the data Calthorpe sent, I could lay out various land configurations containing all three types of TODs. However, it is convenient to visualize the configuration as a circle with a radius of 5,000 feet. The area of the circle would be 1,809 acres, or 2.82 square miles. Inside the circle would be an inner circle with a 2,000-foot radius—the urban TOD described earlier. A third circle with a 2,770-foot radius would consist of one or more neighborhood TODs (figure C-1). These would cover 270 acres, of which 63 percent would be occupied by residential units at a net density of 12 units an acre. These neighborhood TODs would contain more than 2,000 housing units inhabited by 5,100 people.

The space between the 2,770-foot circle and the 5,000-foot circle would consist of a secondary area containing 1,250 acres. About 74

FIGURE C -1. *Combined Transit-Oriented Development*

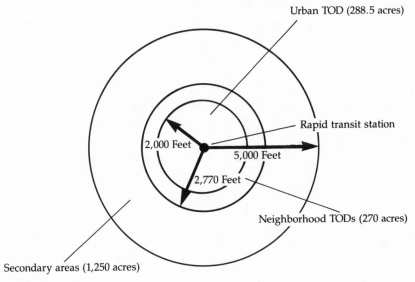

Urban TOD (288.5 acres)

Rapid transit station

2,000 Feet

5,000 Feet

2,770 Feet

Neighborhood TODs (270 acres)

Secondary areas (1,250 acres)

Source: Based on Peter Calthorpe, *The Next American Metropolis* (Princeton University Press, 1993).

percent of it would be occupied by housing at an average net density of 6 units an acre, a total of 5,550 units containing 13,875 people. So the population of the entire 5,000-foot circle would be roughly 23,000 persons in 9,100 units. This combined TOD would thus contain about six times as many residents as an urban TOD alone. It would therefore take one-sixth as many combined TODs as urban TODs to handle any absolute amount of growth.

That implies that the average amount of growth could have been absorbed by about 10.4 combined TODs, and the rapid growth by 23.4 combined TODs. These combined TODs would have to be somewhat farther apart than urban TODs alone because the combined TODs are in circles 10,000 feet across, or just under 2 miles, whereas the urban TODs are in circles only 4,000 feet across. The transit stations at the heart of combined TODs would thus have to be at least 2 miles apart rather than 1.5 miles as in the urban TODs. But this increase in separation would be more than offset by the smaller total number of TODs involved in coping with any given amount of growth.

If the metropolitan area could be served by four radial rapid-transit lines extending outward from the central-city downtown, each line would have to serve about 2.5 combined TODs in its suburbs to accommodate the average amount of suburban growth in large U.S. metropolitan areas during the 1980s. That would require 5 miles of suburban right-of-way for each line, or 20 miles in all. This total is much more consistent with actual lengths of U.S. metropolitan fixed-rail systems than is the requirement for urban TODs alone. Similarly, the total length of right-of-way for very rapid (40 percent) growth would have been 43 miles. Thus it might have been feasible to accommodate all the population growth of the 1980s in combined TODs if large amounts of resources had been devoted to building a rapid transit system linking them together. Whether that investment could have been financed by curtailed spending on highway networks cannot be determined here.

Further Aspects of Coping with Growth

Some further aspects of using TODs to cope with growth are worth discussing briefly. First, my analysis has assumed that all the suburban growth occurring between 1980 and 1990 was shifted into TOD form. However, Calthorpe's approach to urban planning could also be applied to only part of future growth, with the remainder dealt with in more traditional ways. It would surely be more feasible to use TODs in that more limited manner than to make them the only method of dealing with population and economic expansion.

Second, Calthorpe's strategy calls for much higher gross suburban population densities than are typical in American metropolitan areas. Gross population densities of urban TODs laid out as described earlier would have 8,400 people a square mile and combined TODs 8,850 a square mile.[5] Calthorpe's secondary areas have net residential densities averaging 6 units an acre. In the dominant residential pattern many suburbs have 2 or fewer units an acre. Therefore, most U.S. suburban densities are well under 5,000 people a square mile, and many are under 3,000 (see chapter 9).

This means that in most U.S. metropolitan areas, especially newer ones, substituting Calthorpe's TODs for traditional development patterns for any significant part of a metropolitan area's growth would greatly reduce the total amount of land consumed by growth, other things being equal. This outcome would be regarded as desirable by many environmentalists but as undesirable by many owners of vacant land because fewer would benefit from the rising land prices. Their discontent could generate substantial political opposition to the use of TODs to handle any large part of a metropolitan area's growth.

It would also be logical to cluster the new TODs along major highways or fixed-rail routes radiating from the central city's business district. If so, there might be a large amount of vacant land left undeveloped in the pie-shaped gaps between the arteries. But some of the land would be closer to the center that the farthest TODs along the transportation arteries. Enormous economic and political pressure would arise to develop that closer-in land with urban uses laid out in non-TOD patterns highly dependent on autos. This pressure would probably undermine the feasibility of building the farthest-out TODs in the first place. These considerations reinforce the conclusion that it will probably prove politically impossible to incorporate all or even most suburban growth into TOD forms. However, TODs could certainly be used to accommodate a significant share of suburban growth—much more than is being similarly handled now.

Conclusions

Peter Calthorpe's approach to managing urban growth is in no way contradictory to or even inconsistent with the new visions posed by this book. Realistically, it may not be feasible to accommodate all or even most urban growth in the type of transit-oriented developments he advocates. The feasibility of applying them on a large scale is weakened by the high cost of building the rapid-transit links among them that he also advocates. However, his TODs should be viewed as building blocks that could be used to handle some significant part of growth in all the visions described in this book except the unlimited low-density vision.

Notes

Chapter One: Why We Need a New Vision

1. Throughout this book, population growth will be used as a proxy for these other forms of development because it is highly correlated with them and detailed data about it are more readily available.

2. Fannie Mae, "Fannie Mae National Housing Survey 1993," Washington, 1993, pp. 6, 16, 17.

3. These two conditions may seem natural to most Americans, but they are not in the rest of the world. New substandard housing in the form of barrios or shantytowns is the main method of housing the urban poor in most less developed societies. Extensive use of public housing subsidies is a major method of providing housing for the urban poor in many Western European nations. Anthony Downs, "Housing the Urban Poor: The Economics of Various Strategies," *American Economic Review*, vol. 59 (September 1969), pp. 646–51.

4. From 1980 through 1988, the number of cars and trucks in use in the United States increased by 31.9 million, or 22.8 percent; the population increased by 18.3 million, or 8.0 percent. Surfaced road mileage increased by only 4.3 percent. Motor Vehicle Manufacturers Association, *Motor Vehicle Facts & Figures '89* (Detroit, 1989), pp. 28–29, 84; and Bureau of the Census, *Statistical Abstract of the United States: 1989* (Department of Commerce, 1989), p. 7.

5. Data for 1980 from Alan E. Pisarski, *Commuting in America: A National Report on Commuting Patterns and Trends* (Westport, Conn.: Eno Foundation for Transportation, 1987), p. 60. Data for 1990 from Center for Urban Transportation Research, *Florida Demographics and the Journey to Work: A County Data Book* (University of South Florida, 1993), p. 21.

6. Office of Highway Information Management, Federal Highway Administration, "1990 Nationwide Personal Transportation Study: Early Results," Department of Transportation, August 1991, pp. 8–9, 20.

7. For example, the Bay Area Council reported that 38 percent of the 630 respondents in a 1990 poll cited traffic congestion as the area's biggest problem, compared with only 8 percent for each of the three problems ranked next. This 38 percent was up one-third from the 1989 poll. Congestion has been the

most-cited problem for eight straight years. Bay Area Council, *Bay Area Poll* (January 1991).

8. Motor Vehicle Manufacturers Association, *Motor Vehicle Facts & Figures '88* (Detroit, 1988), p. 45.

9. Center for Urban Transportation Research, *Florida Demographics and the Journey to Work*, p. 21.

10. Lack of roadbuilding is only one cause of growing peak-hour traffic congestion. Congestion would undoubtedly have increased significantly from 1980 to 1990 even if many roads had been built. For an in-depth analysis, see Anthony Downs, *Stuck in Traffic: Coping with Peak-Hour Traffic Congestion* (Brookings, 1992), chap. 1.

11. Peter Gordon and Harry W. Richardson, "Trends in Congestion in Metropolitan Areas," paper prepared for the Symposium for the Study on Urban Transportation Congestion Pricing, National Research Council, Washington, June 1993, p. 1.

12. Of all occupied units 64 percent were owner occupied. Bureau of the Census, *Statistical Abstract of the United States: 1992* (Department of Commerce, 1992), p. 716. Also, 64 percent of the entire housing inventory consisted of single-family units. Bureau of the Census, "1990 Housing Highlights: United States," CH-S-1-1, Department of Commerce, July 1991.

13. Author's calculations using data from Ronald B. Mincy, "The Under Class: Changing Concept, Constant Reality," Urban Institute, Washington, May 1993; John D. Kasarda, "Inner-City Concentrated Poverty and Neighborhood Distress: 1970 to 1990," in Fannie Mae, *Housing Policies for Distressed Urban Neighborhoods* (1993), p.20; and Bureau of the Census, "Poverty in the United States: 1990," *Current Population Reports*, series P-60, no. 175 (Department of Commerce, 1991), p. 15. I am greatly indebted to the authors for their assistance.

14. Author's calculations based on data from Bureau of the Census, *Statistical Abstract of the United States: 1992*, p. 8.

15. *Economic Report of the President, January 1993*, table B-30.

16. U.S. public policy does not rely solely on trickle-down to house the poor; the federal public housing program, the federal section 8 subsidy program, and state issuance of federal tax-exempt bonds do finance low-income housing. In 1988 there were 1.45 million low-income public housing units, while in 1989 there were 6.37 million low-income renter households and another 11.5 million with very low incomes. And most public housing units are in central cities. Data on households are from an unpublished tabulation of American Housing Survey data for 1989 done by Carla Pedone of the Congressional Budget Office. Data on public housing units are from Bureau of the Census, *Statistical Abstract of the United States: 1992*, p. 724.

17. For an analysis of the nature and effects of such fees, see Alan A. Altshuler and Jose A. Gomez-Ibañez, *Regulation for Revenue: The Political Economy of Land Use Exactions* (Brookings, 1993).

18. For a detailed analysis of peak-hour road pricing, see Downs, *Stuck in Traffic*, chap. 4. Also see Kenneth A. Small, Clifford Winston, and Carol A.

Evans, *Road Work: A New Highway Pricing and Investment Policy* (Brookings, 1989).

Chapter Two: Factors Affecting Growth

1. Bradley R. Schiller, *The Economics of Poverty and Discrimination* (Prentice-Hall, 1984), p. 64; and Bureau of the Census, *Statistical Abstract of the United States: 1992* (Department of Commerce, 1992), p. 456. Data from 1981 were used because Schiller provides the most recent analysis of poverty among the working poor.

2. Sweden, Germany, and Switzerland have come close to eliminating slums by subsidizing housing and other social services for their low-income households.

3. David Rusk has advocated annexation powers in *Cities without Suburbs* (Washington: Woodrow Wilson Center Press, 1993). He contends that "elastic" cities able to annex surrounding territories easily produce better social outcomes than "inelastic" cities hemmed in by independent jurisdictions. Regardless of whether he is correct, achieving widespread metropolitan governments of the type he espouses is not politically possible in most of the United States. See chapter 9.

4. An externality is a direct relationship between persons or organizations that does not flow through voluntary market transactions. For example, a busy expressway passing near a residential neighborhood bombards that neighborhood with noise and air pollution regardless of the residents' wishes. Urban areas are saturated with externalities because of the close physical proximity of the people and organizations in them. In purely voluntary free market transactions, all the parties involved benefit or they would not participate. But because externalities affect people whether or not they want to be affected, externalities cannot be properly regulated by free market forces alone.

5. The most comprehensive review of the evidence concerning the relationship between ethnicity or race and crime rates was conducted by James Q. Wilson and Richard J. Herrnstein. They concluded that rates of violent crime are certainly much higher among young black men than among young white men. They examined four theories of the causes of this variance: racially different genetic factors, economic deprivation, differences in family behavior patterns, and black hostility to society based on unfair treatment by whites. They concluded that the evidence was not sufficient to determine to what extent, if at all, these factors contributed. See *Crime and Human Nature* (Simon and Schuster, 1985), pp. 466–86.

6. Older homes in some close-in neighborhoods retain high market values because of their convenient locations near the downtown or other amenities such as waterfronts.

7. A few cities have merged with the counties containing them or annexed surrounding territories into a large metropolitan government. These include Indianapolis, Jacksonville, Nashville-Davidson, and Miami. Fewer than a

dozen of the nation's more than 300 metropolitan areas have such governments.

8. State governments have such responsibility if a metropolitan area lies entirely within a single state. But they are also responsible for all other parts of the state. No single entity thus has the welfare of a metropolitan area as its main responsibility.

9. Some urban economists have argued that providing households choices among numerous varied and separate communities is equivalent to creating a quasi-efficient market for certain types of public goods. (Public goods are those that by their very existence are directly available to all citizens equally. Therefore, such goods cannot be paid for through normal price mechanisms, which require the purchaser to put up money before receiving the good. National defense is the classic example of a pure public good.)

Some public goods provided by local governments—streets, schools, parks—are not completely free from potential overuse and congestion; hence they are not pure public goods. Even so, providing consumers with choices of combinations of these and other goods and the taxes that pay for them increases consumer welfare. Therefore, maintaining many and diverse suburbs adds to the welfare of metropolitan residents. See Charles M. Tiebout, "A Pure Theory of Local Expenditures," *Journal of Political Economy*, vol. 64 (October 1956), pp. 416–24. For a thorough discussion of the literature that has developed from Tiebout's hypothesis, see Peter Mieszkowski and George R. Zodrow, "Taxation and the Tiebout Model: The Differential Effects of Head Taxes, Taxes on Land Rents, and Property Taxes," *Journal of Economic Literature*, vol. 27 (September 1989), pp. 1098–1146.

10. They cannot legally exclude members of particular ethnic groups. But they often try to do so through various discriminatory practices, especially concerning the sale or rental of homes.

11. Measuring neighborhood differentiation empirically poses immense methodological problems. Michael J. White attempted to measure important traits in twenty-one large metropolitan areas. He used a complex index called *mean entropy* that indicates the average extent of neighborhood deviation from the composition of the entire metropolitan area for each variable. A score of 50 would indicate complete deviation; a score of zero, no deviation. The variable most differentiated by neighborhood was the proportion of high-rise housing (a score of 46). Second was the presence of group quarters (39); third was race (34); fourth, home values (22); and tied for fifth, rents and housing age (21). Of lesser importance were homeownership (17), percentage of poor persons (11), education (8), and income (7). If housing values and rents are taken to be good measures of socioeconomic status, this index indicates relatively significant neighborhood differentiation consistent with the hierarchy theory. See Michael J. White, *American Neighborhoods and Residential Differentiation* (Russell Sage Foundation, 1987), p. 113. Also see Anthony Downs, *Neighborhoods and Urban Development* (Brookings, 1981), pp. 44–58.

12. Communities move up and down within this hierarchy over time. See Downs, *Neighborhoods and Urban Development*, especially chap. 4.

13. Greg J. Duncan and others, *Years of Poverty, Years of Plenty: The Changing Economic Fortunes of Workers and Families* (Institute for Social Research, University of Michigan, 1984).

14. Bureau of the Census, *Statistical Abstract of the United States: 1992*, p. 20.

15. This point and many ideas in the following section have been taken in part from Paul E. Peterson, *City Limits* (University of Chicago Press, 1981), chap. 3.

16. See Anthony Downs, "Policy Directions Concerning Racial Discrimination in U.S. Housing Markets," *Housing Policy Debate*, vol. 3, no. 2 (1992), pp. 696–704.

17. New York City has raised its tax rates far above those of communities around it to engage in redistributive fiscal policies, on the apparent assumption that its unique traits will prevent businesses and households from moving elsewhere. This policy has contributed to the city government's repeated brushes with bankruptcy and a huge loss of both households and businesses to surrounding jurisdictions.

18. From Douglas S. Massey and Nancy A. Denton, *American Apartheid: Segregation and the Making of the Underclass* (Cambridge: Harvard University Press, 1993), p. 222.

19. Massey and Denton, *American Apartheid*, p. 86.

20. John Yinger, *Housing Discrimination Study: Incidence of Discrimination and Variations in Discriminatory Behavior* (Washington: Urban Institute, 1991).

21. Massey and Denton, *American Apartheid*, pp. 100–03.

22. George C. Galster, "Research on Discrimination in Housing and Mortgage Markets: Assessment and Future Directions," *Housing Policy Debate*, vol. 3, no. 2 (1993), pp. 639–83.

23. Massey and Denton, *American Apartheid*, pp. 88–96; and Reynolds Farley and others, "Continued Racial Segregation in Detroit: 'Chocolate City, Vanilla Suburbs' Revisited," *Journal of Housing Research*, vol. 4, no. 1 (1993), pp. 1–38.

24. Thomas C. Schelling, "A Process of Residential Segregation: Neighborhood Tipping," in Anthony H. Pascal, ed., *Racial Discrimination in Economic Life* (Boston: Heath, 1972), pp. 157–84.

25. Ronald B. Mincy and Susan J. Weiner, "The Underclass in the 1980s: Changing Concept, Constant Reality," Urban Institute, Washington, July 1993, table 7.

26. Massey and Denton, *American Apartheid*, p. 168.

27. This problem is not analyzed in detail in this book because it is the subject of my *Stuck in Traffic: Coping with Peak-Hour Traffic Congestion* (Brookings 1992).

28. Urban Land Institute, "Myths and Facts about Transportation and Growth," Washington, 1989.

29. Regulatory barriers to affordable housing and possible remedies are discussed in detail in Advisory Commission on Regulatory Barriers to Affordable Housing, "Not in My Back Yard: Removing Barriers to Affordable Hous-

ing," Department of Housing and Urban Development, 1991. I was a member of this commission.

30. Whether this is true is a matter of controversy among urban economists. See Alan A. Altshuler and José A. Gomez-Ibañez, *Regulation for Revenue: The Political Economy of Land Use Exactions* (Brookings, 1993).

Chapter Three: Local Growth Management Policies

1. Some urban planners consider local or other growth management policies different from growth control policies. For example, John M. DeGrove with Deborah A. Minass defines growth control as "rigid . . . no-growth or slow-growth programs associated with California cities and counties." But they define growth management as "a commitment to plan carefully for the growth that comes to an area so as to achieve a responsible balance between the protection of natural systems—land, air, and water—and the development required to support growth in the residential, commercial, and retail areas. Growth management is not pro-growth, nor is it anti-growth." *Planning and Growth Management in the States* (Cambridge, Mass.: Lincoln Institute of Land Policy, 1992), p. 1.

For the purposes of analysis in this book, this distinction is not very meaningful. All U.S. localities—even unincorporated portions of metropolitan or rural counties—already have some zoning or other regulations that restrict how their land can be developed. Thus all growth in every locality can be considered managed growth as defined above. But nearly all regulations designed to limit the form or timing of local growth also influence its total amount, at least within any given period. All residential zoning laws place some limits on the number of housing units that can be built in a given area, thereby "controlling" the amount of growth permitted. If a growth management statute slows the pace of growth within a locality, it will divert some growth to other places. That is very similar to a limitation on the first locality's growth during that period. Moreover, determination of whether any program responding to growth problems is "balanced" or "unbalanced" is a highly subjective matter.

Therefore this book does not distinguish between growth management and growth control. It uses the terms interchangeably to mean any policy explicitly intended to influence the form, nature, pace, timing, or amount of growth that occurs within a locality or a metropolitan area.

2. Much of the information about these studies has been taken from William A. Fischel, "What Do Economists Know about Growth Controls? A Research Review," in David J. Brower, David R. Godschalk, and Douglas R. Porter, eds., *Understanding Growth Management: Critical Issues and a Research Agenda* (Washington: Urban Land Institute, 1989), pp. 59–86.

3. Lawrence Katz and Kenneth T. Rosen, "The Interjurisdictional Effects of Growth Controls on Housing Prices," *Journal of Law and Economics*, vol. 30 (April 1987), pp. 149–60.

4. Petaluma adopted stringent limits on how many new housing units could be built there each year. Housing demand was diverted to such nearby localities as Santa Rosa that did not have growth limits. Even so, the prices of new units of a given quality rose somewhat more than those in adjacent communities. But because the annual supply of buildable lots in Petaluma was sharply reduced, builders switched to building higher-priced units. They earned higher profits per lot on larger homes. In addition, the city council skewed its permissions for new projects to favor homes with more amenities and higher quality. Thus the average price of all new housing in Petaluma rose notably. But that increase resulted more from an upgrading of the type of units built than from an increase in the price of each type. See Douglas R. Porter, ed., *Growth Management: Keeping on Target?* (Washington: Urban Land Institute, 1986); and Seymour I. Schwartz, David E. Hansen, and Richard Green, "Suburban Growth Controls and the Price of New Housing," *Journal of Environmental Economics and Management*, vol. 8 (December 1981), pp. 303–20. Fischel, "What Do Economists Know about Growth Controls?" pp. 59–86, postulates that this effect may be smaller than the effects found by Katz and Rosen because Petaluma is much farther from San Francisco's central business district than the localities from which they drew their samples. Fischel believes the effects of growth controls on prices decrease with distance from the metropolitan area's dominant central business district.

5. Peter M. Zorn, David E. Hansen, and Seymour I. Schwartz, "Mitigating the Price Effects of Growth Control: A Case Study of Davis, California," *Land Economics*, vol. 62 (February 1986), pp. 46–57.

6. David Segal and Philip Srinivasan, "The Impact of Suburban Growth Restrictions on U.S. Housing Price Inflation, 1975–1978," *Urban Geography*, vol. 6, no. 1 (1985), p. 15.

7. Paul L. Niebanck, "Growth Controls and the Production of Inequality," in Brower, Godschalk, and Porter, eds., *Understanding Growth Management*, p. 115.

8. Carl F. Neuss, *California and San Diego County: Economies at Risk: The Anatomy of a Failed Growth Management and Housing Policy* (San Diego: Buie Corp., February 1992), p. 36.

9. William A. Fischel, "Comment on Anthony Downs's 'The Advisory Commission on Regulatory Barriers to Affordable Housing: Its Behavior and Accomplishments,'" *Housing Policy Debate*, vol. 2, no. 4 (1991), pp. 1139–60.

10. Arthur C. Nelson pointed out to me that housing prices within a metropolitan area at any given distance from its center tend to rise as the area grows larger. All housing prices in the area can thus be expected to increase somewhat, even corrected for general inflation, as long as the area continues to grow. Nelson believes this effect accounts for some of the housing price increases attributed to growth controls in the studies cited in the text. However, some of those studies used hedonic index techniques that compared prices in different communities, thereby taking this effect into account. I do not believe this point disproves the conclusion that most growth management policies increase housing prices significantly.

11. The median price of existing U.S. single-family homes sold in the last quarter of 1987 was $99,000; see Bureau of the Census, *Statistical Abstract of the United States: 1992* (Department of Commerce, 1992), p. 724. To be able to afford a home with that price, a household should not have to spend more than 28 percent of its income on mortgage payments. This definition of housing affordability is based on two standards. One is the Department of Housing and Urban Development policy that a household should be able to spend 30 percent of its income on housing without suffering a problem of affordability. The second is the established mortgage lending standard that a household should be able to devote 28 percent of its income to making its monthly mortgage payments. If a thirty-year, fixed-rate mortgage covers 75 percent of the purchase price and has an interest rate of 9 percent, the purchaser's payments are $593 a month, or $7,116 a year. That is 28 percent of an annual income of $25,414. If the price of the home increases 5 percent, the total price becomes $103,950; if it increases 10 percent, it becomes $108,900. The incomes necessary to purchase homes of those prices, under the same assumptions, would be $26,685 and $27,955. The number of households in the United States that had incomes between $25,414 and $27,955 in 1990, the latest year for which income distribution data are available, was about 4 million. In 1990 there were 94.31 million U.S. households. Of these, 14.87 million, or 15.76 percent, had incomes between $25,000 and $34,999 in 1990 dollars. Bureau of the Census, "Money Income of Households, Families, and Persons in the United States: 1990," *Current Population Reports*, series P-60, no. 174 (Department of Commerce, 1991), p. 17. If those 14.87 million were evenly distributed among all the incomes between $25,000 and $34,999, then 25.4 percent of them had incomes in the interval between $25,414 and $27,955. And 25.4 percent of 14,865,000 households equals 3,778,000 households. That in turn equals about 4 percent of the 94.31 million total U.S. households.

12. These points are taken from William A. Fischel, "What Do Economists Know about Growth Controls?" p. 81.

13. I am grateful to Edwin Mills for pointing out this relationship.

14. A survey of growth limits adopted by California cities and counties shows that the localities most likely to adopt such limits were not necessarily growing rapidly themselves, but were located in metropolitan areas that were rapidly growing overall. See Madelyn Glickfeld and Ned Levine, "The New Land Use Regulation 'Revolution': Why California's Local Jurisdictions Enact Growth Control and Management Measures," Graduate School of Architecture and Urban Planning, University of California at Los Angeles, June 22, 1990.

15. Katharine L. Bradbury, Anthony Downs, and Kenneth A. Small, *Urban Decline and the Future of American Cities* (Brookings, 1982), pp. 109, 115.

16. A few state governments have imposed uniform growth-related policies on all jurisdictions within their boundaries. But these policies have neither been aimed at nor achieved deliberate control of population growth rates in metropolitan areas.

Chapter Four: Links between Central Cities and Suburbs

1. For example, see Peter F. Drucker, "People, Work, and the Future of the City," in *Managing for the Future: The 1990s and Beyond* (New York: Truman Talley Books, 1993), pp. 125–29. In comments to me, Edwin Mills of Northwestern University argued that all the functions now performed in central cities will be available in the suburbs within two or three decades.

2. Author's calculations using data from Bureau of the Census, *Statistical Abstract of the United States: 1992* (Department of Commerce, 1992), pp. 30–32.

3. Peter F. Drucker, *Post-Capitalist Society* (Harperbusiness, 1993), especially pp. 1–47.

4. Data cited in Mark Alan Hughes and Julie E. Sternberg, "The New Metropolitan Reality: Where the Rubber Meets the Road in Antipoverty Policy," Urban Institute, Washington, December 1992, pp. 10, 12.

5. Stephen Moore and Dean Stansel, "The Myth of America's Underfunded Cities," *Policy Analysis*, no. 188 (February 22, 1993), pp. 8–10.

6. Bureau of the Census, "Money Income of Households, Families, and Persons in the United States: 1990," *Current Population Reports*, series P-60, no. 174 (Department of Commerce, 1991), p. 17.

7. John D. Kasarda, "Inner-City Concentrated Poverty and Neighborhood Distress: 1970 to 1990," in Fannie Mae, *Housing Policies for Distressed Urban Neighborhoods* (1993), p. 20.

8. Bureau of the Census, "Poverty in the United States: 1990," *Current Population Reports*, series P-60, no. 175 (Department of Commerce, 1991), pp. 24, 54–56.

9. Helen F. Ladd and John Yinger, *America's Ailing Cities: Fiscal Health and the Design of Urban Policy* (Johns Hopkins University Press, 1989), p. 85.

10. Ibid., p. 60.

11. Bureau of the Census, *Statistical Abstract of the United States: 1992*, pp. 17, 35–37.

12. If three-dimensional, full color holographic images of meeting participants could be projected from place to place, this limitation might be overcome. But making that advance available at reasonable cost is years away. And just because it can be imagined does not mean it will happen. The Buck Rogers comic strip in the 1930s predicted transportation by personal rocket belts.

13. Where a regional airport occupies a geographically more central site than an area's central city, as does Chicago's O'Hare Airport, facilities clustered around it may become a strong competitor as the locale for face-to-face contacts. But facilities around airports are not nearly as close to each other as those in major regional downtowns, so they are not as likely to generate spontaneous contacts.

14. Data obtained from Donald Starsinik of the Bureau of the Census on January 9, 1992.

15. Henry Buist, "An Analysis of Firm Relocation in a Metropolitan Economy," Ph.D. dissertation, University of Pennsylvania, 1991.

16. Another way suburban homeowners depend on the prosperity of central cities involves capitalization of commuter train and auto access to downtown into the market values of suburban homes. In a study of home prices in Philadelphia suburbs, homes located near commuter train stations and expressways with good access to downtown Philadelphia had higher values than similar homes located farther away. If the economic vitality of downtown Philadelphia were to decline markedly in absolute terms (*not* relative to the vitality of the suburbs), cutting the attraction of commuting to work there, the market values of these suburban homes could fall. See Richard Voith, "Changing Capitalization of CBD-Oriented Transportation Systems: Evidence from Philadelphia, 1970–1988," working paper 91-19, Federal Reserve Bank of Philadelphia, March 1992.

17. Larry C. Ledebur and William R. Barnes, " 'All in It Together': Cities, Suburbs and Local Economic Regions," National League of Cities, Washington, February 1993, p. 4. The R^2 of a one-variable regression linking these two variables was 0.82. However, the authors did not include any other variables in the regression, so this analysis is not a true test of the causal linkages of these two variables.

18. In this discussion, *locality* is used to denote a legally defined political jurisdiction; *community* is used to denote a sociological and economic grouping of persons whose activities are significantly interrelated, regardless of what jurisdictions they live in.

Chapter Five: Urban Decline and Inner-City Problems

1. Katharine L. Bradbury, Anthony Downs, and Kenneth Small, *Urban Decline and the Future of American Cities* (Brookings, 1982), p. 12.

2. Bureau of the Census, *Statistical Abstract of the United States: 1992* (Department of Commerce, 1992), table 37.

3. These sixty-three cities include the twenty-nine largest as of 1990 and forty-five of the largest fifty. Only Portland (Oregon), Albuquerque, Virginia Beach, Omaha, and Toledo were among the fifty largest cities but had minority populations of less than 100,000.

4. The black and Hispanic categories overlap somewhat because *black* is a racial designation and *Hispanic* a linguistic designation. But the number of persons who are both is not large enough to distort conclusions drawn from the data.

5. These figures are based on data from fifty-eight of the cities and their metropolitan areas. They exclude data for the central cities and suburbs of Jackson, Laredo, Albuquerque, Corpus Christi, and Stockton. Together these five contained only 2.8 percent of the total 1990 population of the sixty-three

238   Notes

cities. Data on minority populations in the remaining metropolitan areas are from Bureau of the Census, *Statistical Abstract of the United States: 1992*, p. 34.

6. They lost 14.8 million residents who were neither black nor Hispanic—mostly Asian. They probably lost even more whites. The other groups counted in this category, mostly Asians, undoubtedly increased in number in these cities.

7. For a discussion of many aspects of the underclass, see Christopher Jencks and Paul E. Peterson, eds., *The Urban Underclass* (Brookings, 1991).

8. The population changes in some cities were the result of annexation rather than growth within fixed boundaries. The cities in table 5-3 notably affected by annexation from 1980 to 1990 were Phoenix, Fresno, Birmingham, Baton Rouge, Charlotte, Austin, Houston, San Antonio, Tucson, and Columbus, Ohio. If population gains from annexation are disregarded, Columbus and San Antonio would move from the rapidly growing category to the slowly growing category; Houston would move from the slowly growing to the slowly declining category; and Baton Rouge would show a further population decline but remain in the slowly declining category. Data on annexations are from Joel C. Miller, "Annexations and Boundary Changes in the 1980s and 1990 through 1991," in International City Managers Association, *The Municipal Yearbook: 1993* (Washington, 1993), pp. 101–03. The data are estimates supplied by local governments.

9. Data on the total populations and ethnic composition of individual cities were taken from Bureau of the Census, *Statistical Abstract of the United States: 1991* (Department of Commerce, 1991), table 40.

10. Ronald B. Mincy and Susan J. Wiener, "The Under Class in the 1980s: Changing Concept, Constant Reality," Urban Institute, Washington, July 1993; and Mincy, "Ghetto Poverty: Black Problem or Harbinger of Things To Come?" Urban Institute, Washington, April 30, 1993. Most of the remaining data in this section have come from these two papers.

11. Some of this increase was undoubtedly the result of including a larger sample of census tracts in compiling 1990 data and to slightly different data bases in the two years. However, there was undoubtedly a large increase from 1980 to 1990. For a more detailed discussion, see Mincy and Wiener, "The Under Class in the 1980s."

12. These neighborhoods contained 15.1 percent of the total poor population. But they contained 16.6 percent of all blacks and 10.3 percent of all Hispanics, compared with only 1.9 percent of all whites. Thus the problems generated by concentrations of poverty are much more prevalent among minorities than among whites, even poor whites. Furthermore, 48 percent of all persons living in extremely poor neighborhoods resided in tracts where blacks were a majority of residents, compared with 22 percent living where whites were a majority and 21 percent where Hispanics were a majority.

13. This average was computed by dividing the total number of persons living in extremely poor neighborhoods in the ten cities by the cities' total population.

14. John D. Kasarda, "Inner-City Concentrated Poverty and Neighborhood

Distress: 1970 to 1990," paper prepared for the Fannie Mae 1993 Annual Housing Conference, table 11.

15. Stephen Moore and Dean Stansel, "The Myth of America's Underfunded Cities," *Policy Analysis*, no. 188 (1993), p. 2.

16. Ibid., p. 5.

17. Other problems could be added to this list: drug addiction, dominance of single-parent households, and high frequency of births out of wedlock. But these are essentially encompassed within the four I focus on. I am indebted to Victor Palmieri for suggesting this broader approach to coping with inner-city problems in a talk to a seminar on the twenty-fifth anniversary of the Kerner commission report in Albany, New York, in 1993.

18. The murder rate in Northern Ireland in 1990 was 19.2 per 100,000 residents, so the United States does not have the highest rate among all developed nations. But it has the highest rate among nations not engaged in active revolutionary struggles. Interpol, "International Crime Statistics, 1989–1990."

19. The Bureau of Alcohol, Tobacco, and Firearms estimates that more than 5 million guns are available for sale to Americans each year; 201 million firearms were made available from 1899 to 1989, including foreign imports and net of all gun exports and guns used by the military. Bureau of Alcohol, Tobacco, and Firearms, *ATF News*, May 22, 1991. The total deaths by gunshot includes 14,464 homicides, 18,178 suicides, 1,489 accidental deaths, and 340 deaths from guns with unknown intentions. Data are from Handgun Control, Inc., Washington. More Americans were killed by guns in 1990 than died during the Korean War (1950–53).

20. The handgun murder rate per million residents in 1990 was 42.199 in the United States, 13.497 in Switzerland, 2.562 in Canada, 1.525 in Sweden, 0.704 in Japan, 0.587 in Australia, and 0.380 in the United Kingdom. Data from Handgun Control, Inc., Washington. Population data from Bureau of the Census, *Statistical Abstract of the United States: 1992*, pp. 820–22.

21. Bureau of the Census, *Statistical Abstract of the United States: 1992*, p. 180; and Lynn A. Curtis, ed., *American Violence and Public Policy* (Yale University Press, 1985), p. 235.

22. See Neil Alan Weiner and Marvin E. Wolfgang, "The Extent and Character of Violent Crime in America, 1969 to 1982," in Curtis, ed., *American Violence and Public Policy*, p. 19. See also Jill Smolowe, "Danger in the Safety Zone," *Time*, August 23, 1993, p. 42.

23. John J. DiIulio estimated that "the violent crime rate (number of victimizations per 1,000 resident population for persons 12 years of age and over) for African American men living in [metropolitan central cities] was 61.5, compared to 46.8 for white men. The murder victimization rate for African Americans was about six times the rate for whites, and blacks experienced much higher rates of rape, robbery, and aggravated assault than did whites. . . . In 1991 several big and mid-sized cities set new homicide records, and police related most of the increases to the drug trade." These estimates indicate that a black male older than age 12 living in a central city had one

chance in sixteen of being the victim of a violent crime in a given year; a white male had one chance in twenty-one. The chances were greater for men living in inner cities. John J. DiIulio, Jr., "Crime," in Henry Aaron and Charles L. Schultze, eds., *Setting Domestic Priorities: What Can Government Do?* (Brookings, 1992).

24. According to the FBI, the rate of reported violent crimes per 100,000 residents rose from 597 in 1980 to 732 in 1990, up 22.6 percent. But the rate of victimization by violent crimes per 1,000 persons 12 years or older reported by the National Crime Survey declined from 33.3 in 1980 to 29.6 in 1990, down 11.1 percent. These data imply that the police are learning about a higher percentage of violent crimes now than they did in the past, but the number of crimes per 100,000 people may not be increasing. Bureau of the Census, *Statistical Abstract of the United States: 1992*, pp. 180, 184. Neither measure takes into account crimes involving drug dealing and possession. Since such crimes have undoubtedly increased in the 1980s, it is accurate to conclude that the overall crime rate is at record levels.

25. Bureau of the Census, *Statistical Abstract of the United States: 1992*, p. 456; and Bureau of the Census, "Poverty in the United States: 1990," *Current Population Reports*, series P-60, no. 175 (Department of Commerce, 1991), p. 54.

26. Bureau of the Census, *Statistical Abstract of the United States: 1992*, p. 457.

27. Paul E. Barton and Richard J. Coley, *America's Smartest School: The Family* (Princeton, N.J.: ETS, 1992), pp. 6, 7, 8, 9, 31.

28. Bureau of the Census, *Statistical Abstract of the United States: 1992*, p. 69.

29. Tests given in the Second International Assessment of Educational Progress in 1991 to students from fifteen nations showed that American students' scores on mathematics ranked fourteenth and those on science ranked thirteenth among these nations. The average American mathematics score was 55 compared with the top-ranked South Korean score of 73; the average American science score was 67 compared with the top-ranked South Korean score of 78. Bureau of the Census, *Statistical Abstract of the United States: 1992*, p. 830.

30. Among the fifteen nations participating in the Second International Assessment of Educational Progress, the fewest days of instruction a year were 173 in Ireland, 174 in France, 177 in Hungary, and 178 in the United States. The most were 222 in Taiwan and South Korea, 215 in Israel, 207 in Switzerland, and 204 in Italy. Thus South Korean and Taiwanese students spent 25 percent more days in school than American students. Americans had about as many minutes of in-class instruction each week as children in the nations with the highest amounts. However, 29 percent of U.S. students devoted two or more hours to homework each day, compared with 79 percent of Italians, 41 percent of South Koreans and Taiwanese, and more than 50 percent of students in France, Hungary, Ireland, Israel, Jordan, the former Soviet republics, and Spain. Bureau of the Census, *Statistical Abstract*

of the United States: 1992, p. 830. Neither Japan nor Germany was included in this survey.

31. Gary Orfield, "Urban Schooling and the Perpetuation of Job Inequality in Metropolitan Chicago," in George E. Peterson and Wayne Vroman, eds., *Urban Labor Markets and Job Opportunity* (Washington: Urban Institute Press, 1992), pp. 165, 166, 169.

32. Bureau of the Census, *Statistical Abstract of the United States: 1992*, p. 459.

33. George E. Peterson and Wayne Vroman, "Urban Labor Markets and Economic Opportunity," in Peterson and Vroman, eds., *Urban Labor Markets*, p. 3.

34. Bureau of the Census, *Statistical Abstract of the United States: 1992*, p. 144.

35. Robert B. Reich, *The Work of Nations: Preparing Ourselves for 21st Century Capitalism* (Knopf, 1991).

36. Among blacks they were 69.3 percent in the suburbs and 60.2 percent in cities. Among whites they were 68.2 percent and 65.8 percent. Peterson and Vroman, *Urban Labor Markets*, p. 7.

37. Thomas J. Lueck, "Youth Joblessness Is at Record High in New York City," *New York Times*, June 4, 1993, pp. A1, B2.

38. Gary Orfield, *The Closing Door: Conservative Policy and Black Opportunities* (University of Chicago Press, 1991).

39. Senator Bill Bradley of New Jersey is one of the few who have spoken out about this subject, although he has not argued in favor of race-oriented remedies. See Bill Bradley, "Speech by Senator Bill Bradley on Race and the American City," March 26, 1992.

Chapter Six: Policy Strategies for Large Cities

1. Peter D. Salins, "Cities, Suburbs, and the Urban Crisis," *Public Interest*, no. 113 (Fall 1993), p. 99.

2. Such movement is easiest in metropolitan areas that encompass parts of two or more states. The largest are New York City, Boston, Washington, Chicago, Philadelphia, Portland (Oregon), St. Louis, Memphis, and Charlotte.

3. Data from Peter Reuter cited in John J. DiIulio, Jr., "The Next War on Drugs," *Brookings Review*, vol. 11 (Summer 1993), p. 28.

4. Bureau of the Census, *Statistical Abstract of the United States: 1991* (Department of Commerce, 1991), pp. 34–36.

5. John Harwood, "Republican Party Faces Growing Internal Debate over How to Recapture Tax Issue from Democrats," *Wall Street Journal*, March 3, 1993, p. A16. The polling results were from a *Wall Street Journal*/NBC News poll taken January 23–26, 1993.

6. This group of cities is larger than the group of eighteen classified in chapter 5 as rapidly declining because the latter included only cities with 100,000 or more minority residents. Data are from author's calculations based on Bureau of the Census, *Statistical Abstract of the United States: 1991*, p. 301.

7. Katharine L. Bradbury, Anthony Downs, and Kenneth A. Small, *Urban Decline and the Future of American Cities* (Brookings, 1982), pp. 26–27.

8. Peter Salins advocates general revenue sharing as one of four basic principles in his version of a national strategy for combating urban decline. I agree with his diagnosis of the nature of urban decline and the problems it generates, and I also agree that deteriorating cities need substantial financial aid from the federal government. But I do not think most of that aid should take the form of general revenue sharing, as he suggests. It would not ultimately focus enough federal resources on improving conditions in inner-city neighborhoods. See "Cities, Suburbs, and the Urban Crisis," pp. 91–104.

9. John Kain and Joseph J. Persky, "Alternatives to the Gilded Ghetto," *Public Interest*, no. 14 (Winter 1969), pp. 74–87; and Anthony Downs, "Alternative Futures for the American Ghetto," *Daedalus*, vol. 97 (Fall 1968), pp. 1331–78.

10. *Report of the National Advisory Commission on Civil Disorders* (Bantam, 1968).

11. In 1993 federal legislation, enterprise zones were renamed empowerment zones to give the new Clinton administration pride of authorship, at least terminologically. The concept remains the same.

12. Barry M. Rubin and Craig M. Richards, "A Transatlantic Comparison of Enterprise Zone Impacts: The British and American Experience," *Economic Development Quarterly*, vol. 6 (November 1992), pp. 431–43; and Dan Y. Dabney, "Do Enterprise Zone Incentives Affect Business Location Decisions?" *Economic Development Quarterly*, vol. 5 (November 1991), pp. 325–34.

13. A major obstacle has been a ring of high-rise public housing projects a few miles from downtown Chicago. The concentrations of very poor households there inhibit economic and social redevelopment of the blocks around them. Relocating their residents into private housing or substantially reducing the size of the projects could expedite the long-run success of this inside-out redevelopment. I am indebted to Edward Marciniak for pointing out this relationship.

14. This strategy is not the result of any master plan devised by some ingenious proponent of redevelopment. It has arisen because each redevelopment proposal seemed most feasible if closely linked to established resources in previously redeveloped neighborhoods.

15. In the eighteen cities earlier classified as rapidly declining, an average of 16.8 percent of the residents lived in extremely poor census tracts.

16. This form of targeting was suggested by Frank Raines of the Federal National Mortgage Association.

17. William Julius Wilson, *The Truly Disadvantaged: The Inner City, the Underclass, and Public Policy* (University of Chicago Press, 1987).

18. For a discussion of the sexually exploitative behavior of young men, see Elijah Anderson, "Sex Codes and Family Life among Poor Inner-City Youths," *Annals of the American Academy of Political and Social Science*, vol. 501 (January 1989) pp. 57–78.

19. Cornel West, *Race Matters* (Boston: Beacon Press, 1993), pp. 15, 17.

20. In the Beethoven school project in Chicago, for example, Irving Harris has spent millions of dollars of his own money seeking to improve prenatal and postnatal counseling and care for young women living in a very low income black neighborhood. Yet it has proven extremely difficult to persuade pregnant young women to participate in the program or to get other young women to use contraceptives.

21. This strategy should not emphasize dispersing residents outside poor inner-city areas, as I once advocated in *Opening up the Suburbs: An Urban Strategy for America* (Yale University Press, 1973). The emphasis on dispersal rather than on offering broader housing choices to low-income people has been grossly misinterpreted by some black nationalists. They have accused me of wanting to weaken the political power of minorities in city governments and of emptying inner-city neighborhoods so they could be redeveloped for occupancy by high-income whites. Neither was ever my intention. My objective was simply to help low-income households escape the conditions in concentrated-poverty neighborhoods.

22. *Report of the National Advisory Commission on Civil Disorders*, p. 1.

23. Ronald B. Mincy, "Ghetto Poverty: Black Problems or Harbinger of Things to Come?" Urban Institute, Washington, April 30, 1993, table 3A.

24. James E. Rosenbaum, "Black Pioneers—Do Their Moves to the Suburbs Increase Economic Opportunity for Mothers and Children?" *Housing Policy Debate*, vol. 2, no. 4 (1991), pp. 1179–1213.

25. John Kain has demonstrated that homeownership in general and suburban homeownership in particular are much lower among blacks than among whites with similar incomes, occupations, and socioeconomic status. See "Discrimination in Space: Suburbanization and Black Unemployment in Cities," in George M. von Furstenburg, Bennet Harrison, and Ann R. Horowitz, eds., *Patterns of Racial Discrimination*, vol. 1: *Housing* (Lexington, Mass.: Lexington Books, 1974), pp. 21–53.

26. Rosenbaum, "Black Pioneers," pp. 1179–1213.

27. Mark Alan Hughes and Julie E. Sternberg, "The New Metropolitan Reality: Where the Rubber Meets the Road in Antipoverty Policy," Urban Institute, Washington, 1992.

28. This recommendation coincides with one of Peter Salins's four principles for an effective strategy against urban decline. See "Cities, Suburbs, and the Urban Crisis," pp. 102–04. I agree with another of his four principles: preventing localities from adopting exclusionary land use policies that restrict the entry of low-income households. However, I disagree with his other two principles. Providing federal funding to declining cities in the form of general revenue sharing would permit local officials to divert too much of the money away from inner-city neighborhoods. And devolving fiscal control over local services to individual neighborhoods or city subregions would inhibit subregional cross-subsidization of the expensive public services needed in low-income neighborhoods. Per capita police, fire, and school costs are much higher there for comparable levels of service. And per capita taxable resources in poor areas are much smaller, so letting each neighborhood float on its own

bottom fiscally would produce services of far lower quality in poor areas than in wealthier ones, probably generating an even bigger disparity than now exists.

29. The use of vouchers would raise the issues of who would pay for the transportation and how would schools attracting more students than they could handle decide which ones would attend. Transportation costs could be paid by greatly reducing the busing now required in most big cities for racial balancing, since it has not improved minority educational opportunities much. Several types of arrangements, such as a lottery or some combination of lottery and rules based on school-to-home distances, could be used to allocate scarce school seats.

30. For extensive discussions of continuing discrimination see "Discrimination in the Housing and Mortgage Markets," *Housing Policy Debate*, vol. 3, no.2 (1992).

31. For shocking examples of such inequities see Jonathan Kozol, *Savage Inequalities: Children in America's Schools* (Harper Perennial, 1992).

32. Advisory Commission on Regulatory Barriers to Affordable Housing, *"Not In My Back Yard"*: *Removing Barriers to Affordable Housing* (Department of Housing and Urban Development, 1991).

Chapter Seven: Alternative Visions of Growth

1. For an analysis of how urban growth boundaries work, see Oregon Department of Land Conservation and Development, "Urban Growth Management Study: Summary Report," Salem, Oregon, 1991; and Arthur C. Nelson, "Lessons of Urban Growth Boundary Design and Management," Georgia Institute of Technology, n.d.

2. Judith Kunofsky, "Policy before Planning: Solving California's Growth Problems," Sacramento: Sierra Club, 1991, pp. 12–16. This report also declares that no local government should be compelled to adopt any growth-related policies that its residents do not approve (p. 23). How these two principles can be reconciled in a society in which most people want to reduce densities in their localities is not discussed.

3. Author's calculations using data from Bureau of the Census, *Statistical Abstract of the United States: 1991* (Department of Commerce, 1991), pp. 29–31.

4. Southern California Association of Governments, "Choices for Action: Growth Management Plan, Regional Mobility Plan, Regional Housing Needs Assessment," n.d., p. 2.

5. John Pucher, "Urban Travel Behavior as the Outcome of Public Policy: The Example of Modal-Split in Western Europe and North America," *American Planning Association Journal*, vol. 54 (Autumn 1988), p. 510. In Western Europe the proportion of all urban passenger trips made by automobile ranged from 30.6 percent in Italy to 47.6 percent in Germany and 47.0 percent in France.

6. Ibid. Because the proportion of all trips made by automobiles rose rap-

idly in most Western European nations during the 1980s, it probably surpasses 50 percent in many today.

7. This approach is analyzed in much more detail in Anthony Downs, *Stuck in Traffic: Coping with Peak-Hour Traffic Congestion* (Brookings, 1992), chap. 10.

8. However, shorter average trip lengths are not the same as decreased congestion. In fact, the congestion is often more intense in high-density areas than in low-density ones. Total travel distances are longer in low-density areas, but total time required for travel should be less in higher-density areas.

9. Such a housing allowance is not a completely pure income subsidy because the household must live in a decent-quality unit to receive it. Therefore the subsidy influences the consumption pattern of the household to some extent, rather than simply supplementing overall purchasing power.

10. A federal commission of which I was a member studied this topic and issued a report of its findings. See Advisory Commission on Regulatory Barriers to Affordable Housing, *"Not in My Back Yard": Removing Barriers to Affordable Housing* (Department of Housing and Urban Development, 1991).

11. James E. Rosenbaum, "Black Pioneers—Do Their Moves to the Suburbs Increase Economic Opportunities for Mothers and Children?" *Housing Policy Debate*, vol. 2, no. 4 (1991), pp. 1179–1213.

12. More than one goal from the group concerning provision of housing for the poor could be used simultaneously because some are not mutually exclusive. Thus dual elements in this field of activity are used in both the new visions presented later.

13. A total of 1,440 possible combinations was arrived at by multiplying the number of alternatives in each activity area by those in all other activity areas. However, because more than one alternative might be used simultaneously from some activity areas, more than 1,000 combinations could be formulated from the specific alternatives set forth earlier.

14. There is a strong tension between drawing this boundary close to built-up areas and adequately accommodating rapid growth by setting aside large amounts of vacant land within the boundary. Thus even in theory this model is probably not suitable for fast-growing metropolitan areas.

Chapter Eight: Elements in the Alternative Vision

1. The initial gross density including vacant residential sites would be less than 3,500 persons a square mile (the number would depend on what percentage of residential land was initially vacant). The target density of 7,500 a square mile would apply to the whole area, including formerly vacant sites, which by then would have been fully developed.

2. All the calculations in this section assume that 50 percent of total land area is devoted to housing, which is typical of suburbs.

3. Table 8-4 assumes that the initial gross density of 3,500 persons a square mile was the net result of zero gross density on the initially vacant portions

of the territory concerned and 3,500 persons a square mile on the initially occupied portions. Thus, overall gross density, including initially vacant land, would be less than 3,500 persons a square mile. How much less would depend on what percentage of the residential land was initially vacant and available for development.

4. These two calculations are identical because both assume that all initially occupied residential land would have a gross residential density of 3,500 persons a square mile. Therefore the initial overall gross density (and thus the total population) of the territory containing vacant sites would be lower than that of the redevelopment territory if both were the same size because the latter is assumed to be fully developed, with no vacant sites. But the final populations of both territories would be the same for any given ultimate gross density assumed.

5. This statement compares price changes under these alternatives with the price levels that would prevail under low-density growth.

6. The following discussion is taken with small changes from Anthony Downs, *Stuck in Traffic: Coping with Peak-Hour Traffic Congestion* (Brookings, 1992), appendix C.

7. In metropolitan areas with 3 million or more residents, work trips averaged 11.8 miles in 1990. They averaged 8.7 miles in areas with fewer than 250,000 residents. Federal Highway Administration, "Nationwide Personal Transportation Survey 1990: Travel Behavior Issues in the 90's" (Department of Transportation, 1992), pp. 58, 60.

8. These calculations reflect the fact that the area of a circle (which is the dimension most relevant to population holding capacity) is proportional to the square of its radius (area equals radius squared times 3.1416). But it is the radius that is most relevant to commuting distances.

9. Bureau of the Census, *State and Metropolitan Area Data Book 1991* (Department of Commerce, 1991), pp. xx–xxiii, xl.

10. If this hypothetical metropolitan area were perfectly circular, it would have had a radius of 10.89 miles in 1980. Adding 534,000 people would have increased that radius to 12.9 miles (18 percent) if the addition occurred at 3,500 people a square mile, or to 11.89 miles (9 percent) if the addition occurred at 7,500 a square mile. (These calculations assume that all added development is contiguous and continues the perfectly circular shape.)

11. For example, assume that all single-family developments were built at four units a net acre and all multifamily developments at fifteen a net acre. To obtain an average gross density of 7,500 a square mile, 48.9 percent of all new residential land would have to be built at the higher density. But to attain an average of 3,500, only 3.4 percent would have to be developed at that density. The high-density approach would contain fourteen times as many high-density units.

12. See Oregon Department of Land Conservation and Development, "Urban Growth Management Study: Summary Report," Salem, Ore., July 1991; and Arthur C. Nelson, "Lessons of Urban Growth Boundary Design and Management," Georgia Institute of Technology, n.d.

13. The Puget Sound area encompassing Seattle and Tacoma has already developed such a plan. The plan proposes a hierarchy of centers, including the regional center of downtown Seattle and the five candidate metropolitan centers of Bellevue, Bremerton, Everett, Renton, and Tacoma, plus many smaller ones. See Puget Sound Council of Governments, *Vision 2020* (Seattle, 1990), pp. 20–34.

14. In 1983 at least 68 percent of commuters traveled alone; the percentage is now higher. For 1983 data see my *Stuck in Traffic*, p. 144. Occupancy per vehicle for work trips declined from 1.3 in 1983 to 1.1 in 1990. Federal Highway Administration, "Nationwide Personal Transportation Survey," p. 52.

15. Ibid., pp. 3, 11, 21.

16. Ibid., p. 32.

17. See Downs, *Stuck in Traffic*, pp. 26–34.

18. Institute of Transportation Engineering, "Employer Trip Reduction Programs: How Effective Are They?" Washington, November 1992.

19. About 2.5 percent of commuters residing in suburbs used public transit; 90 percent used private vehicles. Federal Highway Administration, "Nationwide Personal Transportation Survey," pp. 20, 32–33.

20. Boris S. Pushkarev and Jeffrey M. Zupan, *Public Transportation & Land Use Policy* (Indiana University Press, 1977).

21. Downs, *Stuck in Traffic*, appendix D.

22. Federal Highway Administration, *Personal Travel in the U.S.: 1983–1984 Personal Transportation Survey*, vol. 1 (Department of Transportation, 1986), pp. 7–11; and Federal Highway Administration, "Nationwide Personal Transportation Survey," pp. 20, 32–33. In 1989 the proportion of suburban residents who walked to work was 2.2 percent; the proportion who used public transit was 2.5 percent; the proportion who worked at home was 2.2 percent. I estimate that the proportion who used other means was no more than 2 percent. That leaves 91.1 percent driving to work.

23. C. Kenneth Orski, "Evaluating Travel Demand Management Effectiveness," Urban Mobility Corp., Washington, 1991, table 2.

24. Computed at 7 units an acre times 2.5 persons a unit times 320 acres. If only 30 percent of the land is used for housing, gross density could be as low as 3,360 persons. If 70 percent of the land is in housing, the figure would be 7,840.

25. Pushkarev and Zupan, *Public Transportation & Land Use Policy*, pp. 172–73.

26. However, even if barriers to more affordable housing were reduced, builders would not necessarily pass on the resulting savings. Other policies would be necessary to secure that outcome.

27. Specific strategies for reducing regulatory barriers to affordable housing are analyzed in Advisory Commission on Regulatory Barriers to Affordable Housing, *"Not in My Back Yard": Removing Barriers to Affordable Housing* (Department of Housing and Urban Development, 1991).

28. No direct federal housing subsidies for low-income households have ever been made entitlements, although homeownership tax benefits are ex-

tended to all households eligible to claim them. Congress has always shied away from turning federal housing aids into entitlements because of the high cost. Instead, it has limited the funding of the subsidies so that only a few of the households technically eligible for them have actually received them.

Chapter Nine: Offsetting Fragmented Land Use Powers

1. David Rusk, *Cities without Suburbs* (Washington: Woodrow Wilson Center Press, 1993).
2. For a study of bureaucratic resistance to change see Anthony Downs, *Inside Bureaucracy* (Little, Brown, 1967).
3. As Alexis de Tocqueville pointed out more than 150 years ago, "In no country in the world has the principle of association been more successfully used or applied to a greater multitude of objects than in Ameria." *Democracy in America*, vol. 1 (Knopf, 1972), p. 191. This tendency was more recently celebrated in Robert N. Bellah and others, *Habits of the Heart* (Harper and Row, 1985), and Bellah and others, *The Good Society* (Knopf, 1991).
4. Intermodal Surface Transportation Efficiency Act, P.L. 102–240, December 18, 1991, 105 Stat. 1955.
5. This approach was suggested to me by Hugh Mields, Jr., to whom I am grateful.
6. In political theory this is known as the principle of subsidiarity. It states that authority over any policy should be located within the geographic hierarchy of governmental bodies as close as possible to the geographic area in which the policy will be carried out.

Chapter Ten: The Politics of Choosing among Visions

1. Daniel Patrick Moynihan, "Defining Deviance Down," *American Scholar*, vol. 62 (Winter 1993), pp. 17–30.
2. Ibid., p. 26.
3. Quoted in ibid.
4. Of course, it would be possible to define other alternatives, but I believe the limitations of actual conditions in U.S. metropolitan areas would force other alternatives to look a lot like the two just mentioned.
5. The ideas in this section on the decisionmaking process in many respects resemble the guideposts included in Neal R. Peirce with Curtis W. Johnson and John Stewart Hall, *Citistates: How Urban America Can Prosper in a Competitive World* (Washington: Seven Locks Press, 1993), pp. 291–325. However, this section was originally written before Peirce's book was published and before I had read it.
6. The San Francisco Bay Area Council conducts such a poll annually. For

nine straight years, residents declared they believed transportation was that area's most serious problem. See "Transportation Seen as #1 Problem," *Bay Area Poll* (Bay Area Council and KQED, November 1991), pp. 1, 3. More recently they ranked transportation below the need for stronger economic prosperity.

7. Anthony Downs, *An Economic Theory of Democracy* (Harper and Row, 1957).

8. In 2020 the proportion of minority-group members among all persons 18 years of age will be 45 percent. Bureau of the Census, "Population Projections of the United States, by Age, Sex, Race, and Hispanic Origin, 1992 to 2050," *Current Population Reports*, series P25, no. 1092 (Department of Commerce, 1992), pp. xi, xvii.

Appendix A

1. Thomas S. Kuhn, *The Structure of Scientific Revolutions*, 2d ed. (University of Chicago Press, 1970).

2. Robert Fishman, "Megalopolis Unbound," *Wilson Quarterly*, vol. 14 (Winter 1990), pp. 25–48. The term *center focused* is mine, not Fishman's, but it fits his analysis. Fishman did not use the concept of a paradigm shift in his article, or even mention the word *paradigm*. Nevertheless, I am indebted to his thinking and to Ingrid Reed for bringing his article to my attention.

3. See Joel Garreau, *Edge City: Life on the New Frontier* (Doubleday, 1991).

4. I am indebted to Edwin Mills for pointing out this relationship.

5. I have added the term *low-density* to Fishman's *network* to emphasize this aspect of the concept.

6. Fishman, "Megalopolis Unbound," p. 28.

Appendix B

1. Stephen Moore and Dean Stansel, "The Myth of America's Underfunded Cities," *Policy Analysis*, no. 188 (1993), pp. 2, 4, 5.

Appendix C

1. Peter Calthorpe, *The Next American Metropolis: Ecology, Community, and the American Dream* (Princeton Architectural Press, 1993).

2. Ibid., p. 43.

3. This 2,000-foot radius has been used by me in *Stuck in Traffic: Coping with Peak-Hour Traffic Congestion* (Brookings, 1992), appendix D, and by Boris S. Pushkarev and Jeffrey M. Zupan in *Public Transportation & Land Use Policy* (Indiana University Press, 1977).

4. Data for the Washington Metro system are from a telephone interview with Larry Levin, Metro System Office of Planning, December 17, 1993. Data

on the Bay Area Rapid Transit system are from a telephone interview with the Bay Area Rapid Transit System Department of Planning, December 17, 1993.

5. Urban TODs have much higher net residential densities than neighborhood TODs or secondary areas. But this is offset by the smaller proportions of total area in urban TODs devoted to residential uses. Hence the gross density of urban TODs is very similar to that of combined TODs.

Index